ENACTING ATONEMENT

The Narrative Logic of Sacrifice and Sonship in Leviticus

◆◆◆◆◆◆◆◆◆◆◆◆◆◆◆◆◆◆◆◆◆

Roy McDaniel

An imprint of InterVarsity Press
Downers Grove, Illinois

InterVarsity Press
P.O. Box 1400 | Downers Grove, IL 60515-1426
ivpress.com | email@ivpress.com

©2025 by Roy Edmonds McDaniel

All rights reserved. No part of this book may be reproduced in any form without written permission from InterVarsity Press.

InterVarsity Press® is the publishing division of InterVarsity Christian Fellowship/USA®. For more information, visit intervarsity.org.

Scripture quotations, unless otherwise noted, are from The Holy Bible, English Standard Version. ESV© Text Edition: 2016. Copyright © 2001 by Crossway Bibles, a publishing ministry of Good News Publishers. Used by permission. All rights reserved.

The publisher cannot verify the accuracy or functionality of website URLs used in this book beyond the date of publication.

Cover design: Christopher Miller
Interior design: Daniel van Loon
Images: © Jorisvo / iStock Editorial via Getty Images

ISBN 978-1-5140-1252-9 (print) | ISBN 978-1-5140-1253-6 (digital)

Printed in the United States of America ∞

Library of Congress Cataloging-in-Publication Data
A catalog record for this book is available from the Library of Congress.

| 31 | 30 | 29 | 28 | 27 | 26 | 25 | | 13 | 12 | 11 | 10 | 9 | 8 | 7 | 6 | 5 | 4 | 3 | 2 | 1 |

To Becky, my faithful wife and best of friends,

and our children, Micah, Mary Grace, and Luke:

with much love and gratitude, and in the prayer that we all will

be brought home to God through the death and ascension of His Son.

Contents

Acknowledgments — ix

Series Introduction — xi

Introduction: A Particular and Privileged Logic — xvii

1 Setting: Narrative and Theological Contexts — 1

2 Plot: In Search of the Essential Act of Sacrifice — 35

3 Hero: Sacrifice and Sonship — 72

4 Action: Atonement Through the Obedience, Death, and Ascension of the Son — 103

5 Meaning: Jesus Christ and the End of the Story — 154

Conclusion — 185

Appendix: Leviticus, Sacrifice, and Atonement: A (Very) Selective History — 191

Bibliography — 205

General Index — 221

Scripture Index — 225

Acknowledgments

Simply to live is to acquire innumerable debts. To undertake a project like this book, which began with doctoral work at Trinity Evangelical Divinity School, is to acquire further still. Here I wish to acknowledge in a small way some of those who contributed to this work's completion, though not to its faults.

I am grateful to my parents, Thomas and Debra McDaniel, and my in-laws, Jim and Cindy Belin. Without your generosity and prayers the work that resulted in this book would not have been half so enjoyable, if even possible.

I am grateful to faculty members during my time at Trinity Evangelical Divinity School: Graham Cole, Richard Averbeck, Tom McCall, David Luy, Ingrid Faro, Scott Manetsch, James Arcadi, Te-Li Lau, and, most especially, Kevin Vanhoozer. Your wisdom was matched only by your patience, both of which were necessary for me.

I am no less grateful to the fellow students with whom I had the privilege of sharing life and learning at Trinity. Special thanks among them is due to Will Bankston. I count it a great blessing to have a friend so much smarter than I am, yet so gracious. Thank you.

While the research for this project was mostly completed in Deerfield, IL, it was composed in Huntsville, AL, where I gladly serve on the faculty of Westminster Christian Academy. The encouragement and freedom provided by the administration team, particularly Alyssa Knight, made writing this book possible. I have not forgotten.

Finally, words fail to express my gratitude to my wife, Becky, and our three children, Micah, Mary Grace, and Luke. Your daily presence enriches my life and thinking in a way that nothing else could, and your sacrifice in this undertaking was no less than mine. I am forever grateful.

Series Introduction

Studies in Christian Doctrine and Scripture (SCDS)

DANIEL J. TREIER AND KEVIN VANHOOZER

THE STUDIES IN CHRISTIAN DOCTRINE and Scripture (SCDS) series attempts to reconcile two disciplines that should never have been divided: the study of Christian Scripture and the study of Christian doctrine. Old walls of disciplinary hostility are beginning to come down, a development that we hope will better serve the church. To that end, books in this series affirm the supreme authority of Scripture, seeking to read it faithfully and creatively as they develop fresh articulations of Christian doctrine. This agenda can be spelled out further in five claims.

1. We aim to publish constructive **contributions to systematic theology** rather than merely descriptive rehearsals of biblical theology, historical retrievals of classic or contemporary theologians, or hermeneutical reflections on theological method—volumes that are plentifully and expertly published elsewhere.

The initial impetus for the SCDS series came from supervising evangelical graduate students and seeking to encourage their pursuit of constructive theological projects shaped by the supremacy of Scripture. Existing publication venues demonstrate how rarely biblical scholars and systematic theologians trespass into each other's fields. Synthetic treatments of biblical theology garner publication in monograph series for biblical studies or evangelical biblical theology. A notable example is a companion series from IVP Academic, New Studies in Biblical Theology. Many of its volumes have theological significance, yet most are written by biblical scholars. Meanwhile, historical retrievals of theological figures garner publication in monograph series for historical and systematic theology. For instance, there have been entire series devoted to figures such as Karl Barth or the patristic era, and even series named for systematic theology tend to contain figure-oriented monographs.

The reason for providing an alternative publication venue is not to denigrate these valuable enterprises. Instead, the rationale for encouraging constructively evangelical projects is twofold and practical: The church needs such projects, and they form the theologians undertaking them. The church needs such projects, both addressing new challenges for her life in the world (such as contemporary political theology) and retrieving neglected concepts (such as the classic doctrine of God) in fresh ways. The church also needs her theologians not merely to develop detailed intellectual skills but also ultimately to wrestle with the whole counsel of God in the Scriptures.

2. We aim to promote **evangelical** contributions, neither retreating from broader dialogue into a narrow version of this identity on the one hand, nor running away from the biblical preoccupation of our heritage on the other hand.

In our initial volume, *Theology and the Mirror of Scripture*, we articulate this pursuit of evangelical renewal. We take up the well-known metaphor of mere Christianity as a hallway, with particular church traditions as the rooms in a house. Many people believe that the evangelical hallway is crumbling, an impression that current events only exacerbate. Our inspection highlights a few fragmenting factors such as more robust academic engagement, increased awareness of the Great Christian Tradition and the variety of evangelical subtraditions, interest in global Christianity, and interfaces with emergent Christianity and culture. Looking more deeply, we find historical-theological debates about the very definition of *evangelical* and whether it reflects—still, or ever—a shared gospel, a shared doctrine of God, and a theological method that can operationalize our shared commitment to Scripture's authority.

In response, prompted by James 1:22-25, our proposal develops the metaphor of a mirror for clarifying evangelical theology's relation to Scripture. The reality behind the mirror is the gospel of God and the God of the gospel: what is revealed in Christ. In disputes about whether to focus on a center or boundaries, it may seem as if evangelicalism has no doctrinal core. But we propose treating what is revealed in Christ—the triune God and the cross of Christ, viewed in the mirror of Scripture—as an evangelical anchor, a center with a certain range of motion. Still, it may seem as if evangelicalism has no hermeneutical coherence, as if interpretive anarchy nullifies biblical authority. But we propose treating Scripture as *canonical testimony*, a God-given mirror of truth that enables the church to reflect the wisdom that is in Christ. The holistic and contextual character of such wisdom gives theology a dialogic character, which requires an evangelical account of the church's catholicity. We need the wisdom to know the difference between church-destroying heresy, church-dividing disagreements that still permit evangelical fellowship, and intrachurch differences that require mutual admonition as well as forbearance.

Volumes in the SCDS series will not necessarily reflect the views of any particular editor, advisory board member, or the publisher—not even concerning "evangelical" boundaries. Volumes may approach perceived boundaries if their excellent engagement with Scripture deserves a hearing. But we are not seeking reform for reform's sake; we are more likely to publish volumes containing new explorations or presentations of traditional positions than radically revisionist proposals. Valuing the historic evangelical commitment to a deeply scriptural theology, we often find that perceived boundaries are appropriate—reflecting positions' biblical plausibility or lack thereof.

3. We seek fresh understanding of Christian doctrine **through creatively faithful engagement with Scripture**. To some fellow evangelicals and interested others today, we commend the classic evangelical commitment of *engaging Scripture*. To other fellow evangelicals today, we commend a contemporary aim to engage Scripture with *creative fidelity*. The church is to be always reforming—but always reforming according to the Word of God.

It is possible to acknowledge *sola Scriptura* in principle—Scripture as the final authority, the norming norm—without treating Scripture as theology's primary source. It is also possible to approach Scripture as theology's primary source in practice without doing that well.

The classic evangelical aspiration has been to mirror the form, not just the content, of Scripture as closely as possible in our theology. That aspiration has potential drawbacks: It can foster naive prooftexting, flatten biblical diversity, and stifle creative cultural engagement with a biblicist idiom. But we should not overreact to these drawbacks, falling prey to the temptation of paying mere lip service to *sola Scriptura* and replacing the Bible's primacy with the secondary idiom of the theologians' guild.

Thus in *Theology and the Mirror of Scripture* we propose a rubric for applying biblical theology to doctrinal judgments in a way that preserves evangelical freedom yet promotes the primacy of Scripture. At the ends of the spectrum, biblical theology can (1) rule out theological proposals that contradict scriptural judgments or cohere poorly with other concepts, and it can (5) require proposals that appeal to what is clear and central in Scripture. In between, it can (2) permit proposals that do not contradict Scripture, (3) support proposals that appeal creatively although indirectly or implicitly to Scripture, and (4) relate theological teaching to church life by using familiar scriptural language as much as possible. This spectrum offers considerable freedom for evangelical theology to mirror the biblical wisdom found in Christ with contextual creativity. Yet it simultaneously encourages evangelical theologians to reflect biblical wisdom not just in their judgments but also in the very idioms of their teaching.

4. We seek **fresh understanding of Christian doctrine**. We do not promote a singular method; we welcome proposals appealing to biblical theology, the history of interpretation, theological interpretation of Scripture, or still other approaches. We welcome projects that engage in detailed exegesis as well as those that appropriate broader biblical themes and patterns. Ultimately, we hope to promote relating Scripture to doctrinal understanding in material, not just formal, ways.

As noted above, the fresh understanding we seek may not involve altogether novel claims—which might well land in heresy! Again, in *Theology and the Mirror of Scripture* we offer an illustrative, nonexhaustive rubric for encouraging various forms of evangelical theological scholarship:

projects shaped primarily by (1) hermeneutics, (2) integrative biblical theology, (3) stewardship of the Great Tradition, (4) church dogmatics, (5) intellectual history, (6) analytic theism, (7) living witness, and (8) healing resistance. While some of these scholarly shapes probably fit the present series better than others, all of them reflect practices that can help evangelical theologians to make more faithfully biblical judgments and to generate more creatively constructive scholarship.

The volumes in the SCDS series will therefore reflect quite varied approaches. They will be similar in engaging one or more biblical texts as a key aspect of their contributions while going beyond exegetical recital or descriptive biblical theology, yet those biblical contributions themselves will be manifold.

5. We promote scriptural engagement **in dialogue with catholic tradition(s)**. A periodic evangelical weakness is relative lack of interest in the church's shared creedal heritage, in churches' particular confessions, and more generally in the history of dogmatic reflection. Beyond existing efforts to enhance understanding of themes and corpora in biblical theology, then, we hope to foster engagement with Scripture that bears on and learns from loci, themes, or crucial questions in classic dogmatics and contemporary systematic theology.

Series authors and editors will reflect several church affiliations and doctrinal backgrounds. Our goal is that such commitments would play a productive but not decisive hermeneutical role. Series volumes may focus on more generically evangelical approaches, or they may operate from within a particular tradition while engaging internal challenges or external objections.

We hope that both the diversity of our contributor list and the catholic engagement of our projects will continually expand. As important as those contextual factors are, though, these are most fundamentally studies in Christian *doctrine* and *Scripture*. Our goal is to promote and to publish constructive evangelical projects that study Scripture with creative fidelity and thereby offer fresh understanding of Christian doctrine. Various contexts and perspectives can help us study Scripture in that lively way, but they must remain secondary to theology's primary source and soul.

We do not study the mirror of Scripture for its own sake. Finding all the treasures of wisdom in Christ to be reflected there with the help of Christian doctrine, we come to know God and ourselves more truly. Thus encountering God's perfect instruction, we find the true freedom that is ours in the gospel, and we joyfully commend it to others through our own ministry of Scripture's teaching.

Introduction

A Particular and Privileged Logic

LIKE IT OR NOT, Leviticus is in the biblical canon. It is the common judgment of the church, led by the Spirit, that God has given Leviticus for our instruction. On a traditional doctrine of biblical inspiration, this means that God himself speaks to us in Leviticus. And if that is so, then the conclusion follows that, given the book's contents, God speaks to us there about atonement. In its own voice, Leviticus proclaims Jesus' work of atonement, the reality of what he has accomplished to bring us back to God. We are given knowledge of Christ in Leviticus. We should receive it.

Perhaps I am already claiming too much, and too quickly. Should we not rather say that Leviticus anticipated Christ, but anticipation is not revelation? Levitical sacrifice was indeed a metaphor that the early church used for understanding the accomplishment of Christ. But it was just that, a metaphor, and one among many. What's more, with each metaphor we must be mindful of both the similarities and the dissimilarities. The obedience unto death of Christ may have been similar to Levitical sacrifice, but it was obviously dissimilar as well. We should beware, then, of making too much of the sacrificial metaphor when considering the work of Christ.

Much of that may be true. It is not true, however, that Levitical sacrifice is a metaphor that the early church just happened to have at hand. It is not true that Christ's apostles used the imagery and language of Levitical sacrifice solely because of their Jewish context. The Levitical cult had been given by God.[1] As

---

[1] Throughout, I will use the word *cult* to refer to the system of rituals for approaching and worshiping God prescribed in Leviticus. Connotations of a secret, sectarian, and false religion are not intended.

I will argue below, it was given by God so that God's people might know the mystery of Christ (even if they could not yet name him) and his saving sacrifice. The Levitical cult was not just "a convenient metaphor for illuminating certain aspects of the atonement, but instead offers a particular and privileged logic under which the atonement may be made sense of."[2] That kind of claim is bound to be contentious. Consequently, its merit is probably best substantiated by demonstration. Thus, I submit this book.

This book intends to contribute to the doctrine of atonement by offering a theological exegesis of Levitical sacrifice, specifically the burnt offering (as prescribed in Lev 1:1-9).[3] It is concerned with what is sometimes called the *mechanism* of atonement, the rationale by which, to put it crudely, atonement "works." It presses into the details of the Levitical prescriptions for the burnt offering out of the conviction that, by God's providential ordering, something of the meaning of Christ's atoning work is disclosed to the church therein. Ultimately, it argues that the burnt offering teaches that atonement is made by way of what we might call filial satisfaction: Jesus makes satisfaction for sins as he enacts his identity as Son in and through his incarnate self-offering.

Such a work requires care, both close attention to the biblical text and sound theological reflection. A healthy dose of methodological awareness is therefore necessary. To that end, this introduction lays out the trajectory of the book and puts some important methodological guidelines in place.

The Case for Filial Satisfaction in Outline

This work offers a theological interpretation of the Levitical prescriptions for the עֹלָה, usually translated as "burnt offering," found in Leviticus 1.[4]

---

[2]Stephen R. Holmes, "Death in the Afternoon: Hebrews, Sacrifice, and Soteriology," in *The Epistle to the Hebrews and Christian Theology*, ed. Richard Bauckham et al. (Grand Rapids, MI: Eerdmans, 2009), 249.

[3]My reasons for focusing on the burnt offering will be explained more fully later in this introduction and again in chap. 4. For now, it is enough to say that the burnt offering is an atoning offering, at least according to Lev 1:4, and that it is simultaneously paradigmatic for the Levitical cult. The entire movement of the cult is summed up in this offering, and the result is atonement. The burnt offering is therefore uniquely suited to serve our understanding of how Christ fulfills the cultic way of atonement. And, in my judgment, it is underresearched. Thus, a robust theological reading of the burnt offering that speaks to the Christian doctrine of atonement seems needed.

[4]"Ascension offering" is often considered the better translation. It corresponds well to what happens in this offering: the entire victim ascends to the altar, and the smoke of its burning

Introduction   xix

Specifically, it seeks to identify the mechanism of atonement implicit in the prescriptions for this offering. As it reflects on the text of Leviticus 1:1-9, it employs some of the categories of narrative analysis—the categories of setting, plot, hero, action, and meaning. This approach, I believe, is invited by the text itself. Leviticus is a narrative, the continuation of the larger and theologically loaded narrative of Genesis–Exodus, and the meaning of Levitical ritual unfolds only when we read its instructions in light of that narrative. The categories of setting, plot, hero, action, and meaning highlight the point that Levitical ritual was an enactment of the pentateuchal story and its theology.[5] They therefore allow us to approach the text with the whole of that story and its theology in view, which in turn allows for a rich and canonically sensitive reading of the burnt offering.

Part of the contribution of this study lies in its focus on the burnt offering. One might question the decision to focus on the burnt offering; it is not often seen as important for atonement in the Levitical cult. One might think the sin and guilt offerings would be the more obvious choices here, as both are occasioned by the need for atonement due to some specific transgression. In defense, I have rather a lot to say and will reserve much of it for chapter four, when I finally give attention to Leviticus 1:3-9, in which we meet the ritual instructions for the burnt offering head-on. But here I should mention the primary reason for my focus on the burnt offering, which is the way the burnt offering seems to "encompass the whole ritual movement in itself."[6] The Levitical cult, in its various offerings, was a ritual expression of humanity's return to God, a movement back to the holy and blessed presence of God, and so a movement that required atonement. As the details of

---

ascends into heaven. See Roland de Vaux, *Studies in Old Testament Sacrifice* (Cardiff, UK: University of Wales Press, 1964), 27. It also appears to be true to the Hebrew term for this offering, which probably means "ascending." See Gordon Wenham, *The Book of Leviticus*, New International Commentary on the Old Testament (Grand Rapids, MI: Eerdmans, 1979), 52. I have chosen, however, to stick with the translation "burnt offering" in most instances, since this translation also highlights what, as we will see in a later chapter, is an essential element of the offering and is more customary.

[5]Frank H. Gorman, *Divine Presence and Community: A Commentary on the Book of Leviticus*, International Theological Commentary (Grand Rapids, MI: Eerdmans, 1997), 5.

[6]Michael L. Morales, "Atonement in Ancient Israel: The Whole Burnt Offering as Central to Israel's Cult," in *So Great a Salvation: A Dialogue on the Atonement in Hebrews*, ed. Jon C. Laansma, George H. Guthrie, and Cynthia Long Westfall, Library of New Testament Studies 516 (London: T&T Clark, 2019), 33.

Leviticus 1:1-9 will show, the עֹלָה was a summation of that movement with all its discrete steps along the path of return.⁷ All other offerings mentioned in Leviticus were to some extent enfolded into the burnt offering and can be thought of as accompaniments to the burnt offering. The burnt offering was the "fundamental sacrifice," and "all the other sacrifices . . . are virtually incorporated into it."⁸ Surely, then, this offering is worthy of attention and worthy of being treated as an atoning offering.

In my study of this offering, I move more or less verse by verse through Leviticus 1:1-9, attending to what can be thought of as the story of Levitical sacrifice. As my reading progresses, a thesis emerges. The mechanism of the burnt offering, I argue, is one of satisfaction and recapitulation through filial substitution—or, more concisely, one of filial satisfaction. At the heart of the burnt offering is an act of substitution. The substitute, importantly, is one who ultimately proves to be a true son of God. By the substitution of this true son in place of the offeror (who fails to be son), God is satisfied and the offeror is restored, having the guilt and corruption of his original sin forgiven and cleansed. There is in this offering both forgiveness and healing, correction and perfection. There are, in other words, notes of both satisfaction and recapitulation in the burnt offering and in Christ's fulfillment thereof, and both are important to the mechanism of atonement in this offering.⁹

Further, I argue that, according to Leviticus 1:1-9, it is ultimately Christ's identity as the incarnate Son of God that allows him to accomplish the work of atonement. Seeing Christ's atoning work through the lens of the burnt

---

⁷Michael L. Morales, *Who Shall Ascend the Mountain of the Lord? A Biblical Theology of the Book of Leviticus*, New Studies in Biblical Theology (Downers Grove, IL: InterVarsity Press, 2015), 123.
⁸John Kleinig, *Leviticus* (St. Louis: Concordia, 2003), 40.
⁹"Correction and perfection" is a gloss given to Irenaeus's concept of recapitulation in Eric Osborne, *Irenaeus of Lyons* (Cambridge: Cambridge University Press, 2001), 97-98. Osborne states that, according to Irenaeus's usage, "recapitulation, summing up, does four things. It corrects and perfects; it inaugurates and consummates a new humanity." Importantly, he continues, Irenaeus does not separate the redemption and perfection of humanity, an emphasis that grows out of his insistence that one and the same God is the Creator and Redeemer of humanity. Even when I do not always use the language of recapitulation in later chapters, partly because of the intimidating complexity of the concept (which Osborne also highlights), the basic idea of recapitulation as correction and perfection is often applicable to my argument.
By using the shorthand "filial satisfaction," I am to some degree emphasizing satisfaction over recapitulation. That emphasis comes out of my reading of the details of the burnt offering. Nevertheless, I do not wish to lose sight of the concept of recapitulation. As I hope my exposition of the story of sacrifice makes clear, the notion of recapitulation should be understood to be embedded in the word *filial*.

offering allows us to see more clearly how it is that his sacrifice extends from his identity, that is, how his *person* is the key to his *work*. The same point can be made from exegesis of the New Testament, of course. But it cannot be made in quite the same way. It is not merely the case that the New Testament "cast[s] light on the dark shadows of the Old [Testament]," though, in many respects this is true. But it is also true that "the New [Testament] finds a needed deepening and elaboration from the Old [Testament]."[10] The Levitical witness adds something unique to our understanding of the work of Christ, and it is the purpose of this book to highlight something of that uniqueness.

This study, I hope, will therefore not only illuminate the meaning of the Levitical burnt offering but also make a contribution to our understanding of the doctrine of atonement by showing why offering himself in sacrifice was fitting for the incarnate Son, and why the incarnate Son's sacrifice would be atoning. The burnt offering demonstrates that the efficacy of Christ's atoning sacrifice lies in the depths of the central Christian mystery, the perfection and plentitude of God's triune life.[11] It makes this demonstration in a unique way. Thus, it enriches our understanding of the mystery of atonement.

The argument will proceed in the following manner. Beginning with consideration of the Levitical cult as a whole, chapter one will give its attention to Leviticus 1:1 and consider the setting of Levitical sacrifice. Here I will identify the ways in which the opening sentence of Leviticus recalls the narrative and theological context of YHWH's call to Moses from the tent of meeting, and I will begin to note how our reading of the burnt offering might be influenced by the character of YHWH and the history of his dealings with Israel as recounted in Genesis–Exodus. In chapter two, I begin to advance my thesis more directly by outlining what I believe to be the plot of Levitical sacrifice. Acknowledging that the Levitical offerings in general and the burnt offering in particular were presented with a variety of motives and on diverse occasions, I will argue that the procedural order of Levitical

---

[10] Gary A. Anderson, *That I May Dwell Among Them: Incarnation and Atonement in the Tabernacle Narrative* (Grand Rapids, MI: Eerdmans, 2023), 194.

[11] For reflection on this theme, see John Webster, "'It Was the Will of the Lord to Bruise Him': Soteriology and the Doctrine of God," in *God Without Measure*, vol. 1, *God and the Works of God* (London: T&T Clark, 2016), 152.

sacrifice nevertheless gives us the outline of a single plot running throughout the cult, a plot of return to God through death. I will also argue that this plot is uniquely visible in the burnt offering, which serves as a summary of the cultic movement. Chapter three will then add to the argument of chapter two by identifying the hero of the Levitical story. There, I will argue that, as Leviticus envisions it, it is specifically the son of God who returns to God through death in sacrifice, and I will further argue that Leviticus 1 shows us something of why it was so fitting for the eternal Son to make this return by the offering of his own body.

In chapters four and five I will give full attention to the burnt offering itself and the way in which Jesus Christ fulfills the mechanism and movement of atonement therein. In chapter four, I offer a reading of Leviticus 1:3-9. I suggest that the burnt offering was given as a means of atonement for the offeror's original sin, the guilt and corruption that disqualifies him for the presence and service of the LORD. Further, as I follow the movements of the ritual and its culmination in God's delighted reception of the offering as a "pleasing aroma," I present the proposal that the burnt offering effected satisfaction and recapitulation through filial substitution. Chapter five follows from this argument. I note a number of ways in which the New Testament, especially Hebrews, applies the logic of the burnt offering to the atoning work of Christ, and I press my case that the burnt offering leads us to see the work of Christ as an enactment in human flesh of his eternal relationship to God the Father. I will then conclude with a brief word on what I believe this study accomplishes.

Before proceeding along these lines, however, it will be helpful to say a few things about some of the theological convictions informing my work.

THEOLOGICAL PROLEGOMENA

Given the outline of this book, there are several matters that need attention at the outset.

Typology. First, a word on my understanding of typology is necessary. The argument of this book depends on treating the burnt offering as a type of the greater, single, eternally effective atoning sacrifice offered by Jesus Christ. To identify the Levitical sacrifices as types of the sacrifice of Christ is a long-standing tradition in Christian theology. The typological relation

Introduction   xxiii

has not always been clearly defined, however. Following Benjamin Ribbens, I read the Levitical sacrifices as prospective, sacramental types of the sacrifice of Christ. Here, *prospective* is opposed to *retrospective*. In the latter, the typological relation is constructed as a way of making sense of something new; the new (the antitype) is construed as analogous to the old (the type) so that we may more easily appropriate it. In the former, the typological relation is anticipated in the old, which is appointed as a prophetic witness to the new.[12] Ribbens argues that the author of the epistle to the Hebrews, contrary to what is sometimes claimed, treats the Levitical sacrifices prospectively. The sacrifices of the old covenant were ordained by God as a prophetic pattern that Christ would fulfill.[13] If that is so, then the Levitical cult was something more than a conceptual tool the New Testament church happened to have at hand for understanding the work of Christ.[14] Instead, as said above, it is by God's design a "particular and privileged logic under which the atonement [accomplished by Christ] may be made sense of."[15] Thus, the logic of Leviticus's atoning sacrifices, insofar as it can be discerned, can and should inform our understanding of the atoning logic at work in the life, death, and resurrection of Christ, what I am calling the mechanism of atonement.

As Ribbens adds, however, the Levitical types are not only prospective but also sacramental types of the work of Christ. This too will inform my reading of the burnt offering. To say a type is sacramental is to say that it is divinely appointed to represent or picture the antitype and that it derives efficacy from the antitype.[16] In Ribbens's words, "God established [the Levitical sacrifices] as a means of achieving the efficacy achieved in the heavenly sanctuary," that is, the efficacy of the priestly work of the risen and ascended Christ.[17] Positing a derivative yet real atoning efficacy of the

---

[12] Benjamin J. Ribbens, *Levitical Sacrifice and Heavenly Cult in Hebrews* (Boston: de Gruyter, 2016), 15, 14.
[13] Ribbens, *Levitical Sacrifice and Heavenly Cult*, 162.
[14] Contra, e.g., Ingolf U. Dalferth, "Christ Died for Us: Reflections on the Sacrificial Language of Salvation," in *Sacrifice and Redemption: Durham Essays in Theology*, ed. Stephen W. Sykes (Cambridge: Cambridge University Press, 1991), 302.
[15] Holmes, "Death in the Afternoon," 249.
[16] In my understanding, it is especially the derivative efficacy of Levitical sacrifice that warrants the label "*sacramental* types." Something of the efficacy of the signified (Christ's offering) was present in the sign (Levitical offerings).
[17] Ribbens, *Levitical Sacrifice and Heavenly Cult*, 230.

Levitical sacrifices is significant for the way we read those sacrifices, for it grants an integrity to the Levitical rituals that might otherwise be denied, an integrity that makes studying the details of those rituals meaningful for the doctrine of atonement.

The opposite of a "real" efficacy in this case would be the kind of efficacy implied by the Scotist doctrine of acceptation. According to this doctrine, there is no inherent value in sacrifice, either that of Christ or of the Levitical cult. What gives sacrifice its efficacy is the (arbitrary) will of God to accept it. In this case, there is no logic inherent in sacrifice, at least not one that God would recognize and honor. To be sure, there is a grain of truth in this view; it warns us against the idea that sacrifice has power *over* God. However, this need not mean that sacrifice could not have an efficacy *from* God that has an ontological basis in the creative and redemptive acts of God.[18] What I argue in this study is that Levitical sacrifice had an efficacy derived from the sacrifice of Christ, the efficacy of which was not itself without ontological basis in God's creative act through the Son. Recognizing this sacramental efficacy of Levitical sacrifice, along with its prospective typological function, gives consideration of the efficacy of the burnt offering a significance for understanding the sacrifice of Christ that it would not otherwise hold.

Atonement. Second, a word on the definition of atonement. A problem sometimes encountered in conversations around atonement is that we do not always use the term consistently or even agree on what it means. Sometimes, the term is used more or less as a synonym for *reconciliation.* Eleonore Stump provides an example. With a nod to the etymological origin of the term in Tyndale's neologism, "at-one-ment," Stump registers her intention to employ the term in a "more neutral sense," that is, in a sense that connotes "the resumption of friendly relations" and avoids the idea of "placating an offended God by the gift of a bloody sacrifice." Stump therefore writes the

---

[18]Here I am borrowing an argument from Oliver O'Donovan, *Resurrection and Moral Order: An Outline for Evangelical Ethics,* 2nd ed. (Grand Rapids, MI: Eerdmans, 1994), in which he argues that the choice between a divinely revealed ethic and one with an ontological basis in creation (which consists of living "with the grain of creation") is a false choice (19). The same can be applied to sacrifice. Levitical sacrifice was not only appointed by God but was also a proper response to creation on the part of Israel, a means of living in accord with the structures of the world. This is seen most clearly when we consider sacrifice as an act of gratitude.

Introduction   XXV

word as "at onement" at times "in an effort to call attention to the broader meaning of the term."¹⁹

Other thinkers would take issue with Stump on this point, noting that, with all proper theological qualifications set in place, the placation of God is, traditionally, precisely what *atonement* means. To speak of atonement is to presuppose that there is a real obstacle to reconciliation, namely, sin and its accompanying guilt. Atonement is an act that somehow negates or compensates for sin and thereby effects reconciliation. Thus, Oliver Crisp: "[Atonement] is about the reconciling of two parties that are estranged, especially God and human beings. But there is more to it than that. It also has the connotation of reparation, that is, the repairing of some breach, the restitution of some wrong done."²⁰ On this definition, atonement is not reconciliation but that which opens the door to reconciliation. Atonement is the compensation for an offense that allows for reconciliation.

Not surprisingly, more technical definitions are offered by biblical scholars, particularly those with interest in the Old Testament's sacrificial system. The debate most relevant to this study concerns the definition of a Hebrew term often translated as "atonement," כִּפֶּר. In recent decades, this debate has largely been driven by the work of Jacob Milgrom, a Jewish scholar who has argued that in Leviticus, כִּפֶּר refers to the purification of the sanctuary and sancta from the defilement of sin. Impurity was directly harmful only for the sancta, Milgrom argues, not for persons. When the sanctuary was polluted, it threatened to drive God "out of his sanctuary and out of [the Israelites'] lives." Accordingly, a purification rite was needed if God would continue to dwell with his people. It is the action of this sort of rite that is denoted by כִּפֶּר. The verb therefore means "to purify" or "to purge," and, importantly, the direct object of this verb is always a (sacred) thing, never a person.²¹

Milgrom's work has elicited a strong and varied response, much of which has come by way of appreciative critique. Roy Gane, a student of Milgrom's, has argued that, contrary to Milgrom's analysis, persons can in fact be the

---

[19] Eleonore Stump, *Atonement* (Oxford: Oxford University Press, 2018), 7.
[20] Oliver Crisp, *Approaching the Atonement: The Reconciling Work of Christ* (Downers Grove, IL: IVP Academic, 2020), 15.
[21] Jacob Milgrom, *Leviticus 1–16: A New Translation with Introduction and Commentary*, Anchor Yale Bible 3 (New Haven, CT: Yale University Press, 2009), 43, 1080, 1040.

object of כִּפֶּר in Levitical rituals. Gane demonstrates that both physical impurities and moral faults are purified from offerors by rites of atonement and that the purification effected by such rites can mean the removal of guilt.[22] Jay Sklar has added that the purification of sinners has a ransoming effect. He garners biblical evidence to show that sin both pollutes and endangers the sinner, since impurity provokes God's wrath. Atonement is therefore both a "purifying ransom" and a "ransoming purgation."[23] In other words, Sklar is saying that there are notes of both compensation and cleaning in the Hebrew כִּפֶּר.[24]

In my judgment, Gane and Sklar point in a helpful direction. Accordingly, I define atonement as an act of cleansing and compensation that qualifies a sinner for the presence and service of God. Similar to Stump's contention, I hold that atonement is that which allows us to draw near to God and live in union with him. This much can be seen, I believe, in Leviticus itself. A good example is found in the consecration of the priests in Leviticus 8. There we read that Aaron and his sons present sin offerings for atonement as part of their consecration. Indeed, consecration and atonement are tightly bound together in this ceremony; in Leviticus 8:15, we read that the altar was consecrated "to make atonement for it." Atonement and devotion to God—both life in his presence and employment in his service—seem to go hand in hand.

Nevertheless, Crisp seems to be right in insisting that atonement is not merely the union between God and human beings but that which is done to bring about that union. Leviticus seems to confirm this on every page. While atonement is clearly the gift of God in Leviticus, it is nevertheless mediated through rituals that, God insists, must be carried out in a particular way. The impression given at all times is that there are real obstacles to communion between humanity and God that must be dealt with in a precise manner. Most often, the manner of dealing with the obstacles created by sin has to do with either cleansing or compensation, or perhaps both. Take the sin

---

[22]Roy Gane, *Cult and Character: Purification Offerings, Day of Atonement, and Theodicy* (Winona Lake, IN: Eisenbrauns, 2005), 106-43.

[23]Jay Sklar, *Sin, Impurity, Sacrifice, Atonement: The Priestly Conceptions*, Hebrew Bible Monographs 2 (Sheffield, UK: Sheffield University Press, 2005), 182.

[24]At least as it is used in Leviticus and other priestly texts. There is debate about whether כִּפֶּר has a consistent meaning outside the priestly text, about which one may consult the forthcoming study of Chad Hardy of Trinity Evangelical Divinity School.

offering, for instance. It is clearly presented in order to cleanse or purify on some occasions (e.g., when offered for ritual impurity after childbirth). But it can also seem to take on the connotation of "compensation," as in Leviticus 5:5-7, when it is said to be offered for an אָשָׁם, an offering of reparation.[25] This note of compensation is in line with Sklar's definition of atonement, which I am amending slightly. My suggestion is that cleansing and compensation are the means by which sin was negated and the sinner was qualified for God's presence. Thus, in what follows I will consider atonement to be an act of compensation and cleansing that qualifies a sinner for the presence and service of God.

The mechanism of atonement. Third, a word about the language of the "mechanism" of atonement. Gustaf Aulén objects that the concern with the mechanism of atonement evident in the "Latin theory" is rationalistic and at odds with the more "dramatic" account of the New Testament.[26] J. I. Packer sympathizes, noting that Reformed orthodoxy, preoccupied with *how* atonement is made, sometimes treated the doctrine of atonement "more like a conundrum than a confession."[27] To others, *mechanism* might easily connote an impersonal or even technological process, a manipulation of forces; atonement might be thought to depend on a religious technique, as in pagan religions, not on the love of God, as the Christian gospel claims.

Despite these objections and the valid concerns expressed therein, I take concern with describing the mechanism of atonement to be an exercise of "faith seeking understanding," the end of which is to "take delight in the understanding and contemplation" of the truths we confess.[28] In my understanding, "the mechanism of atonement" is shorthand for "the logic or rationale of atoning efficacy." Why does sacrifice make atonement? If that is a legitimate question, then so also is investigation into the mechanism of atonement.

---

[25]This is how Milgrom has translated אָשָׁם, and many scholars have followed his lead. "Compensation" is how the ESV translates it. The same term is later translated as "guilt or reparation offering."

[26]Gustaf Aulén, *Christus Victor: An Historical Study of the Three Main Types of the Idea of Atonement*, trans. A. G. Hebert (repr., Eugene, OR: Wipf & Stock, 2003).

[27]J. I. Packer, "What Did the Cross Achieve?," *Tyndale Bulletin* 25 (1974): 5.

[28]Anselm, *Why God Became Man*, in *Anselm of Canterbury: The Major Works*, ed. Brian Davies and G. R. Evans (Oxford: Oxford University Press, 1998), 1.1 (265).

To be sure, we should be on guard here. The mystery of atonement is not unreasonable or irrational. But it is, in an important sense, beyond reason, *suprarational*. T. F. Torrance is not wrong when he asserts, "The nature of [Christ's] work was unutterable. . . . The innermost mystery of atonement and intercession remains mystery."[29] When considering the work of redemption, then, we must heed Hilary's warning that "these deeds of God, wrought in a manner beyond our comprehension, cannot, I repeat, be understood by our natural faculties," and we must beware of judging God's work by "the limits which bound our common reason."[30]

What Hilary's and Torrance's warnings should alert us to, however, is the mistake of trying to solve the "problem" of the doctrine of atonement, not legitimate endeavors to clarify its mystery. As Thomas Weinandy has argued, the error of heretics has often come in treating the mysteries of the faith as problems to be solved. Weinandy points to the example of Arius, who resolved the "problem" of affirming both God's unity and the Son's deity but did so at the cost of undermining the latter, thereby dissolving the mystery of the incarnation. Denial of some revealed truth, Weinandy argues, is the inevitable outcome of treating theological mysteries as problems to be solved, and this is why some theologians rightly show caution when it comes to explaining how it is that Christ has made atonement: better to silently rejoice in the mystery than explain away its reality. Nevertheless, silence is not always the only option. It is possible to *clarify mysteries* without solving problems, to gain insight that yields clearer understanding while deepening, not dissolving, the recognition of mystery.[31] As Joshua McNall states, "Mystery and mechanism must 'kiss' within atonement doctrine, as they do with the New Testament."[32] It is in this spirit that I look into the mechanism of atonement, endeavoring to sharpen, to however small a degree, our vision of the mystery of atonement.

---

[29] Thomas F. Torrance, *Atonement: The Person and Work of Christ*, ed. Robert T. Walker (Downers Grove, IL: IVP Academic, 2009), 2.

[30] Hilary of Poitiers, *On the Trinity*, ed. W. Sanday, trans. E. W. Watson and L. Pullen, in *A Select Library of Nicene and Post-Nicene Fathers of the Christian Church*, Second Series, ed. Philip Schaff and Henry Wace (Grand Rapids, MI: Eerdmans, 1989), vol. 9, 1.13.

[31] Thomas Weinandy, *Does God Suffer?* (Notre Dame, IN: University of Notre Dame Press, 2000), 33-35, 36.

[32] Joshua McNall, *The Mosaic of Atonement: An Integrated Approach to Christ's Work* (Grand Rapids, MI: Zondervan, 2019), 141.

A final (and important) note here: when considering the mechanism of atonement, it is necessary to make a distinction between mechanisms of accomplishment and mechanisms of relationship.[33] When we make the confession that Christ died for our sins, we claim both that Christ has done something remarkable and that he has done it for "us." Christ has acted, and he has acted for me. Both an achievement and a relationship are thus implied, and both are necessary for atonement. The importance of this distinction is that the identification of a mechanism of atonement requires us to give account of both the achievement and the relationship: What, exactly, has Christ accomplished, and what does it have to do with me? Shortcomings in accounts of atonement can often be exposed by noting how an account fails to answer one of these questions. For example, Aulén's *Christus Victor* account seems to fail to give a satisfactory account of the mechanism of relationship, since it does little to explain how Christ's victory becomes the Christian's victory. It may also fail to give a satisfactory account of the mechanism of achievement, since the victory as Aulén describes does not seem to address the obstacle of our guilt. One might disagree with each of these examples, of course. But regardless, the point holds that both an achievement and a relationship are required for vicarious atonement, and in this study I will be concerned with both.

Satisfaction. Next, it is necessary to indicate what is meant by *satisfaction*. Traditionally, the concept of satisfaction has legal overtones.[34] Satisfaction has reference to God's justice and to his law. The law stipulates what God is owed; sin is a failure to give what is owed; satisfaction is made by some sort of payment of this debt.[35] While I do not wish to diminish the tradition of

---

[33]Perhaps this terminology could be improved. But the general idea is that vicarious atonement, a proposition to which Christian theology is committed, requires both that the vicar represent another and that he actually accomplish something on behalf of that other. Both the relationship and the achievement are essential, and yet they are clearly distinct from one another. This distinction, I believe, can help clarify what we mean when we speak of a mechanism of atonement.

[34]It is often pointed out that the language of satisfaction was largely introduced into Christian theological vocabulary by Tertullian, who had been a lawyer and therefore drew on the language and concepts of Roman jurisprudence in his thinking about penance (the original context of the language of satisfaction). See, e.g., Trevor Hart, *In Him Was Life: The Person and Work of Christ* (Waco, TX: Baylor University Press, 2019), 117.

[35]This is, of course, Anselm's way of construing satisfaction, but it is one he holds in common with much of the Christian tradition.

thinking of satisfaction as a legal concept, I do believe we can speak of other aspects of satisfaction besides the legal.[36] And, in fact, the text of Leviticus invites us to consider those other aspects. Specifically, these aspects are the aesthetic (something that elicits God's delight) and the teleological (something that realizes or represents the fulfillment of God's purposes for creation). Regarding the aesthetic, I will note in chapter four that God promises to receive the burnt offering with what seems to be an expression of delight, which would indicate that the burnt offering is something more (though not necessarily less) than a payment.[37] If so, then it seems that the burnt offering made atonement as something that delighted God on behalf of the offeror; and so too did the self-offering of Jesus.[38]

We can be more even confident, I believe, in affirming a teleological aspect of satisfaction. In a study of the concept of satisfaction in medieval theologians, J. Patout Burns states, "Satisfaction involves three aspects of the sin of Adam: the insult shown to God, the injury done to man, and the punishment imposed for sin." He clarifies that the "injury done to man" may be considered as "God's loss of the elect who were to fill the heavenly city, or as man's own loss of his eternal goal, or as the disorder introduced into the universe by the corruption of human nature." For many medieval theologians, then, the concept of satisfaction included the idea of restoration, and it even gave a nod to the fulfillment of the human telos, as evidenced by a statement from Alexander of Hales: "The satisfier must re-establish human nature's relationship to God as its goal, which was

---

[36]Trevor Hart, in an essay on satisfaction, argues that if we are to take seriously God's decision to entrust the message of salvation to the "limits, potential, and variability" of human language, then we should be willing to consider whether a word such as *satisfaction* might mean "something more and other than the first theological users of the term were able to appreciate" (*In Him Was Life*, 116-17). I want to be very careful here, as I think Hart's suggestions can potentially take us far off course. Nevertheless, I do think it is worth considering whether *satisfaction* as we use it in the doctrine of atonement can mean more than a strict satisfaction of justice, and I suggest possibilities for what more it could mean in this study.

[37]For the delight of the recipient is often what distinguishes gift from payment. See Ephraim Radner, "Practice Without Purpose," *First Things*, March 2023, 71-72. The insistence that the burnt offering makes satisfaction in a way not encompassed by the concept of payment also fits with the fact that the burnt offering seems to be used as a gift of thanksgiving to God on some occasions.

[38]Hart makes an interesting argument that that satisfaction given to God in Jesus' self-offering stems from "the reciprocation of [God's] own holy love from the creature's side," along with a creaturely reflection of the divine nature and character (*In Him Was Life*, 140-41).

disrupted by Adam's sin."[39] The medieval theologians seem to be suggesting that God is satisfied when his good purposes for creation are realized.[40] In this, I believe, we should follow them.

In summary, we can say that Christ's sacrifice "satisfies not only God's justice but the sum total of God's perfections," including the wisdom by which he appoints human beings to their telos and the love by which he determines that telos to be communion with himself.[41] The key to this satisfaction, I will argue, is Christ's filial obedience, which honors God's law, images God's goodness, and honors God's intentions for humanity. Thus, it is a distinctively filial account of satisfaction that I will be offering in what follows.

Theological exegesis. Finally, a word on theological exegesis. "Theological exegesis" is notoriously difficult to define.[42] But its presuppositions, intuitions, and habits can be described in the following way.

A theology of exegesis. First, theological exegesis depends in no small part on a *theology of* exegesis. This requires a word on the ontology of Scripture. A theological presupposition at work throughout this study is that Scripture—by which I mean the sixty-six books of the Old and New Testaments that Protestants accept as canonical—is the covenantal self-revelation of the triune God. To label these books as the self-revelation of God is to identify their ultimate origin: they are inspired by God. The Holy Spirit spoke through the prophets who penned these books, so that the result of the process of authorship (however complicated that might have been) is not merely a human word about God but God's address to humanity. It is by the

---

[39] J. Patout Burns, "The Concept of Satisfaction in Medieval Redemption Theory," *Theological Studies* 36, no. 2 (May 1975): 286, 294.

[40] See Adam J. Johnson, "Atonement: The Shape and State of the Doctrine," in *T&T Clark Companion to Atonement*, ed. Adam J. Johnson (London: Bloomsbury T&T Clark, 2017), 3: "The mission of Jesus involves overcoming the reality and consequences of sin while simultaneously bringing to completion God's creative purposes." In another work, Johnson affirms that the work of "bringing to completion" should also be considered an act of satisfaction, since it satisfies "God's intention to share with us the divine life"; Adam J. Johnson, *Atonement: A Guide for the Perplexed* (London: Bloomsbury T&T Clark, 2015), 132.

[41] Kevin J. Vanhoozer, "Redemption Accomplished: Atonement," in *The Oxford Handbook of Reformed Theology*, ed. Michael Allen and Scott R. Swain (Oxford: Oxford University Press, 2020), 488.

[42] The best introduction to theological exegesis of which I am aware is Daniel Treier, *Introducing Theological Interpretation of Scripture: Recovering a Christian Practice* (Grand Rapids, MI: Baker Academic, 2008).

will of the God who desires to reveal himself to humanity that these books say what they say, and it is by that same will that they have been given to the church for the sake of its knowledge of God. They are therefore to be received as the very Word of God (see 1 Thess 2:13).[43]

To label the canonical books as covenantal is to identify their role and scope. In the canonical books, God speaks to his church for the sake of binding it to himself in covenant. God has "commissioned just these texts to play a vital and authoritative role in the triune economy of covenantal communication whereby the Lord dispenses his light (i.e., revelation, knowledge, truth) and life (i.e., redemption, fellowship, salvation)."[44] Presenting Jesus Christ (the "ultimate content" of Scripture) to his church in words inspired and empowered by the Spirit for that task, God the Father pours out his grace for his church in the pages of the canon, making them Holy Scripture.[45] The canon belongs to "the economy of trinitarian, covenantal self-communication and communion;" it is "one of the preeminent means whereby the triune God communicates himself to us and holds communion with us." Scripture's role, then, is covenantal: "communicative fellowship" between God and his people.[46] And so too is Scripture's scope: God's presentation of Jesus Christ, through whom we are reconciled to God and bound to him in covenant.[47]

Importantly, the same role and scope is to be affirmed of the books of both the Old and New Testaments. Both Testaments, and each book therein, are authorized by God as witnesses to Jesus Christ. This affirmation is of no small importance for how a book such as Leviticus is to be read. If Leviticus is Christian Scripture, a text in which God presents Christ to us, then it should be read as a guide to Christian faith and practice. And if this is so, then, as Christopher Seitz argues, the Old Testament must be read as something more

---

[43]John Frame has called this the "personal word model" of Scripture. See Frame, *The Doctrine of the Word of God*, vol. 4 of *A Theology of Lordship* (Phillipsburg, NJ: P&R, 2010), 3-7.

[44]Kevin J. Vanhoozer, "Holy Scripture," in *Christian Dogmatics: Reformed Theology for the Church Catholic*, ed. Michael Allen and Scott R. Swain (Grand Rapids, MI: Baker Academic, 2016), 44.

[45]See J. I. Packer, *God Has Spoken* (Downers Grove, IL: InterVarsity Press, 1979), 97. Packer defines Scripture as "God the Father preaching God the Son in the power of God the Holy Ghost." Vanhoozer describes Christ as the "ultimate content" of Scripture ("Holy Scripture," 31).

[46]Scott Swain, *Trinity, Reading, and Revelation: A Theological Introduction to the Bible and Its Interpretation* (London: Bloomsbury T&T Clark, 2011), 7, 9.

[47]Vanhoozer, "Holy Scripture," 39.

than "background literature for the NT." Seitz notes, "The Christian church at its origin received the Scriptures of Israel as the sole authoritative witness.... These Scriptures taught the church what to believe about God: who God was; how to understand God's relationship to creation, Israel, and the nations; how to worship God; and what manner of life was enjoined in grace and in judgment." Though the church read the Old Testament in accord with the apostolic testimony, that testimony did not negate or dilute the distinctive theological contribution of the Old Testament. Because the God revealed to us in Jesus Christ truly spoke in the Old Testament, Seitz reasons, the Old Testament has its own integrity as a witness to Christ, a witness that does not wholly depend on the use the New Testament makes of the Old Testament.[48] The Old Testament "retains its theological voice as a witness to the Triune God." While the Old Testament, to be sure, should always be read *with* the New Testament, we should beware of "maximal coordination" of the Old Testament and New Testament, which inevitably results in the loss of the Old Testament's "discrete voice" as a witness to Jesus Christ. If it is to be honored as Christian Scripture, then the Old Testament must be allowed to make its own (Christian) theological voice heard. It must, that is, be allowed to function as a "major doctrinal source for Christian reflection on God."[49]

A Christian reading of Leviticus is therefore not wholly dependent on the New Testament's use of Leviticus. So, as Christian Scripture, when Leviticus speaks about atonement, it is speaking ultimately of the atoning work of Christ, even if it is doing so by way of shadowy figures. Importantly, it is not necessarily saying the exact same thing the New Testament says about the atoning work of Christ, even when the New Testament draws on Levitical rituals and imagery. What Leviticus means for our understanding of the work of Christ is not reducible to what the epistle to the Hebrews says about the Day of Atonement, for example. More to the point of the present study, the significance of the עֹלָה for Christian atonement theology may go beyond connections made in the New Testament between the עֹלָה and the work of Christ. We

---

[48]Christopher R. Seitz, *The Character of Christian Scripture: The Significance of a Two-Testament Bible* (Grand Rapids, MI: Baker Academic, 2011), 11, 17. Seitz is here, as elsewhere, repeating the arguments of Brevard Childs, who made much of the "continuing integrity of the Old Testament witness" to Jesus Christ. See Childs, *Biblical Theology of the Old and New Testaments: Theological Reflection on the Christian Bible* (Minneapolis: Fortress, 1992), 78.

[49]Seitz, *Character of Christian Scripture*, 21, 62, 90.

have room to develop the typological relationship to a greater degree than the New Testament does. To be sure, the New Testament's use of the Old Testament sets the trajectory for our own reading of the Old Testament. It does not, however, exhaust the meaning of the Old Testament for the Christian church.

The exegesis found in the following pages will be theological in that it reads Leviticus in light of the preceding. That is, it reads Leviticus as a word from the triune God and about the triune God for the sake of the church's theological instruction.[50] This means it will be somewhat less concerned about questions that often preoccupy historical-critical scholars, though it will not ignore them altogether. Specifically, it will be less concerned with hashing out the nature of the influence of other ancient Near Eastern cultures on Israel's rituals than historical-critical scholars justifiably are, not because the question is unimportant but because the more pressing theological question concerns the witness of Leviticus to the being and act of God. For the same reason, this work's exegesis will be less concerned with questions of the text's composition history than historical-critical scholars and more concerned with the current form of the text God has given the church means for our knowledge of Jesus Christ.

Making theological sense of Levitical ritual. From this, one can see that this work's exegesis of Leviticus will find common cause with much premodern Christian exegesis; it will seek to read Leviticus as a very Christian book. Nevertheless, this study will not read much like a premodern commentary of Leviticus 1. Specifically, I will not follow the premodern tendency to read Leviticus as a book of isolated symbols, the referents of which are primarily the virtues of a Christian soul.[51] My intention is not to disparage such readings, which played an important role in the church for many, many years. However, as Ephraim Radner suggests, premodern readings too often led to a reduction of the Levitical text to either a "handbook of Christian tropes" (when it is read through a medieval sacramental lens) or a shabbily arranged collection of moral allegories (when read with Protestant concerns).[52]

---

[50]This reflects my conviction that theological interpretation is better thought of as a set of governing assumptions concerning the nature and ends of exegesis than as an exegetical method.
[51]For examples, see Joseph T. Lienhard, ed., *Exodus, Leviticus, Numbers, Deuteronomy*, Ancient Christian Commentary on Scripture Old Testament 3 (Downers Grove, IL: IVP Academic, 2001).
[52]Ephraim Radner, *Leviticus*, Brazos Theological Commentary on the Bible (Grand Rapids, MI: Brazos, 2008), 24.

What I pursue in these passages is therefore something different from most premodern exegesis. Following scholars such as Frank Gorman and Michael Morales, I will emphasize the role of the narrative context of Leviticus in understanding Levitical ritual.[53] The meaning of a ritual act prescribed in Leviticus is seldom explicated in the text. But that does not mean it is inexplicable. The ritual acts and symbols are not arbitrary but are dense with meaning derived from the worldview of the community, a worldview determined by the mighty works of God in Israel's election and redemption.[54] Gorman argues that Leviticus stands as the center of the pentateuchal history and "looks back" to four moments in the pentateuchal narrative: the creation of the cosmos, the promise to Abraham, the exodus from Egypt, and the ratification of the covenant at Sinai. The rituals of Leviticus are a "means of actualizing and 'bodying forth' the story" told in Genesis and Exodus, and the offerings can be read as means of "enacting" creation, holiness, and covenant, the major themes of the pentateuchal story as Gorman understands it.[55] While I will make my own proposals about how the text of Leviticus recalls this narrative in its ritual prescriptions, I nevertheless follow Gorman's lead in asserting that the ritual for the burnt offering recapitulates the narrative of Genesis–Exodus and that the church's reading of this ritual as a "word of life" depends on our ability to read it as such.[56]

As said above, however, the best argument for the kind of reading I am proposing is in its demonstration. And so it is to the text of Leviticus 1 that I now turn.

---

[53]Frank H. Gorman, *Ideology of Ritual: Space, Time and Status in the Priestly Theology*, Journal for the Study of the Old Testament Supplement Series 91 (Sheffield, UK: Sheffield Academic Press, 1990); Gorman, *Divine Presence and Community*; Morales, *Who Shall Ascend*.

[54]To speak of the worldview of the ancient Israelite community is to raise the question of the role of the ancient Near Eastern background. I believe Leviticus communicates a worldview that is not simply a reflection of its ancient Near Eastern context but is instead shaped by the saving acts and speech of God. Consequently, it is a worldview that in important respects is shared by authors of the NT and even the postapostolic church. We might even say that while the world picture of Leviticus is largely that of the ancient Near Eastern, the worldview of Leviticus is a Christian worldview. For this distinction, see C. John Collins, *Genesis 1–4: A Linguistic, Literary, and Theological Commentary* (Phillipsburg, NJ: P&R, 2006), chap. 10. In the Levitical sacrifices, both the worldview and world picture of ancient Israel are operative. But they are not identical, and the worldview does not depend on the world picture for its cogency.

[55]Gorman, *Divine Presence and Community*, 4-5. *Enacting* is Gorman's term and seems to be a near synonym of *actualizing* (Gorman, *Divine Presence and Community*, 5).

[56]Gorman, *Divine Presence and Community*, xi.

ONE

Setting

Narrative and Theological Contexts

WHAT, EXACTLY, WAS LEVITICAL SACRIFICE? And how did it "work"?[1] As previously noted, these questions carry significant weight in the Christian doctrine of atonement. If Levitical sacrifice did indeed typify the saving work of Christ, then Christ has somehow done (perfectly) what Levitical sacrifice did (imperfectly). The logic of atonement in Levitical sacrifice, if we can speak of such, is the logic of atonement in the life, death, and resurrection of Jesus.

This, I am convinced, is a Christian line of thought. But it is one that encounters an immediate problem. The problem is that any logic that might be present in Levitical sacrifice is far from obvious. Leviticus gives

---

[1] Two quick notes are necessary. First, I use the phrase "Levitical sacrifice," here and throughout, as a shorthand way of referring to the system of sacrifices and offerings prescribed for Israel in the Pentateuch. "Levitical offering" would perhaps serve better here since the sacrifices of Leviticus were actually particular kinds of offerings. But it seems more consistent with modern usage to use *sacrifice* instead of *offering* as a shorthand. Second, it must be recognized that my question concerns *Levitical* sacrifice, not religious sacrifice in general. Contrary to many anthropologists of the last two centuries or so, and in part because of their varied proposals, I am not confident that it is possible to explain the origin and meaning of all religious sacrifice. Even if such an explanation were possible, what I am interested in here is the testimony of Leviticus, not a generalized account of humanity's religious practices. General theories of sacrifice are interesting and are relevant to my concerns in this study; though I believe this system was prescribed by God, it nevertheless shares something in common with the sacrificial practices of other peoples. However, the discontinuities between the sacrifices of Israel and surrounding nations were sharp, and were so by divine intention; to some degree, it seems God intended to correct their idolatrous sacrificial practices through the Levitical cult. Further, it is the text of Leviticus, not a scholarly reconstruction of the sources and development of ancient Israel's cultic practices, that God has given the church as canonical. The rituals and assumptions of other cultures may be informative, then, but should not displace sustained attention to the text of Leviticus and its interpretation by the prophets of the OT and NT.

only the sparsest explanations as to the efficacy of its offerings; in fact, it is not always easy to discern what exactly happened in its rituals. And, however clear it all might have been to ancient Israel with their lived experience of sacrificial worship, much of the meaning of Levitical ritual is opaque to modern readers.[2] Perhaps, then, making an effort to understand Christ through the cult appears naively idealistic; a nice thought, but impractical.

I admit the seriousness of the problem. However, Scripture offers us more interpretive help for Levitical sacrifice than we often realize. First, we do, at least, have the text of Leviticus itself. Even if details as to meaning are sparse, Leviticus nevertheless explains the sacrificial procedures to all the people; Moses was to speak the instructions of Leviticus to "the people of Israel" (Lev 1:2). Elsewhere in the ancient Near East, such knowledge was reserved for the priestly class alone. Leviticus, by contrast, was to be a "textbook for all Israel."[3] The church is therefore invited to consider the inner workings of Levitical sacrifice and to search out its theology through this text.

Second, we do well to remember that Leviticus is not a standalone text but is presented to us as the continuation of the pentateuchal narrative. Levitical sacrifice, it has been suggested, was a means of "bodying forth" the story of Israel as told in the Pentateuch, a story of "creation, promise, redemption, and covenant."[4] The narrative context of Leviticus, and the theological context that that narrative generates, should therefore serve as guides for interpreting Levitical ritual and be allowed to bring to the fore certain concepts that guide our attempt to discern a logic of atonement in the burnt offering.[5]

---

[2]That Levitical rituals all might have been clear to ancient Israel is a commonly made claim. See, e.g., Gordon Wenham, "The Theology of Old Testament Sacrifice," in *Sacrifice in the Bible*, ed. Roger T. Beckwith and Martin J. Selman (repr., Eugene, OR: Wipf & Stock, 2004), 77.

[3]Jacob Milgrom, *Leviticus 1–16: A New Translation with Introduction and Commentary*, Anchor Yale Bible 3 (New Haven, CT: Yale University Press, 2009), 144.

[4]Frank H. Gorman, *Divine Presence and Community: A Commentary on the Book of Leviticus*, International Theological Commentary (Grand Rapids, MI: Eerdmans, 1997), 5. By "bodying forth," Gorman seems to mean something like reenacting. The ritual as a whole, with all its participants, objects, and movements, was a symbolic repetition of Israel's history with YHWH.

[5]Gorman, *Divine Presence and Community*, 7. I distinguish the narrative and theological context here. But in truth they are one and the same. The God of Israel, the God of the church, is a God who acts in history and is thereby known. The book of Exodus illustrates this point well, as God first reveals his name, YHWH, and then reveals the meaning of that name through all he does to deliver Israel and enter into covenant with it.

As I have stated, it is my conviction that the burnt offering "represented the core, and perhaps even the summation, of the entire sacrificial system."[6] The burnt offering was the "fundamental sacrifice," the offering that "encompasses the whole ritual movement in itself."[7] It can therefore rightly be called "the paradigmatic offering in the Hebrew Bible," the offering that "represents the purest form of divine service," and "the main sacrifice of the Israelite cult."[8] If this is so, then consideration of the narrative context of Leviticus is necessary for understanding this offering, an offering in which the story of Israel was ritually summarized.

In other words, if we are to understand the story of the burnt offering, we must understand its setting. Setting is simply "the background against which action takes place." Setting is composed of time and place, of course, but also the occupations and habits of the characters along with their "general environment."[9] Setting is therefore indispensable to understanding a story: as a word cannot be rightly understood outside its context, neither can an action or a sequence of actions that make up a story. This might be especially true of ritual action. Roy Gane emphasizes that ritual actions have no inherent meaning, demonstrating that the same action can have more than one meaning, depending on the context.[10] Sometimes this notion is used to distinguish the meaning of Israelite sacrifice from that of its Canaanite neighbors: even when Israel *did* the same thing as their neighbors at the altar,

---

[6]Michael L. Morales, *Who Shall Ascend the Mountain of the Lord? A Biblical Theology of the Book of Leviticus*, New Studies in Biblical Theology (Downers Grove, IL: InterVarsity Press, 2015), 123.
[7]John Kleinig, *Leviticus* (St. Louis: Concordia, 2003), 40; Michael L. Morales, "Atonement in Ancient Israel: The Whole Burnt Offering as Central to Israel's Cult," in *So Great a Salvation: A Dialogue on the Atonement in Hebrews*, ed. Jon C. Laansma, George H. Guthrie, and Cynthia Long Westfall, Library of New Testament Studies 516 (London: T&T Clark, 2019), 28.
[8]James W. Watts, "Olah: The Rhetoric of Burnt Offerings," *Vetus Testamentum* 66, no. 1 (2006): 125, 132; John E. Hartley, *Leviticus*, Word Biblical Commentary 4 (Grand Rapids, MI: Zondervan, 2015), 17.
[9]Hugh Holman and William Harmon, *A Handbook to Literature*, 6th ed. (New York: Macmillan, 1992), 440.
[10]Roy Gane, *Cult and Character: Purification Offerings, Day of Atonement, and Theodicy* (Winona Lake, IN: Eisenbrauns, 2005), 4-6. Gane's example: the sevenfold sprinkling of blood on the Day of Atonement, which serves to purge the inner sanctum of impurity and also to reconsecrate the outer altar. Purgation and consecration are related but distinct concepts. So, this action had related but distinct meanings, based on the context in which it occurred. Gane goes on to warn his readers against a kind of illegitimate totality transfer of ritual action; "the danger is interpretive leveling by importing meaning from one context to another." Like words, it seems that ritual actions can have a given range of meaning depending on context.

it does not follow that they necessarily meant the same thing.[11] Setting, in short, is determinative of meaning.

If that is so, then much depends on understanding the setting of Levitical sacrifice. Chiefly, this means understanding its theology. This is so because, as just noted, the occupations and habits of characters is a major component of setting, and there is no more important character in Leviticus than God. But this is also so because of the preoccupation with theology inherent in all Levitical ritual. As Milgrom states, "Theology is what Leviticus is all about. It pervades every chapter and almost every verse. It is not expressed in pronouncements but embedded in rituals. Indeed, every act, whether movement, manipulation, or gesticulation, is pregnant with meaning."[12] To understand Levitical ritual is to understand Levitical theology—and, to some extent, vice versa. To understand the burnt offering, then, we must understand something of the God who both prescribed and received this offering.

The aim of this chapter is therefore to set the background for my reading of the burnt offering in later chapters by attending to the narrative context of Leviticus. It seeks to do so through a commentary on Leviticus 1:1 that gives particular attention to the way this opening verse recalls the narrative of Genesis–Exodus. In the course of that commentary, I will begin to highlight concepts crucial to understanding Levitical sacrifice as a whole. Most importantly, however, I will call attention to the way this opening verse characterizes the God who speaks to Moses and summons Israel to himself. In doing so, I hope to establish the theological setting of the burnt offering in a way that will illumine my reading of the ritual and its testimony to the atoning work of Christ.

LEVITICUS 1:1: A COMMENTARY

וַיִּקְרָא אֶל־מֹשֶׁה וַיְדַבֵּר יְהוָה אֵלָיו מֵאֹהֶל מוֹעֵד לֵאמֹר

The LORD called Moses and spoke to him from the tent of meeting, saying . . .[13]

---

[11] For examples of how the Israelite worldview affected the meaning of their sacrificial practices, and ruled out some potential meanings or ritual action, see Milgrom, *Leviticus 1–16*, 42-43.
[12] Milgrom, *Leviticus 1–16*, 42.
[13] Throughout, citations of the Hebrew text follow *Biblia Hebraica Stuttgartensia: With Werkgroep Informatica, Vrije Universiteit Morphology* (Bellingham, WA: Faithlife, 2006).

The opening sentence of Leviticus carries in its syllables the weight of a theological world. Two brief reflections reveal something of that weight.

First, it should not be overlooked that Leviticus opens with divine speech. This is no rare occurrence. Throughout the biblical narrative, the God of Israel shows himself to be a God who speaks. This certainly holds true for Leviticus, a book in which nearly every verse is a record of divine speech (Lev 8–10 being the main exception). The frequency of divine speech, however, does not diminish the weight of the divine voice. God's speech reveals Godself. Through his word, including that of Leviticus, God addresses his covenant people from the depths of his love and holiness. This proposition in itself affects the way we read Leviticus and what we might see in its pages. "If the words here are the words of God who reveals his very self, then we are called through the words themselves into an encounter with God."[14] A Christian reading of Leviticus therefore requires that we read with the "existential openness" and "full imaginative seriousness" of those who stand before God.[15]

Second, as mentioned above, the divine speech at the beginning of Leviticus puts the book in a narrative context; Leviticus continues a conversation that has already begun. Leviticus is not simply and purely law; rather, it is "law within a narrative context."[16] And that narrative is theologically loaded. In the narrative context of Leviticus, the book of Exodus in particular, we are constantly confronted with the identity, character, and purposes of the one who reveals himself as God Almighty. Here we meet the holiness, justice, and compassion of Israel's God; here we are confronted with claims of this God's absolute and universal supremacy. And here we are called to consider what it is that this God intends to do with the world and with us.

Most immediately, Leviticus 1:1 directs us back to Exodus 40:34-38, where the LORD is said to fill the newly erected tabernacle with the glory

---

[14]Ephraim Radner, *Leviticus*, Brazos Theological Commentary on the Bible (Grand Rapids, MI: Brazos, 2008), 35.

[15]These concepts come from R. W. L. Moberly, *The God of the Old Testament: Encountering the Divine in Christian Scripture* (Grand Rapids, MI: Baker Academic, 2020), 5-10. Importantly, Moberly notes that such a reading requires a close reading of the text and a second naiveté that "must be located downwind of the insights of modern learning."

[16]Gordon Wenham, *The Book of Leviticus*, New International Commentary on the Old Testament (Grand Rapids, MI: Eerdmans, 1979), 7.

of his presence.¹⁷ Here God comes to dwell among his people so that he might be with them as their God (Ex 29:45). But as we will see, God's filling of the tent is not an unexpected event; it is rather the fitting end of the exodus. By recalling this event, Leviticus thus shows itself to be the sequel of Exodus and invites us to read its divine utterances as a continuation of the exodus narrative, which itself continues the story of creation and election found in Genesis.¹⁸

Reading with "imaginative seriousness," we might now ask ourselves: What does this God have to say to us?

וַיִּקְרָא—"And He Called"

Leviticus begins with the Hebrew word וַיִּקְרָא, commonly translated "and he called." Here the divine voice calls out, seeking a response.

Commentators have sometimes made much of the character of this call. Mark Elliot notes a tendency in Jewish exegetes to hear in it a note of affection.¹⁹ Thus Jonathan Sacks, following the medieval rabbi Rashi: "*Vayikra* is a call uttered in love"; "it is the language of invitation, friendship, love."²⁰ Such a reading seems justified since it fits with what is undeniably one purpose for the tabernacle—YHWH's loving presence among his people. In the tabernacle, the Lord will dwell among the people of Israel and be their

---

¹⁷Milgrom, *Leviticus 1–16*, 134. It seems appropriate to me to use both the Tetragrammaton (YHWH) and the honorific "the Lord" when referring to the divine name given to Israel in Exodus. YHWH reminds us that the God of Israel is not a generic deity. He has particular attributes and a particular history that might cut against our assumptions about who God should be and what he should do. "The Lord," on the other hand, is appropriate for the Christian claim that YHWH, God of Israel, is no tribal deity of an ancient people in whom we might be interested for purely historical reasons. He is rather the living God, worthy of all reverence and obedience and trust, who presents his grace to us in Jesus Christ and calls for our response. Use of "the Lord" also respects the Jewish tradition of referring to the divine name by a reverential substitute, a tradition Jesus himself seems to have followed. See Richard Bauckham, *Who Is God? Key Moments of Biblical Revelation* (Grand Rapids, MI: Baker Academic, 2020), 49-55.

¹⁸Wenham, *Leviticus*, 49; Gorman, *Divine Presence and Community*, 5; Jay Sklar, *Leviticus*, Tyndale Old Testament Commentaries (Downers Grove, IL: IVP Academic, 2014), 27; Philip Peter Jenson, *Graded Holiness: A Key to the Priestly Conception of the World*, Journal for the Study of the Old Testament Supplement Series 106 (repr., London: T&T Clark, 2021), 211. Interestingly, Jenson argues for reading Leviticus as part of a continuous narrative that runs all the way from Genesis to Kings.

¹⁹Mark W. Elliot, *Engaging Leviticus: Reading Leviticus Theologically with Its Past Interpreters* (Eugene, OR: Cascade Books, 2012), 2. Cf. Radner, *Leviticus*, 39.

²⁰Jonathan Sacks, *Leviticus: The Book of Holiness*, Covenant and Conversation: A Weekly Reading of the Jewish Bible (New Milford, CT: Maggid Books and the Orthodox Union, 2015), 61, 16.

God. Indeed, for just this reason, the LORD delivered Israel from Egypt (Ex 29:45-46). In this house, YHWH will meet with Israel; to this house, Israel will come to "gaze upon the beauty of the LORD" (Ps 27:4) and rejoice in his goodness (Ps 43:3-4), to worship the LORD and be blessed by him (Ps 132; cf. 1 Sam 1). The joy and blessing of YHWH's presence mark the remainder of Leviticus 1, as the LORD holds out the promise of atonement, acceptance, and divine joy to those who approach the altar (Lev 1:3-9). In his call to Moses, the LORD invites Israel to enter into the joy of their Master.

As much as this call is an invitation uttered in love, however, it is also a summons uttered with divine authority.[21] In YHWH's call to Moses, there rings a note of "solemnity," emphasizing the weight of the forthcoming revelation.[22] Such solemnity fits the context of YHWH's glory descending on and filling the tent. Sklar notes that God's call to Moses from the tent, with subsequent deliverance of law, continues a pattern begun in Exodus: God descends (on Sinai in Exodus, here into the tent), God calls to Moses (Heb. קרא), then God issues his law through Moses (see Ex 19:20; 24:16).[23] When the pattern is repeated in the opening of Leviticus, it sets a distinctive tone, reminding us of the absolute authority and supremacy of the God who calls to Moses.

The LORD's call therefore elicits a holy fear—a mix of gratitude, awe, and obedience. This holy fear becomes the affective ideal for Levitical sacrifice. At the altar, appearing before their King, Israel was to "serve the LORD with fear, and rejoice with trembling" (Ps 2:11). Such a response would serve well to reflect the nature of Israel's relationship to God: it is a divinely initiated covenant, in which they are bound by both law and love to the God who has made them his own. We are reminded of that covenant as we keep reading.

אֶל־מֹשֶׁה—"TO MOSES"

Not to be overlooked is that YHWH issues the call of Leviticus 1:1 אֶל־מֹשֶׁה, "to Moses." This, too, reminds us of the weight of the divine encounter. At

---

[21]"And he summoned" is a common translation of וַיִּקְרָא in Lev 1:1; see, e.g., Milgrom, *Leviticus 1–16*, 133.
[22]Wenham, *Leviticus*, 49.
[23]Sklar, *Leviticus*, 86.

Sinai, Israel speaks to Moses and says, "Why should we die? For this great fire will consume us. If we hear the voice of the LORD our God any more, we shall die. . . . Go near and hear all that the LORD our God will say, and speak to us all that the LORD our God will speak to you" (Deut 5:25, 27). The LORD's presence, the people realize, is dangerous, and they ask Moses to intercede.

Moses' mediation. That Israel would ask Moses to intercede is unsurprising. Moses is at this point the leader of Israel in every sense—political, military, and religious. In Exodus, he has been introduced as the prophet of YHWH and deliverer of Israel. Through Moses, God freed Israel from the tyranny of Pharaoh and the false gods of Egypt. Through Moses, God has led Israel through the wilderness, providing them with "bread from heaven" (Ex 16:4) and water from the rock (Ex 17:6), and giving them victory over Amalek (Ex 17:8-13). And, most remarkably of all, through Moses, the LORD has now descended to meet with Israel at Mount Sinai and established his covenant with them.

God's summons to Moses from the tabernacle can therefore be seen as the culmination (at this point) of his history with Israel. It represents the purpose of the exodus and the fulfillment of God's promise to Abraham. As Frank Gorman states,

> The Exodus from Egypt took place in order that Yahweh might dwell in the midst of the people of Israel (cf. Exod. 6:2-8). The tabernacle is an expression of the future God anticipates in redeeming Israel from the slavery and oppression of Egypt. This text also recalls the promise made to the ancestor (Gen. 17:8: "I will be their God"). Thus, the tabernacle is a partial but concrete actualization of the ancestral promise, and as the divine dwelling place it is a manifestation of the promise actualized and redemption realized.[24]

The descent of God's glory to the tent of meeting thus contains the whole of his dealings with Israel to this point. As Israel approaches him there, God's redemptive acts are not only remembered but participated in. At the altar, Israel will enjoy the fruit of their election and redemption.

The Mosaic covenant. To recall Moses' role as mediator, of course, is to recall the covenant that typically bears his name. Of all the events narrated

---

[24]Gorman, *Divine Presence and Community*, 12.

in Exodus, it is probably the solemnization of the Mosaic covenant, recounted in Exodus 19–24, that is most prominent in the setting of Leviticus. In fact, this covenant might be seen as the very purpose of everything that happened at the tabernacle. Directly after the solemnization of the covenant, God commands a sanctuary be built so that he might dwell among Israel (Ex 25:1-9). The implication seems to be that this sanctuary, known as the tent of meeting or tabernacle, will perpetuate the experience of that covenant ceremony.[25] Reflection on that ceremony therefore sheds light on what it was that YHWH was calling Israel to at the tabernacle.

When YHWH leads Israel to Mount Sinai after the exodus (Ex 19:1-2), he makes his covenant proposal through Moses.[26] "You yourselves have seen what I did to the Egyptians," he reminds Israel, "and how I bore you on eagles' wings and brought you to myself. Now therefore, if you will indeed obey my voice and keep my covenant, you shall be my treasured possession among all peoples, for all the earth is mine; and you shall be to me a kingdom of priests and a holy nation" (Ex 19:4-6). YHWH, who has already shown great love and faithfulness toward Israel in redeeming them from Egypt, now calls Israel into a more formalized covenant relationship. Israel will be YHWH's beloved people—his "treasured possession"—as they have been since the call of Abram (Gen 12:1-3). Now, however, Israel will exist not only as a family but as a nation. No longer will they be formally defined by descent from Abraham alone but by the law of YHWH their king and the land he will give them.[27]

Israel accepts YHWH's covenant proposal with a pledge of obedience: "All that the Lord has spoken we will do" (Ex 19:8). It is then, after Israel's pledge, that YHWH comes to dwell in their midst on Sinai "in a thick cloud" (Ex 19:9). From the fire and cloud on Sinai, YHWH declares the terms of the covenant to Israel—the law, with its moral, ceremonial, and civil aspects (Ex 20:1–23:19)—and promises to give them the land of Canaan, where he will bless and protect them (Ex 23:20-33).

---

[25]Morales, *Who Shall Ascend*, 96.
[26]Umberto Cassuto, *A Commentary on the Book of Exodus*, trans. Israel Abrahams (Jerusalem: Magnes, 1967), 227.
[27]William J. Dumbrell, *Covenant and Creation: A Theology of the Old Testament Covenants* (repr., Carlisle, UK: Paternoster, 2000), 99.

After Moses repeats to the people the commandments of YHWH, and after they again pledge their obedience (Ex 24:3), the newly established covenant is celebrated in breathtaking fashion. Moses writes down the words of YHWH, builds an altar at the foot of the mountain, and commands that burnt and peace offerings be offered to YHWH. Moses then reads the words of YHWH, and the people respond yet again with a pledge of obedience, this time more emphatically: "All that the Lord has spoken we will do, and we will be obedient" (Ex 24:7). Following this final pledge, Moses throws the blood of the slain offerings onto the people, declaring it "the blood of the covenant that the Lord has made with you in accordance with all these words" (Ex 24:8). Then, most remarkably of all, God shows himself to Israel and communes with them on the mountain. After Moses throws the blood of the covenant onto the people, "Moses and Aaron, Nadab, and Abihu, and seventy of the elders of Israel went up, and they saw the God of Israel. . . . And he did not lay his hand on the chief men of the people of Israel; *they beheld God, and ate and drank*" (Ex 24:9-11).

The whole of this covenant ceremony informs our understanding of Levitical sacrifice, and there are at least three important conclusions that may be drawn from it, which I will note here and further develop below. First, that the tabernacle was meant to perpetuate this event suggests that, as Gorman states, Levitical ritual was "a means of enacting the covenant relationship."[28] The promise of the covenant—that God will be Israel's God, that they will be his people—was to be realized in the Levitical cult. By their offerings, Israel was to acknowledge God's covenant lordship, his electing and redeeming grace, and respond to it with their own pledge of covenant loyalty.

Second, while the meaning of Levitical sacrifice cannot be reduced to a legal transaction (as I will argue below), the setting of Levitical sacrifice was nevertheless charged with concern for God's law. The law of God was a fundamental concern at the altar. This concern was concretized by the fact that, as Israel approached God in the tabernacle, they stood before this law as summarized in the Ten "Words" or Commandments. Waltke notes that the Ten Words of the covenant were placed in the ark of the covenant, the

---

[28]Gorman, *Divine Presence and Community*, 5.

symbolic throne of YHWH on which he resided in the holy of holies. The
Lord's personal presence in the tent was therefore tied to his law. In fact, we
can think of this law as "an expression of God himself. The [commandments] are part of God's identity, a central part of God's self-revelation."[29] To
draw near to this God in sacrifice therefore required walking in the way of
righteousness prescribed by the law given at Sinai.

Third, and perhaps most importantly, in the covenant ceremony on
Mount Sinai, we get a glimpse of the telos of Levitical sacrifice: holy communion with God, even beatific vision. The most remarkable scene in Exodus's account of the covenant ceremony is the ascent of Moses, Aaron, and
the elders up the mountain, where they eat and drink with God and see his
glory. To this point in Exodus, the danger of God's presence on the
mountain has been emphasized. As his glory dwells in the cloud on
the mountain, YHWH repeatedly warns Moses to allow no one to come
near the mountain. Israel was not allowed to touch the mountain, nor to
"break through to the Lord to look" (Ex 19:21). The promised consequences
are severe: the Lord will "break out against them" (Ex 19:24). Now, however,
after the application of sacrificial blood, Israel is able to draw near to God,
to dwell in his presence and even "behold" (Heb. חָזָה) him.[30] The sacrifice
at Mount Sinai grants access to God's glory and presence and even what
seems to be a prefiguration of the beatific vision. Where such a vision would
previously have been fatal, it was graciously granted to Israel after the application of sacrificial blood.

If the tabernacle really was an extension of the Sinai experience, then we
might expect the Levitical offerings to share a similar telos. And that in fact
is just what we find in Leviticus 9, the text that tells of the inauguration of
the Levitical cult and that likely depicts the usual procedural order of Levitical offerings.[31] There we read that sacrificial worship culminated in the
peace offering, an offering that consisted of a shared meal between the Lord,
his priests, and the offeror. Once the first peace offering was presented and

---

[29] Bruce K. Waltke, *An Old Testament Theology* (Grand Rapids, MI: Zondervan, 2011), 413.
[30] It is helpful to note the way in which Moses' act of throwing blood on the people anticipates the priests' later throwing of blood at the tabernacle. Most often, that blood will be thrown on the altar of burnt offering, not people. Still, there seems to be a clear parallel: in each case, the throwing of blood, whether on persons or objects, purifies (or sanctifies).
[31] A. F. Rainey, "The Order of Sacrifices in Old Testament Ritual Texts," *Biblica* 51, no. 4 (1970): 497.

the Levitical order of worship completed for the first time, the people were granted the vision of God: "The glory of the LORD appeared to all the people" (Lev 9:23). As the fire of the LORD came out from the tent to consume the offerings, the people responded by shouting (either for joy or fear) and falling on their faces (Lev 9:24).³² The divine fire confirmed that YHWH was indeed dwelling in the midst of Israel and receiving their worship.³³ But it also revealed the telos of Levitical sacrifice: the vision of God. Just as it was at Sinai, so it was in the tabernacle: the sacrifices of the Mosaic covenant led to the vision of God and communion with him in a shared meal.

That Levitical sacrifice held out the promise of the vision of God and a secure dwelling in his glory will be important to my reading of the burnt offering. For now, however, there is more to say about the theological context of Levitical sacrifice, in particular about the identity of the God whom Israel beholds and to whom they draw near in the tabernacle.

יְהוָה—"YHWH"

As we continue reading, Leviticus 1:1 makes explicit the identity of the one calling to Moses from the tent: יְהוָה ("YHWH"). This is the God who blessed the patriarchs, spoke to Moses, and delivered Israel out of Egypt. Here again, we are pointed back to the exodus narrative, especially as it bears on the identity of Israel's God.

The revelation of the Name. Of prime importance in the exodus narrative (and the entire canon) is the revelation of the name יְהוָה in Exodus 3. As Moses is tending his father-in-law's sheep, he comes to "the mountain of God," where the angel of the LORD appears to him "in a flame of fire" (Ex 3:1-2). This fire indwells a thornbush, and though the bush seems to burn, it is not consumed. When Moses, fascinated by "this great sight," turns aside to observe it more thoroughly, God calls to him, commanding him "take your sandals off your feet, for the place on which you are standing is holy ground" (Ex 3:3-5). As the LORD identifies himself as "the God of your father, the God of Abraham, the God of Isaac, and the God of Jacob," Moses

---

³²Sklar, *Leviticus*, 154.

³³Gorman, *Divine Presence and Community*, 63. "The fire is divine fire in which the LORD reveals his glory." Robert D. Macina, *The Lord's Service: A Ritual Analysis of the Order, Function, and Purpose of the Daily Divine Service in the Pentateuch* (Eugene, OR: Pickwick, 2019), 82.

Setting

hides his face, "for he was afraid to look at God" (Ex 3:6). As Moses stands before the flame, simultaneously frightened and allured, the Lord announces his intention to deliver Israel from their oppression under Pharaoh and to do so through Moses' agency.[34] Moses hesitates, expressing doubt as to his own fitness as well as his ignorance of this God's name.[35] The Lord then responds to Moses:

> "I am who I am." And he said, "Say this to the people of Israel, 'I am has sent me to you.'" God also said to Moses, "Say this to the people of Israel: 'The Lord, the God of your fathers, the God of Abraham, the God of Isaac, and the God of Jacob, has sent me to you.' This is my name forever, and thus I am to be remembered throughout all generations." (Ex 3:14-15)

In this name, the Lord reveals something of his character. According to the customs of the ancient Near East, "the meaning of an object's name indicates its nature and determines its characteristics."[36] In Scripture, a name often "expresses a person's essence and identity and the meaning of this person's life." Since the God of Israel has a name, "he is not an anonymous force."[37] The Name that God gave Moses in the burning bush thus revealed who he was in himself—his nature or essence.[38] It also revealed something of who he would be *for Israel*. This name "expressed the nature and operations of God, and [assured Israel] that God would manifest in deeds the nature expressed in his name."[39] It therefore denoted his "enacted identity, God's sheer, irreducible particularity of *this* One who is and acts *thus*."[40] The name יְהוָה

---

[34]Moberly, *God of the Old Testament*, 56.

[35]It is unclear whether Moses was confessing his ignorance of the Name itself or of the meaning of the Name. Dumbrell notes that the Name is found around 116 times in between Gen 12:1 and Ex 3:12, with 40 times coming from the lips of the patriarchs (*Covenant and Creation*, 83). It is possible, Dumbrell admits, that these occurrences of the Name are all anachronisms (many take this view, including Moberly, *God of the Old Testament*, 67). It has also been proposed that while Israel previously knew the Name, Moses, who grew up in the courts of Egypt, did not (67). Dumbrell chooses to follow J. A. Motyer in holding that while the Name was known to the patriarchs, "it is now in the Exodus period that the significance of the name Yahweh is communicated" (*Covenant and Creation*, 83).

[36]Cassuto, *Commentary on the Book of Exodus*, 37.

[37]*The Catechism of the Catholic Church, with Modifications from the* Editio Typica (New York: Doubleday, 1997), 203.

[38]Thomas Aquinas, *Summa Contra Gentiles*, book 1, *God*, trans. Anston C. Pegis (Notre Dame, IN: University of Notre Dame Press, 1975), 1.22.10.

[39]C. F. Keil and F. Delitzsch, *Commentary on the Old Testament*, vol. 1, *The Pentateuch* (repr., Peabody, MA: Hendrickson, 2011), 287.

[40]John Webster, *Holiness* (Grand Rapids, MI: Eerdmans, 2003), 36.

"summarizes a history," a history that is grounded in God's eternal attributes and was still unfolding as he called to Moses from the burning bush.[41]

It is this name that Israel remembered at the altar and this name that was said to dwell in the tent (Deut 12:11-12). Calling on this name in the tabernacle, Israel would remember the divine attributes and mighty acts attached to the name YHWH. Surely the identity of YHWH, then, has something to say about the meaning of the burnt offering.

Yet, what exactly does this name reveal? Who is the God who calls out to Moses from the tent of meeting? Given the way the presence and character of יְהוָה dominate the setting of Leviticus, it is appropriate to reflect on the Name at length.

The meaning of the Name: Mystery. As much as anything else, the name יְהוָה speaks to the mysterious nature of the God of Israel. "This divine name is mysterious just as God is mysterious. It is at once a name revealed and something like the refusal of a name, and hence it better expresses God as what he is—infinitely above everything that we can understand or say."[42] The mystery of God is evident both in the name יְהוָה and in the way that name was revealed to Moses.

Commenting on the giving of the Name in Exodus 3, R. W. L. Moberly calls attention to the uniqueness of the fire that symbolizes the divine presence. Here and elsewhere (notably Ex 19), Moberly notes, the fire that symbolizes God's presence blazes yet does not consume. To say the least, this is unusual. The divine fire of Mount Sinai is "intrinsically unlike regular fire," a point that speaks to the unique and mysterious nature of the God who appears in the flame. Fire itself, Moberly states, is "symbolically suggestive" of a reality that simultaneously attracts and repels, and that "by its nature cannot be grasped or readily controlled by humans."[43] How much more a fire that burns without consuming? The imagery of the burning bush points to something beyond human comprehension and control.

---

[41] As Christopher J. H. Wright, *The Mission of God: Unlocking the Bible's Grand Narrative* (Downers Grove, IL: IVP Academic, 2006), says beautifully, the name YHWH refers to "a very specific, named and biographied God" (54). "Summarizes a history" is the language of Peter J. Leithart, *The Ten Commandments: A Guide to the Perfect Law of Liberty* (Bellingham, WA: Lexham, 2020), 46.

[42] *Catechism of the Catholic Church*, 206.

[43] Moberly, *God of the Old Testament*, 55-56.

The mystery symbolized in the burning bush is likewise present in the Name itself. The translation of the longer form of the Name (Heb. אֶהְיֶה אֲשֶׁר אֶהְיֶה) is notoriously difficult. The verbal form is imperfect and could therefore be taken as either continuous present or future. Context usually forces the decision one way or the other, but not in this case. So, in addition to the usual English rendering "I am who I am," another possible translation is "I will be who I will be," and it is probably not possible to choose between these alternatives on the basis of the verbal form alone.[44] This difficulty in itself makes the Name somewhat elusive.[45]

Whichever translation one prefers, however, this construction remains odd as a name. The Name is doubtless significant—the text's repetition of the Name and the way it attaches the Name to God's solemn promises of deliverance make that clear. But the nature of its significance is not immediately obvious. Classical commentators, sensitive to the Name's play with the verb "to be," were inclined to see the Name as a metaphysical statement, identifying God as most real and true Being. The Name, on this reading, identifies Israel's God as the one who possesses being in and of himself, not derivatively, and who is the ground of existence for all else. Thus Origen: "All things that exist derive their share of being from him who truly exists, who said through Moses, 'I am that I am.'"[46] Contemporary exegetes, on the other hand, tend to see this name not as a metaphysical statement but as a pledge; the Name means, above all, that God will show himself and prove his faithfulness by his future grace toward Israel. "I AM WHO I AM" therefore has the force of "I will be with you" or "I am who I am for you."[47] It is meant to denote consistency and dependability, not the "Being" of classical metaphysics.[48]

---

[44]Moberly, *God of the Old Testament*, 71.
[45]Many commentators, on this basis, see the Name as the refusal of a name. By providing Moses with the name "I am who I am," God was refusing to be labeled and therefore controlled by Israel. For example, Bauckham, *Who Is God?*, 41.
[46]Origen, *On First Principles* 1.3.6; as quoted in Joseph T. Lienhard, ed., *Exodus, Leviticus, Numbers, Deuteronomy*, Ancient Christian Commentary on Scripture Old Testament 3 (Downers Grove, IL: IVP Academic, 2001). For another classic example of this kind of reading, see Gregory of Nyssa, *The Life of Moses*, ed. and trans. Abraham J. Malherbe and Everett Ferguson, Classics of Western Christianity (Mahwah, NJ: Paulist, 1978), 60 (2.23).
[47]Waltke, *Old Testament Theology*, 366.
[48]R. Allen Cole, *Exodus*, Tyndale Old Testament Commentaries (Downers Grove, IL: InterVarsity Press, 1973), briefly and admirably lays out these alternatives (26).

Certainly, the modern trend to take the Name as a statement about YHWH's forthcoming faithfulness to Israel is warranted and makes for edifying reading. The LORD did indeed enact this name through his redemptive works on Israel's behalf, thereby proving his faithfulness, justice, and sovereignty in his triumph over Pharaoh. In this way, the Name promised God's "loving faithfulness" to Israel, about which I will say more below.[49] However, even if a metaphysical reading such as Origen's does not capture everything there is to say about the Name, the construction "I AM WHO I AM" nevertheless seems to point to YHWH's "ontological incomparability." Michael Allen remarks on what is perhaps the most peculiar feature of this name, its lack of "referential matrix." When God identifies himself in Exodus 3:14, he does so without reference to any other reality. The name God reveals to Moses is "self-reflexive" and should be understood, at minimum, as a statement on divine uniqueness.[50] The God manifest in the burning bush, who later dwells in the tabernacle, cannot be classified with any other reality, even in the broadest terms, but is ontologically unique.[51] Even in his self-revelation, then, he remains mysterious, beyond our grasp, as he is beyond comparison.

The meaning of the Name: Aseity. The ontological uniqueness denoted by the Name appears also to entail God's aseity, or self-existence. Whatever else the self-reflexive name "I AM WHO I AM" might mean, it undoubtedly suggests YHWH's absolute independence. This God, defined by nothing besides himself, is therefore determined by nothing else and dependent on nothing else. Rather, he possesses his life and being in and of himself. The Septuagint famously translated YHWH as Ὁ ὤν, "the One who is," a rendering that scholars today tend to see as "less a translation than an interpretation."[52] But even if that is the case, it does not necessarily mean that the Septuagint misleads us. The God who appears in the fire on Sinai is exquisitely alive, a flame that burns without dependence on fuel. In his

---

[49]Bauckham, *Who Is God?*, 43.
[50]"The Bible's primary way of signaling God's uniqueness is by way of God's proper name, YHWH." Scott R. Swain, *The Trinity: An Introduction*, Short Studies in Systematic Theology (Wheaton, IL: Crossway, 2020), 29.
[51]Michael Allen, *Sanctification*, New Studies in Dogmatics (Grand Rapids, MI: Zondervan, 2017), 57.
[52]Moberly, *God of the Old Testament*, 82.

everlasting vitality, YHWH is truly the One "who is and who was and who is to come" (Rev 1:4).

Even if the Name in its context of origin did not entail all that classical Greek philosophy meant by "Being" and participation, that does not mean the text does not lend itself to such a reading. Hilary of Poitiers famously saw in the name YHWH the pure, supreme existence standing behind all things that his philosophical pursuits had led him to believe necessary for making sense of the world.[53] Moberly notes that while Hilary's reading may go beyond what was envisaged in the text's context of origin, it is not for that reason an illegitimate interpretation. Given the Christian recontextualization of the text, and the intellectual context in which Hilary was reading it, we can fairly judge that Hilary saw "some genuinely possible implications of Exodus 3 in its depiction of God's self-revelation to Moses as the God who can be known yet is beyond knowledge, as the living God who can cause Hilary to be alive."[54] The revelation of the divine name in Exodus 3 invites the kind of metaphysical reading Hilary (and so many other classical exegetes with him) gave it.

The exodus narrative reveals a God who is preeminently *alive*. This God is eternal, active, alert, and incomparably mighty. YHWH hears the cries of his oppressed people, remembers his ancient covenant, and acts in the vitality of his immeasurable strength—showing himself at every point to be the living God, in contrast to the deities of Egypt. At no point is he dependent or limited, at no point is the exercise of either his mercy or his might constrained by anything outside himself. On him, rather, all things depend, and by him are all things constrained. This God possesses life in himself and possesses it to a degree unmatched by any living thing. He alone is YHWH, the one who most truly *is*.

The meaning of the Name: Incomparability and sovereignty. The rest of the Pentateuch likewise insists that YHWH alone is God—unmatched, inimitable, incomparable. In the "priestly" voice of the creation account of Genesis 1, for example, YHWH is exalted as supreme: he alone is Creator, making all things from nothing, unrivaled, and without dependence on any coeternal principle. As the sole Creator of heaven and earth, alone eternal,

---

[53] Hilary, *On the Trinity* 1.5.
[54] Moberly, *God of the Old Testament*, 86.

YHWH is set apart from all other reality. He cannot be classed or categorized alongside his creatures but is set apart from all else by an "infinite qualitative distinction."[55] This God is singular, incomparable, Wholly Other. While not unknown to his people, he remains incomprehensible.

In Exodus, too, God's incomparability is emphasized. For example, when YHWH plagues Egypt with frogs, Pharaoh summons Moses and Aaron and asks them to plead with YHWH to take the frogs away. Moses agrees to do so but asks Pharoah to specify a time for the frogs to be removed. His reasoning: when Pharaoh sees the frogs die out on the day he requested, he will know "that there is no one like the LORD our God" (Ex 8:10). In the plagues, the LORD was not only making war on Egypt but showing Israel and Egypt alike he had no rivals; there was none like YHWH.

This much seems also to be entailed by the divine name. In all the plagues, and in his great act of delivering Israel from Egypt, God will act so that "the Egyptians shall know that I am the LORD" (Ex 7:5). The implication of this statement is that the name YHWH is not wholly incomprehensible to the Egyptians. When they learn that Israel's God is YHWH, they will learn his absolute sovereignty—that he alone is the God who accomplishes all his will and that there is no other. The name YHWH, it seems to be assumed, clearly enough denotes that singular sovereignty.

As the God who perfectly possesses life and gives life as he will, the one who accomplishes all his holy will as he sees fit, the God of Israel is unique. Thus, as noted above, he is not definable by reference to any other reality. He might be *imaged* by created reality—he manifests himself in fire; he plays the role of warrior (Ex 15:3); he is "Most High" and "Almighty"; he is a rock in the wilderness. These analogies, however, should be read with a recognition that whatever likeness these realities may have to God, there is always a greater unlikeness.[56] The self-reflexive name of God, as Allen puts it, reminds us that even when God reveals himself, he remains Wholly Other.

---

[55] As Thomas Aquinas argues, in *Summa Theologica* 1.3.5, God, as the principle of all being, is without genus.

[56] As it is said in the canons of the Fourth Lateran Council, 1215, canon 2: "Between the Creator and the creature there cannot be a likeness so great that the unlikeness is not greater." H. J. Schroeder, *Disciplinary Decrees of the General Councils: Text, Translation and Commentary* (St. Louis: B. Herder, 1937), 236-96, https://sourcebooks.fordham.edu/basis/lateran4.asp.

By his gracious self-disclosure, we know God in truth; yet we always know him as Holy, Incomparable Mystery.

The meaning of the Name: Holiness. Closely related to the mystery, aseity, and sovereignty of God is his holiness. In the Lord's self-manifestation through the fire for the burning bush, this holiness is revealed. As Moses approaches the blaze—an approach that informs Israel's approach at the altar—the Lord warns Moses, "Do not come near; take your sandals off your feet, for the place on which you are standing is holy ground" (Ex 3:5). Richard Bauckham notes how striking the occurrence of the word *holy* is here. "If one were reading through the Bible from the beginning, this is the first time [since Gen 2:3] one would encounter the word 'holy.'"⁵⁷ Given how often *holy* and *holiness* appear in the rest of the Pentateuch, this is remarkable. God's holiness, it seems, is tightly bound up with the name יְהוָה.

Moral and majestic holiness. The concept of divine holiness, central to the drama of Exodus and Leviticus, is rich and difficult. It has sometimes been defined as moral purity, the absolute righteousness of God's will and ways.⁵⁸ This could even be considered a "classical" definition of divine holiness.⁵⁹ In much Christian theology, God's holiness has been considered "a general term for the moral excellency of God."⁶⁰ It has been considered synonymous with his righteousness, his "incorruptible rectitude and justice."⁶¹

Certainly, moral excellence is one aspect of God's holiness, one that elicits our worship: "Infinite purity, even more than infinite knowledge or infinite power, is the object of reverence."⁶² To reduce God's holiness to moral purity, however, does not fully account for the witness of Scripture, a point that has been widely argued in the past century or more.⁶³ In Scripture, God's

---

⁵⁷Bauckham, *Who Is God?*, 37. Genesis 2:3, rendered in English, reads, "So God blessed the Sabbath day and made it holy." *Holy* appears here in a verbal form, however, so perhaps Bauckham can be taken as correct if the search is restricted to nominal and adjectival forms, as his statement might be read.
⁵⁸Bavinck notes the tendency to associate holiness with moral perfection and purity in the early Reformed theologians. See Herman Bavinck, *Reformed Dogmatics*, vol. 2, *God and Creation*, ed. John Bolt, trans. John Vriend (Grand Rapids, MI: Baker Academic, 2004), 216.
⁵⁹Allen, *Sanctification*, 47.
⁶⁰Charles Hodge, *Systematic Theology*, vol. 1, *Theology* (Peabody, MA: Hendrickson, 2013), 413.
⁶¹Francis Turretin, *Institutes of Elenctic Theology*, vol. 1, *First Through Tenth Topics*, ed. James T. Dennison, trans. George Musgrave Giger (Phillipsburg, NJ: P&R, 1992), 235 (3.19.1).
⁶²Hodge, *Systematic Theology*, 1:413.
⁶³Bavinck could state, "At present everyone acknowledges that the concept of holiness in the Old and New Testaments expresses a relation of God to the world," not just his moral purity. Herman

holiness marks all he is and does.[64] It refers not only to his negative relation to sin—he is both free from any stain of injustice and rightly opposed to all evil—but also to all his relations to his creatures, and even the quality of his own self-contained life. "Talk of God's holiness," says John Webster, "denotes the majesty and singular purity which the triune God is in himself and with which he acts towards and in the lives of his creatures."[65] Holiness speaks of the moral perfection of God, to be sure, but does so as this perfection is enfolded into the totality of God's majesty.

Holiness is not simply one divine attribute among many but the brilliant perfection of the LORD's unbounded goodness, simple in nature yet varied in effects.[66] "YHWH is not called holy because of an immediately conspicuous attribute. He is rather called holy in a comprehensive sense, in connection with every revelation that impresses us with his deity."[67] Holiness, we might say, is that which "consummates and harmonizes all other divine characteristics." Better, "Holiness points especially to the undivided glory of God in all God's diversely good qualities."[68] God's holiness is thus his uniqueness; we may again refer to his "ontological incomparability."[69] "Holiness just is the Mystery, the Immanence and Sovereign Aseity of God; It is the Hidden and Infinite Majesty of the One Lord."[70] In this sense, God's holiness is his singular "capacity and right to arouse our reverent awe and wonder."[71]

Bavinck, *Reformed Dogmatics*, vol. 1, *Prolegomena*, ed. John Bolt, trans. John Vriend (Grand Rapids, MI: Baker Academic, 2003), 216. Allen, writing in recent years, makes a similar observation—it is rare today to find a theologian who treats holiness exclusively as a moral attribute (*Sanctification*, 51).

[64]Geerhardus Vos, *Biblical Theology: Old and New Testaments* (Grand Rapids, MI: Eerdmans, 1948), 266: "[Holiness] is not really an attribute to be coordinated with the other divine attributes distinguished in the divine nature. It is something coextensive with and applicable to everything that can be predicated of God: He is holy in everything that characterizes Him and reveals Him, holy in goodness and grace, no less than in His righteousness and wrath."

[65]Webster, *Holiness*, 41.

[66]For brilliance as an image for God's holiness, see Allan Coppedge, *Portraits of God: A Biblical Theology of Holiness* (Downers Grove, IL: InterVarsity Press, 2001), chap. 5.

[67]Bavinck, *Reformed Dogmatics*, 2:220.

[68]Thomas C. Oden, *Classical Christianity: A Systematic Theology* (New York: HarperCollins, 1992), 64.

[69]John Frame, *The Doctrine of God*, vol. 2 of *A Theology of Lordship* (Phillipsburg, NJ: P&R, 2002), 28; Allen, *Sanctification*, 68.

[70]Katherine Sonderegger, *Systematic Theology*, vol. 2, *The Doctrine of the Holy Trinity: Processions and Persons* (Minneapolis: Fortress, 2020), 27.

[71]Frame, *Doctrine of God*, 28. I do not mean to imply that holiness is attributed to God only insofar as he is related to his creatures; he is holy eternally, apart from creation, in and of himself. Yet

It may be best, then, to define divine holiness simply as that which distinguishes God as God. In a sense, each divine attribute attests God's uniqueness. God is simple; there is no distinction between his essence and existence or attributes. Each attribute of God "designates the totality of the being of God under some particular aspect," so each divine attribute reveals God as unique.[72] Yet holiness is the name we give that majestic uniqueness. When YHWH reveals himself as "majestic in holiness, awesome in glorious deeds, doing wonders," he prompts the rhetorical question, "Who is like you, O Lord?" (Ex 15:11).

Triune holiness. On a Christian reading of Leviticus—one convinced that the God of the Old Testament is the God of the New Testament, the God who is eternally and unchangeably Father, Son, and Spirit—we can say that the holiness revealed in the fiery theophany is the holiness of Father, Son, and Spirit. "God is holy in his triune being and activity." This, according to John Webster, determines what Christian theology can and must say about God's holiness. The triune nature of God's holiness (along with the history of the enactment of his holy name) makes his holiness something concrete and particular. "God is not simply holy mystery, the nameless and voiceless whence of some sense of the numinous, and ineffable and indefinite deity."[73] Rather, God's holiness is structured by his triune being.

Recently, motivated in part by concerns similar to Webster's, Katherine Sonderegger has argued that "holiness is the conceptual name for the Triune Mystery." "Trinity," conversely, "is the conceptual unfolding of the Superabundant Holiness of God."[74] Interestingly, Sonderegger argues this claim by reflecting on the holy fire of Exodus and Leviticus, an image she believes corresponds to the mystery of the divine procession.[75] "Here we are shown in the sacrificial cultus a perfectly general property of the Holy One: He is altogether Fire, and His Life is an Exceeding Weight of Glory whose Inner Core is Molten Flame. Out of this Luminous Cloud, His Combustion pours forth." In this "combustion," she explains, we see an image of the *exitus et*

---

that eternal holiness is recognized in large part by the impression of awe it leaves on God's creatures.
[72]Webster, *Holiness*, 37.
[73]Webster, *Holiness*, 32, 36.
[74]Sonderegger, *Systematic Theology*, 2:84, 27.
[75]Importantly for Sonderegger, this procession is one.

reditus of God's inner life.⁷⁶ Sonderegger notes that the "doctors of the church spoke eagerly of Divine Fire when they considered the Holy Processions. Nicaea itself sums up the Divine Life: God from God, Light from Light." She notes also Rowan Williams's appeal to "the fittingness of fire as idiom for Trinitarian development: the flame passed from torch to torch, say, can extend itself without division or diminution; the second flame is fully fire yet distinctly its own light and heat."⁷⁷ She thus speaks of "the Procession, the Divine Fire that just is God in Act . . . the Fiery Descent of the Son, His Generation, which is Fire blazing forth from the Holy of Holies." Significantly for our present purposes, Sonderegger even goes so far as to say that the order of the divine life is one of sacrifice. The divine procession is self-offering and return, the descending flame of divine self-gift answered by ascending smoke. God is not just Molten Flame but "Molten Gift." All this, Sonderegger claims, is the way the priestly voice of the Pentateuch teaches the Trinity.⁷⁸

Sonderegger happily admits that her reading of the text, like (as she judges) the doctrine or the Trinity itself, is "speculative." That is, it is a confident, dogmatic exegesis that closely attends to Scripture in order to search out "the principal truths of [Christian] doctrine; high truths and mysteries."⁷⁹ Some points of exegesis will not be persuasive to all, not even to those sympathetic to her approach to the text. Regardless of how one assesses her reading, however, she is making an important claim about divine holiness. Similar to Webster, Sonderegger argues that divine holiness is not the impression left on us by his raw, undifferentiated power. Nor does it merely denote the subjective effect of standing before sheer mystery, as Rudolf Otto's *The Idea of the*

---

⁷⁶Sonderegger, *Systematic Theology*, 2:434, 458.
⁷⁷Sonderegger, *Systematic Theology*, 2:434; referencing Williams's *Tokens of Trust* (Louisville, KY: Westminster John Knox, 2007), 68-72.
⁷⁸Sonderegger, *Systematic Theology*, 2:452, 465, 27-33.
⁷⁹Sonderegger, *Systematic Theology*, 2:xxvii. The term *speculative* might raise suspicions in some of Sonderegger's readers. Some, too, will be concerned with the novelty of her reading—though she clearly has something of a precedent in the works of Hans Urs von Balthasar. But while some may believe there is little to justify Sonderegger's reading of the divine fire of Exodus-Leviticus as a witness to divine procession, it seems to me that this move cannot be wholly dismissed. The mystery and wonder of the divine fire in Exodus and Leviticus does indeed seem to correspond to the mystery and wonder of God's own inner life. On that basis, I believe that Sonderegger's effort at such a speculative reading is justified, even if the reading itself is more difficult to assess.

Holy might lead us to believe. Rather, God's holiness is something particular. It is an *order*, the trinitarian structure of God's "Infinite Boundedness." And as any order implies an ethic, so too does the order of God's inner life as Father, Son, and Spirit. The structure of God's inner life reveals "the Processional Life of God as *ethical*, as Goodness." "There is nothing in God," she insists, "in His Majestic Inwardness, that is not an expression of His Sublime Righteousness."[80] Even the holiness of God's triune life, and even when considered apart from his creatures, would therefore contain some notion of moral good, or at least a ground for such a notion.

Perhaps, then, even if God's holiness should not be reduced to his moral excellence, we can say that it never leaves behind the notion of moral excellence. Holiness is always more than righteousness but never less. In this way, God's holiness can be the principal of his judgment against sin, as Scripture seems to make it, without being made synonymous with righteousness.[81]

The meaning of the Name: Steadfast love. Finally, we should draw attention to the way the name YHWH communicates God's steadfast love. In Exodus 5, having been commissioned by God to lead Israel out of Egypt, Moses announces God's will to Israel: "Thus says the Lord, the God of Israel, 'Let my people go, so that they may hold a feast to me in the wilderness'" (Ex 5:1). Pharaoh responds in a way that sets the stage for further revelation of the Name through the plagues that will follow—"Who is the Lord, that I should obey his voice and let Israel go? I do not know the Lord, and moreover, I will not let Israel go" (Ex 5:2). Pharaoh's disregard for God is followed (as is so often the case) by brutality; he increases his demand on Israel by withholding the straw needed to make bricks. The people see they are in trouble, and they despair.

In Exodus 6:2-13, in response to Israel's discouragement, God provides something of his own commentary on the name he gave to Moses. God sends Moses to Israel with words that unfold the significance of his name.

> I am the Lord, and I will bring you out from under the burdens of the Egyptians, and I will deliver you from slavery to them, and I will redeem you with an outstretched arm and with great acts of judgment. I will take you to be my people, and I will be your God, and you shall know that I am

---

[80] Sonderegger, *Systematic Theology*, 2:85, 380, 347.
[81] Herman Bavinck, *Reformed Dogmatics*, 2:220.

the LORD your God, who has brought you out from under the burdens of the Egyptians. I will bring you into the land that I swore to give to Abraham, to Isaac, and to Jacob. I will give it to you for a possession. I am the LORD. (Ex 6:6-8)

The threefold repetition of "I am YHWH [i.e., the LORD]" in this passage is surrounded by pledges of God's covenant love and faithfulness (on which he had made good by the time of Leviticus). According to his own testimony in these verses, the God of Israel will show himself to be "YHWH your God" when he redeems Israel from Egypt, takes them to be his own (i.e., makes a covenant with them at Sinai), and keeps the promise he made to their fathers to give them the land of Canaan. When YHWH fulfills his covenant promise, Israel will know the significance of his name.

The same notes of divine love and faithfulness were sounded earlier in Exodus 3. When God first speaks to Moses from the burning bush, he identifies himself by reference to his covenant beneficiaries; he is "the God of Abraham, the God of Isaac, and the God of Jacob" (Ex 3:6). He then announces his remarkable compassion for Israel, whom he already regards as his beloved: "I have surely seen the affliction of *my people* who are in Egypt and have heard their cry because of their taskmasters. *I know their sufferings*, and I have come down to deliver them out of the hand of the Egyptians and bring them up out of that land into a good and broad land. . . . The cry of the people of Israel has come to me" (Ex 3:7-9). When Moses tells the elders of Israel of YHWH's appearance and intent to rescue them, he is similarly to announce YHWH as the God who has made promises to Israel's fathers and who now promises himself again. Per God's instruction, he is to gather the elders and tell them, "The LORD, the God of your fathers, the God of Abraham, of Isaac, and of Jacob, has appeared to me, saying, 'I have observed you and what has been done to you in Egypt, and I promise that I will bring you up out of the affliction of Egypt to the land of the Canaanites . . . a land flowing with milk and honey'" (Ex 3:16-17). Here again, the revelation of the name YHWH is bound up with God's promise, faithfulness, and mercy to Israel.

The name of YHWH therefore denotes, in addition to all that was said above, his "pragmatic presence"; YHWH is "I am who I am for you [Israel]."[82]

---

[82]Waltke, *Old Testament Theology*, 366.

The name YHWH indicates both something of the eternal, infinite being of God and the good news that this eternal and infinite God has given himself to Israel in covenant. As God explains the meaning of his name to Moses, he explains that he is "the absolute God of the fathers, acting with unfettered liberty." The Name "precluded any comparison between the God of Israel and the deities of the Egyptians and other nations, and furnished Moses and his people with strong consolation in their affliction, and a powerful support to their confidence in the realization of His purposes of salvation made know to the fathers."[83] YHWH, in short, is "he who makes good on his promises"—as the exodus narrative will prove and as Israel will gladly celebrate at the altar.[84] This God is both "he who is," who is superlatively existent, and "he who is with his creatures in mercy and faithfulness."[85]

The Name and Levitical sacrifice. Given all that has been said about the character of the Lord and the meaning of his name, it seems appropriate to state here what all this means for our reading of Levitical sacrifice.

First, and most obviously, the God revealed in the narrative of Genesis and Exodus, identifying himself as YHWH, is not a God who is in need and can therefore be manipulated. YHWH is not a pagan god, dependent on the world and the service of his people. Instead, YHWH's aseity means that, properly speaking, YHWH cannot be acted on by his creatures. As we saw above, the self-reflexive character of YHWH's name indicates an absolute independence from all other reality. YHWH, the Creator and sustainer of all, is supremely existent, having all life in and of himself and deriving nothing from his creatures. And, as Thomas Weinandy argues, this strong Creator-creature distinction implied by the Name grounds a proper doctrine of divine impassibility. YHWH, Weinandy comments, always shows himself to be "wholly other than the created order," even as he is constantly and lovingly active in the created order.[86] In other words, YHWH's relation to the world, given his eternality and self-existence, is necessarily marked

---

[83]Keil and Delitzsch, *Pentateuch*, 287.
[84]Christopher R. Seitz, *The Elder Testament: Canon, Theology, Trinity* (Waco, TX: Baylor University Press, 2018), 93.
[85]Cassuto explains the sense of the name YHWH as "It is I who am with My creatures in their hour of trouble and need" (*Commentary on the Book of Exodus*, 38).
[86]Thomas Weinandy, *Does God Suffer?* (Notre Dame, IN: University of Notre Dame Press, 2000), 56.

by a beneficent "outsideness," akin to the relation between an author and the author's characters. Importantly, this outsideness entails neither apathy nor impotence. Rather, it allows for a mode of presence and activity in the life of the character that would otherwise be impossible.[87]

The impassibility of God does not deny all reciprocity in the covenant relation between YHWH and his creatures. It does mean, however, that any such reciprocity is strictly asymmetrical. As I will argue later in this study, God intended to receive something from his people in sacrifice. But this reception on God's part did not meet a material (or quasi-material) need in God, nor did it have a material (or quasi-material) effect on God. I propose, then, that instead of thinking of Israel acting on YHWH by Levitical sacrifice, we should think of Levitical sacrifice as a means of YHWH acting on his people. At the altar, while Israel did indeed present their gifts to the Lord, it was more truly the Lord who was giving gifts to Israel, extending to them a creaturely fellowship—we might even say participation—in his own life and holiness.[88] If we hold to a trinitarian understanding of holiness, like that of Webster, we might even say that such fellowship in God's life and holiness would mean creaturely participation in God's intratrinitarian love. This, a gift greater than which cannot be conceived, is surely not something we could achieve for ourselves; divine grace alone could be the cause of such a wonder. This assertion does not mean that Israel was passive at the altar; the individual Israelites who routinely brought near their offerings selected their offerings from their livestock, led them to the tent, and slaughtered them at the altar. What it

---

[87]Kevin J. Vanhoozer, *Remythologizing Theology: Divine Action, Passion, and Authorship* (Cambridge: Cambridge University Press, 2010), 324-29. See also 54: "God is able to establish such intimate relationships [with his people] only because he is the Wholly Other. To make God less than wholly other does not make him more personal, loving, and compassionate, but rather he would be less personal, loving, and compassionate. If God were not the Wholly Other, he could not be the Creator, the Savior, and the Holy One capable of the intimate presence and the dynamic actions that these designations disclose."

[88]Andrew Davison, *Participation in God: A Study in Christian Doctrine and Metaphysics* (Cambridge: Cambridge University Press, 2019), helpfully notes that, at least in the Thomistic conception, creaturely participation in God is "form-determined." In other words, what a creature receives from God is determined by the nature (i.e., limits) of the creature. The key is that we remain thoroughly creaturely in this participation. We do not by this participation take on the infinite quality of the divine nature but receive from that nature all that we can while remaining the finite, particular creatures God has made us to be. Our created essence limits what we can receive of God, yet it also allows us to receive from God in a particular way.

does mean, however, is that whatever efficacy sacrifice may have had was ultimately due to God's agency, which worked through Israel's cult. Levitical sacrifice was a means of God acting in and for his people in the steadfast love denoted by his name.[89]

Second, the character of YHWH means that, if sacrifice was really to be a means of Israel drawing near to God and uniting themselves to him in covenant union, then sacrifice in some way must have included some means of addressing the demands created by the holiness and righteousness of God. In other words, it must have been accepted by God as *satisfaction and sanctification*. Throughout the pentateuchal narrative, the presence of God creates a crisis for Israel. This is evident at Mount Sinai, where Israel shrank back from God in fear, begging Moses to intercede (Ex 20:19). It is also evident in Numbers, which describes the appointment of the Levites as a means of protecting the congregation of Israel from the danger of the Lord's presence (Num 8:19) and which speaks time and again of the appearance of the Lord's glory in the context of judgment; at least four times in Numbers, "the glory of the Lord appeared" to Israel to enact judgment (see Num 14:10; 16:19, 42; 20:6). The Lord thus appears to Israel in his immutable holiness and righteousness, and this often endangers Israel.

The character of the Lord creates two demands for those who would draw near to God: that they be made compatible with divine holiness and that they be made righteous in regard to the divine law.[90] In other words, as we read in Psalm 15:1, it is the one who is blameless (before the law) who may "sojourn in [the Lord's] tent." And, as we read in Psalm 24:3-4, the one who is clean and pure (i.e., compatible with divine holiness) shall "stand in his holy place." Sacrifice, therefore, serving as it did to qualify Israel for the presence and service of the Lord, must have addressed matters of both satisfying the divine law and sharing in the divine holiness. Somehow, sacrifice effected both legal blamelessness and cultic purity before God. How each of these was effected by Levitical sacrifice—and, ultimately, the

---

[89]This point is well-argued in Macina, *Lord's Service*, 14-35.

[90]Notably, this line of reasoning brings to the table the theological terms *justification* and *sanctification* in my reading of Levitical sacrifice. And, equally notably, it makes each term as important as the other.

sacrifice of Christ—is the crucial question. For now, it is enough to note that the notions of blamelessness before divine justice and consecration each have an important place in sacrificial atonement.[91]

מֵאֹהֶל מוֹעֵד—"FROM THE TENT OF MEETING"

At last, we read in Leviticus 1:1 that the voice calling out to Moses, the voice of YHWH, issued forth מֵאֹהֶל מוֹעֵד, "from the tent of meeting." The tent, too, shapes our understanding of what was happening in Levitical sacrifice.

Most basically, the tent can be conceived of as YHWH's palace among Israel.[92] Jay Sklar describes how the tent from which YHWH calls to Moses was designed not as a mere dwelling but as a throne room. "The tent's royal overtones," states Sklar, "should not be missed: like a palace, it was decorated with costly materials. . . . The ark within the Most Holy Place was the Lord's 'footstool' (1 Chr. 28:2), while the carved cherubim on top of the ark served as his royal 'throne' (2 Sam. 6:2)." When the people of Israel come to the tent, they therefore come to "stand before" their King, offering their praise and presenting themselves for service.[93] In the tent, the LORD is enthroned among his people.

But to this basic picture we should add that the tent recalls both Mount Sinai and the Garden of Eden and that the purpose of each was being partially, temporarily realized in the tent. The tent stood as symbol for all God's

---

[91] Part of what motivates this point is the tendency among some scholars—biblical scholars and systematic theologians alike—to downplay legal concerns in their accounts of sacrifice and atonement. John Goldingay, for instance, opposes a "framework of law" to a "framework of worship," and argues that sacrifice assumed the latter. See Goldingay, "Old Testament Sacrifice and the Death of Christ," in *Atonement Today: A Symposium at St. John's College, Nottingham*, ed. John Goldingay (London: SPCK, 1995), 10. Consequently, he argues, sacrifice may be understood as vicarious cleansing but not vicarious punishment. Even if Goldingay is right, his argument seems faulty based on the importance of the divine righteousness in the Pentateuch and of God's law at the tent.

[92] Milgrom discusses "a rabbinic source that speaks of two tents," one located outside the camp (as Num 11:24-27 seems to say) and one at the very center of the camp (as in Num 2:17; *Leviticus 1–16*, 140). According to this source, the function of the tent outside the camp was oracular—it was a place for Moses to receive divine revelation—while that of the tent at the center of the camp was cultic. Biblical scholars often advance a similar line of argument based on the two names for the tent, the "tent of meeting" and the "tabernacle." Following Morales, it seems best to see these two names as referring to distinct functions of one tent. This construal even guides Morales's reading of the text: "We may understand the movement of Leviticus as the drama of how the dwelling of God, the [tabernacle], becomes a tent of meeting" (*Who Shall Ascend*, 110).

[93] Sklar, *Leviticus*, 87, 37.

good purposes for his people. As the LORD calls to Moses from the tent, those purposes are recalled and thereby etched into the setting of Levitical sacrifice.

A portable Sinai. For a number of reasons, the tent of meeting, otherwise known as the tabernacle, can be considered a "portable Sinai."[94] Like Sinai, the tent of meeting is the site of YHWH's presence and revelation.[95] Morales notes the way in which Exodus creates a verbal link between YHWH's presence on Sinai and his later presence in the tent. Just as the glory of YHWH is said to "dwell" (from Heb. שָׁכַן) on Sinai in Exodus 24:16, so in Exodus 25:8, after the covenant celebration on Sinai is complete, God commands that a sanctuary be built that he might "dwell" (again from Heb. שָׁכַן) among the people of Israel. The same Hebrew root, in fact, is used to denominate that sanctuary in Exodus 25:9, מִשְׁכָּן, translated "tabernacle."[96]

YHWH's dwelling in the tent, moreover, will be symbolized by fire and cloud, just as it was on the mountain. As "the cloud covered" the mountain in Exodus 24:15 (וַיְכַס הֶעָנָן אֶת־הָהָר), so "the cloud covered" the tent of meeting in Exodus 40:34 (וַיְכַס הֶעָנָן אֶת־אֹהֶל מוֹעֵד). As the summit of Sinai blazed with the fire of God's glory, so is the tabernacle's altar of burnt offering "ablaze with [God's] fiery presence."[97]

The parallels are even more striking when seen in light of the structural similarities between Sinai and the tent. Milgrom explains how the tripartite division of the tent, with differing grades of holiness, corresponds to that of the mountain. The similarities he notes are remarkable.

> Mount Sinai is the archetype of the Tabernacle, and is similarly divided into three gradations of holiness. Its summit is the Holy of Holies; God's voice issues forth from there (Exod 19:20) as from the inner shrine (Exod 25:22; Num 7:89); the mountaintop is off limits to priests and layman alike (Exod 19:24b), and its very sight is punishable by death (Exod 19:21b), and so with its Tabernacle counterpart (cf. Lev 16:2 and Num 4:20); finally, Moses alone is privileged to ascend to the top . . . just as, later, the high priest is permitted entry to the inner shrine. . . . The second division of Sinai is the equivalent of the outer shrine, marked off from the rest of the mountain by

---

[94]Sklar, *Leviticus*, 86.
[95]Sklar, *Leviticus*, 86.
[96]Morales, *Who Shall Ascend*, 96.
[97]Morales, *Who Shall Ascend*, 97, 100.

> being enveloped in a cloud.... Below the cloud is the third division.... This is where the altar [is] erected (24:4). It is the equivalent of the courtyard.

Milgrom concludes, "The blazing summit, the cloud-covered slopes, and visible bottom rim [of the mountain] correspond to Tabernacle divisions."[98]

Thus, according to Morales, "the significance of Mount Sinai gets transferred to the tabernacle." Through the tabernacle and its cult, "Sinai is not merely remembered but *relived*—recreated and re-experienced." As they did at Sinai, Israel will approach the holy presence of YHWH at the tabernacle. As they did at Sinai, Israel will know and acknowledge YHWH as their God at the tabernacle. And, as they did at Sinai, Israel will learn the will of YHWH at the tabernacle. From the ark of the covenant, housed in the most holy place, God will reveal his commands.[99] As the Lord says of the ark in Exodus 25:22, "There I will meet with you [Moses], and from above the mercy seat ... I will speak with you about all that I will give you in commandment for the people of Israel." The tent of meeting, the site of Levitical sacrifice, holds in its boundaries the "heart of the covenant," namely, "God's real and visible presence."[100] As such, it was an extension of Sinai.

A return to Eden. The tabernacle, however, was not only an extension of Sinai—the place where God communed with his beloved and enacted his covenant with them. It was also a symbolic return to the Garden of Eden, to the place where God had wished to dwell among his creatures as their Father, to receive their worship and extend his blessing, to enact his covenant with all creation.

The similarities between the tabernacle and the Garden of Eden begin with parallels between the construction of the tabernacle in Exodus 35–40 and the construction of the cosmos in Genesis 1. Jon Levenson shows how both accounts are marked by the authority and efficacy of God's word; cosmos and tabernacle alike are constructed by a "perfect realization of divine commandments." Both, too, are marked by the beautifying presence of God's Spirit; the same Spirit that hovered over the face of the waters when God built the cosmos also endowed Bezalel the son of Uri with skill,

---

[98]Milgrom, *Leviticus 1–16*, 143.
[99]Morales, *Who Shall Ascend*, 95, 98–99.
[100]Wenham, *Leviticus*, 17.

intelligence, and craftmanship as he built furnishings for the tent.¹⁰¹ And both follow a pattern of construction and consecration: in Genesis, God blesses his creatures and sanctifies the seventh day upon completion of his work (Gen 1:31; 2:3); in Exodus, Moses blesses the people and consecrates the tabernacle when its construction is complete (Ex 39:43; 40:9-11). Levenson concludes that Israel's tabernacle was conceived as a microcosm, and the cosmos "as a macro-temple."¹⁰²

Morales notes other links between the cosmos and the tabernacle: the use of the Hebrew word מָאוֹר ("light") in Genesis 1:14-16 to denote the sun, moon, and stars, the same word used of the lamps in the tabernacle; the liturgical significance assigned to those lights in Genesis 1:14; the emphasis on wisdom in the construction of each (see Prov 3:19-20; Ex 31:3); the likening of God's creative act to pitching a tent (Ps 104:2; Job 9:8; Is 40:22). He too concludes that "the cosmos is a large temple; the temple is a small cosmos."¹⁰³

If the cosmos is a large temple, Morales continues, then Eden, as described in Genesis 2–3, was "something of an archetypal holy of holies—the place of most intimate communion and fellowship with YHWH God." This is the interpretation of Jubilees 8:19: "And he [Noah] knew that Eden was the holy of holies and the dwelling of YHWH." And this interpretation proves a valid one. The description of YHWH "walking" in Eden (Gen 3:8) is matched by a description of God walking among Israel in the tabernacle (Lev 26:12; see Deut 23:14); Eden's eastward orientation is likewise matched by that of the tabernacle. And the fruitfulness of Eden is matched by "the fullness of life associated with the tabernacle, including the menorah as a stylized tree of life."¹⁰⁴

Morales goes on to explain that Eden, like Sinai, should be understood as the mountain of God, a "cultic mountain." Ezekiel 28:13-14 speaks of Eden as "the garden of God . . . the holy mountain of God." Further, Genesis 2:10-14

---

¹⁰¹Jon D. Levenson, *Creation and the Persistence of Evil: The Jewish Drama of Divine Omnipotence* (Princeton, NJ: Princeton University Press, 1988), 84. Leveson is unsure that the "spirit/wind of God" in Gen 1:2 means anything other than "a great wind." He notes, however, that "the absence of the term anywhere between the two texts [of Gen 1:2 and Ex 35:30] suggests the homology of world building and temple building, which is the burden of my argument here." Cf. Morales, *Who Shall Ascend*, 40-41.
¹⁰²Levenson, *Creation and the Persistence of Evil*, 85-86.
¹⁰³Morales, *Who Shall Ascend*, 41-42.
¹⁰⁴Morales, *Who Shall Ascend*, 51-52.

describes a "spring-fed river that runs through the garden and then flows *down* from Eden . . . suggesting a locale that corresponds well with a mountain summit."[105] Within the lush boundaries of that mountaintop garden, Adam served as priest. Morales notes that Adam's work in the garden is described as priestly service. Translations often relate that Adam was commanded by God to "work" and "keep" the garden in Genesis 2:15.[106] But a better rendering of this command might be "to worship and obey," and at any rate, the Hebrew terms employed are "used together elsewhere in the Pentateuch only to describe the duties of the Levites pertaining to the tabernacle (Num 3:7-8; 8:26; 18:5-6)." Adam's failure to fulfill his priestly vocation led to his exile from Eden, a fate paralleled by Israel's expulsion from YHWH's holy presence in the Babylonian exile. This point further strengthens the parallel between Eden and YHWH's later sanctuaries.[107]

If Eden was the original abode of God among his creatures, Morales reasons, then the tabernacle and its cult are God's invitation to return to Eden, the place where God's grace and glory dwell.[108] In the call of Leviticus 1:1, therefore, God is calling Adam back home.

The tent, with all its rich symbolism, therefore brings a key concept into the setting of Levitical sacrifice. In addition to strengthening the concept of covenant that has been so prominent in this exegesis, it also sets firmly in place the concept of creation. Levitical sacrifice was not only a covenantal act, one in which the goal of the covenant relationship was realized. It was also meant to be a supremely creaturely act, one in which God's purposes in creation were in some measure realized. This is all the more apparent in the sacrifice of Christ, through which God's purposes for the world are being completed; through the death and resurrection of Christ, God is working out his "plan for the fullness of time, to unite all things in him, things in heaven and things on earth" (Eph 1:10). This association between sacrifice and God's purposes in creation is significant, for it ultimately allows us to see the work of Christ as "fundamentally positive, constructive, and lifegiving," even if "it contains within it an essentially negative, destructive, and

---

[105] Morales, *Who Shall Ascend*, 52.
[106] This is the ESV's rendering. The RSV employs the verbs *till* and *keep*; other major English translations are similar.
[107] Morales, *Who Shall Ascend*, 53-55.
[108] Morales, *Who Shall Ascend*, 75-108.

deadly element."[109] YHWH, it seems, wishes Israel to return to Eden, and wishes that they receive the perfecting blessing of the beatific vision. And he has brought this about—not only for Israel but for all who call on the name of Christ—in the sacrifice of his incarnate Son.

Sacrifice and Recapitulation in the Narrative Context of Leviticus

This chapter has attended to the setting of Levitical sacrifice, that is, the narrative context of Leviticus. It has been especially concerned with the character of the God who calls out to Moses and this history of this God's dealings with the nations of Israel. For this God himself is the primary feature in the setting of the story told by Levitical sacrifice. The history of his mighty works, and what those works say about his intentions for Israel, form the background against which the action of burnt offering is intelligible.

In surveying that background, it is important not to rush to conclusions about the nature of atonement in the burnt offering. We have yet to consider important questions, such as those about the themes, plot, and hero of Levitical sacrifice, all of which give depth to our understanding of the cultic story. Nevertheless, we can already see that the story is moving in a certain direction. That direction is marked out by the terms *satisfaction* and *recapitulation*. The setting of the burnt offering is heavy with concern for God's law and judgment, on the one hand, and God's purposes for his people, Israel, on the other. The God who calls us to Moses is a God who keeps his promises, whose integrity will not be compromised. As he has given a law, so he will uphold it and the righteous judgment it requires. And as he has called Israel to a particular purpose, so he will see that that purpose is fulfilled. In other words, we are already led to expect that if Israel is to answer this summons and come to God at the altar, it will mean both the satisfaction of divine justice and the recapitulation—the correction and perfection—of the offeror.

Satisfaction and recapitulation are therefore already emerging as two components of the mechanism of atonement. This, of course, fits with the thesis I identified in my introduction: the burnt offering proclaims the

---

[109] Adam J. Johnson, "Atonement: The Shape and State of the Doctrine," in *T&T Clark Companion to Atonement*, ed. Adam J. Johnson (London: Bloomsbury T&T Clark, 2017), 8-9.

promise of atonement by means of satisfaction and recapitulation through filial substitution. But these terms need more content before we rush to theological conclusions. In particular, if "satisfaction" is to be more than a mere label—if the concept is really to shed light on the work of Christ, really to give us theological insight—then it needs filling out. And there is no other way to fill it out than by continuing to pay close attention to the Levitical story. We need to continue the instructions for the burnt offering and what they might mean for our understanding of Christ's work of atonement.

Plot

In Search of the Essential Act of Sacrifice

דַּבֵּר אֶל־בְּנֵי יִשְׂרָאֵל וְאָמַרְתָּ אֲלֵהֶם אָדָם כִּי־יַקְרִיב מִכֶּם קָרְבָּן לַיהוָה מִן־הַבְּהֵמָה מִן־הַבָּקָר וּמִן־הַצֹּאן תַּקְרִיבוּ אֶת־קָרְבַּנְכֶם׃

> Speak to the people of Israel and say to them, When any one of you brings an offering to the LORD, you shall bring your offering of livestock from the herd or from the flock.
>
> LEVITICUS 1:2

"MYSTERY," WRITES MATTHIAS JOSEPH SCHEEBEN, "is generally defined as a truth concerning which we know that it is, but not how it is; that is, according to the usual explanation, we know that the subject and the predicate are connected, but we are unable to determine and perceive the manner of the association." This is not to say, Scheeben clarifies, that when it comes to the Christian faith, the mystery lies "only in the *How*, not in the *That*," for even the *that* of Christianity (e.g., Trinity, incarnation, atonement) is unanticipated by human reason and knowable only by divine revelation. Nevertheless, it is often in pondering the *how* of the central claims of the Christian faith that we become especially aware of mystery, for it is the *how* that "we cannot adequately express with our rational concepts."[1] The *that* of Christianity may be above us, something we could not have

---

[1] Matthias Joseph Scheeben, *The Mysteries of Christianity*, trans. Cyril Vollert, SJ (New York: Herder & Herder, 1946), 12 (with n8), 13.

deduced or even imagined without the preaching of the gospel. But the *how* of Christianity, Scheeben asserts, is beyond us, something we cannot fully grasp and articulate with our limited conceptual and linguistic resources.

Scheeben's words should be taken as a cautionary note, one that is particularly instructive at this point in the current study. In the last chapter, I made claims about the *that* of Levitical sacrifice: *that* Levitical sacrifice was ordained by God as a means of approaching God, *that* it was an expression of covenant faithfulness, *that* it was in some way a fulfillment of God's intentions for creation, *that* it was an act of consecration. The stated purpose of my study, however, concerns the *how* of Levitical sacrifice—specifically, the mechanism of atonement in the burnt offering and its fulfillment in Christ. From this point forward, it is the *how* that will receive most immediate attention. Some might see this as a fool's errand: if, as Scheeben says, our rational concepts fail at this point, then what is there to say? However, the fact that rational concepts fail to explain *all* of a mystery does not mean that they fail to explain *any* of a mystery. And in Christian theology, every bit of clarity we can gain into the mystery of Christ should be cherished.

Continuing my narrative analysis of Levitical sacrifice, the present chapter will give its attention to the plot of Levitical sacrifice. Plot, as I will explain, is not just a sequence of events—a narrative's movement from beginning to middle to end. Rather, plot is a sequence of causes and effects—a determination of how one event or act of a narrative gives rise to another or the principle by which a narrative moves from beginning to middle to end. My aim here is thus to identify what we can call the "essential act" of sacrifice, that which moves the narrative enacted at the Levitical altar from its beginning to a fitting end. This is no easy task, and the plot identified in this chapter is not intended to be taken as an exhaustive explanation of how Levitical sacrifice (and the sacrifice of Christ) "worked." Still, the effort to clarify the plot of sacrifice is a necessary one, for it is here, in discerning some kind of cause and effect in sacrifice, that the mystery of sacrifice is most squarely confronted. It is here too that the disagreements are the strongest.

After a brief word on plot, this chapter will proceed to argue on the concept of plot that the plot of Levitical sacrifice, a plot fulfilled in the sacrifice of Christ, is one of "return." This plot is layered—there are multiple returns, and each return implies or depends on another.[2] As God calls from the tent, Israel returns to the LORD and his presence; as he commands, they return obedience; as he gives graciously, they return sacrificial gifts in gratitude. Importantly, however, this return is not without conflict; there is in sacrifice a struggle between life and death. The return of sacrifice thus becomes a *return through death*. This return is made possible only by the life-giving grace of God.

The argument of this chapter depends on exegesis of Leviticus 1:2, along with other selected passages. Before getting to that exegesis and the argument that follows from it, however, a brief word on why the concept of plot helps us read Levitical sacrifice in general and the burnt offering in particular.

PLOT AND LEVITICAL SACRIFICE

Plot, action, and authorship. First, a definition. According to Aristotle, plot is a "single, whole, and complete" action that gives a narrative its structural unity or integrity. Plot, as stated above, is not synonymous with narrative: a narrative is a sequence of events, but a plot is a sequence of events in a causal relationship directed to some end. That end is the resolution of some conflict; "without conflict, plot hardly exists."[3] Therefore, in Aristotle's famed definition, plot consists of a beginning, middle, and end. The beginning is that which "does not itself follow anything by causal necessity, but after which something naturally occurs." The middle flows "naturally" out of the beginning and propels the narrative toward its end. And, in the end, the single, unified action of the whole arrives at a fitting conclusion.

Our assessment of a plot's soundness might be understood in terms of how natural or necessary we judge the relationship of cause and effect to be; events should be bound by a relation of *propter hoc* ("on account of this")

---

[2]As I will be arguing throughout, the "return" at the altar can be thought of in terms of covenantal reciprocity. Through sacrifice, Israel drew near to God's presence, honored his loving lordship (divine fatherhood), and acknowledged his faithfulness. As each aspect of Israel's cultic return is discussed below, the covenantal context should be remembered; a legal-relational connotation is intended.

[3]Hugh Holman and William Harmon, *A Handbook to Literature*, 6th ed. (New York: Macmillan, 1992), 360-61.

and not merely *post hoc* ("after this").⁴ Necessity in plot can be complex and is dependent on a number of factors, not least of which is the character of the different agents involved in the action. Critics therefore speak of a plot of character in addition to plot of action. Nevertheless, some sense of necessity (or fittingness) should be discernible in plot. The different episodes of a narrative should be joined by some principle of relationship so that the episodes make up one whole and continuous action. "The structural union of the parts [should be] such that, if any one of them is displaced or removed, the whole will be disjointed and disturbed."⁵

Plot can therefore be considered "an intellectual formulation about the relations among incidents and is, therefore, a guiding principle for the author and ordering control for the reader."⁶ This, I suggest, is precisely what we want when we peer into the mysteries of Levitical sacrifice. The conviction of this study is that God authored Levitical sacrifice and that in doing so he gave it some guiding principle, so that Levitical sacrifice is not wholly irrational. There is, then, some unifying principle in Levitical sacrifice that offers us an "ordering control" for interpretation, if we can discern it. Of course, discerning a unifying principle that runs throughout the Levitical ritual and constitutes a logical arrangement is precisely the problem that underlies this study.⁷ I suggest, however, that thinking of this problem as an issue of plot can provide clarity for our investigation.

Beginning, middle, and end. We can start by thinking in terms of the beginning, middle, and end of Levitical sacrifice, which sets a helpful trajectory for our inquiry. In chapter one, I argued that Leviticus 1:1 reveals both the beginning and end of sacrifice. A bit more reflection on each is necessary here, followed by attention to what I call the mysterious middle.

---

⁴Thus Aristotle; Holman and Harmon, *Handbook to Literature*, 360-61. This account of plot, of course, is contested. In some postmodern authors, a disregard for logical relationship between events is evident; the conclusion of Sartre's *Nausea* is an example.
⁵Holman and Harmon, *Handbook to Literature*, 361.
⁶Holman and Harmon, *Handbook to Literature*, 361.
⁷By stating that plot is a logical arrangement, I do not mean to say that all action in a plot (including that of the Levitical cult) is logically determined by a foundational set of axioms. The language of *fittingness* is more appropriate to the logic I have in mind than that of *necessity*. My analysis of the cultic plot intends to show why each action fits in the context of the whole and that the whole is meaningful, not that each act in the sequence is in some strict sense necessary.

Beginning. As we saw earlier, Leviticus opens with YHWH calling out to Moses from the tent of meeting. In this call, we hear both a summons and an invitation: YHWH calls to Israel both as Master to servant and as Father to son. A note of affection might be heard in this call; it is "a call uttered in love," issued in "the language of invitation, friendship, [and] love."[8] This, to use Aristotle's language, is the beginning of Levitical sacrifice, in that it both initiates the action and "does not follow anything by causal necessity" but is the ground of all that follows.[9] In theological terms, it is a call of grace, as the Lord speaks to Israel of his own initiative and with the intent to do them good.

The gracious nature of this call is all the more evident when we consider its timing, a point not previously mentioned. Many readers of Leviticus over the centuries have found it noteworthy that the Levitical legislation concerning sacrifice comes soon after the golden calf incident of Exodus 32. Often, they have taken this as proof that God's command to offer animal sacrifice was an accommodation to Israel's moral and religious immaturity or weakness. Israel had proven their stubborn proclivity toward idolatrous sacrificial practices. God, wise and patient, therefore allowed them to present sacrifices to himself so that he might gently and effectively correct them.[10] In some early Christian writers, this view is combined with the idea that Levitical sacrifice was meant to point Israel to the coming Christ.[11] In either case, what comes through clearly is that the Levitical legislation was an act of divine mercy. When the Lord calls out from the tent of meeting, he is calling out as one who has already proven to be "a God merciful and gracious, slow to anger . . . forgiving iniquity and transgression and sin" (Ex 34:6-7). Though only recently betrothed, Israel has already broken covenant with YHWH and "corrupted themselves" (Ex 32:7) with an idol. And, to be sure, the Lord disciplines Israel in response, sending "a plague on the people, because they made the calf" (Ex 32:35). Nevertheless, he demonstrates his mercy by renewing the covenant with Israel and inviting them

---

[8]Jonathan Sacks, *Leviticus: The Book of Holiness*, Covenant and Conversation: A Weekly Reading of the Jewish Bible (New Milford, CT: Maggid Books and the Orthodox Union, 2015), 61, 16.
[9]Holman and Harmon, *Handbook to Literature*, 361.
[10]E.g., Maimonides, *The Guide for the Perplexed*, 2nd ed., trans. M. Friedländer (New York: Dover, 1956), 3.32 (322-24).
[11]E.g., Justin Martyr, *Dialogue with Trypho* 22.

once again into his presence. The tabernacle is erected soon after this incident (in the apparent timeline of Exodus). When YHWH invites Israel to the tent of meeting, he offers friendship to a people who have proven quick to forget and betray him. Soon after they make the golden calf, Israel is commanded to leave Sinai, the place where they had met the Lord, suggesting that their idolatry has made them unfit for the presence of the Lord. When the Lord invites them to the tent of meeting, he is therefore inviting a return to Sinai, as represented by the tent, by means of sacrifice.

Here, then, the plot of Levitical sacrifice begins: in YHWH's merciful call to sinners, summoning them to return. There is no necessity behind this call; the Lord is not bound by anything external to himself, and not even by his covenant with Israel, since they have already broken it. All that compels this call is the Lord's determination to be gracious, to share the riches of his own holy life with a people he has created and consecrated for himself, however much they might refuse to receive it. From this gracious call, heard in the words of Leviticus 1:1, all else in Leviticus follows—a good reminder that Levitical sacrifice was first and foremost something God offered to Israel, and only on that basis was it something Israel offered to God.[12]

End. If the plot of Levitical sacrifice begins with grace, it ends in glory. It has been noted already that, according to Leviticus 9, the sacrificial service culminated in a vision of God's glory. After Aaron presented the Levitical offerings in order for the first time and emerged from the tent of meeting to bless the people, "the glory of the Lord appeared to all the people" (Lev 9:23). As at Mount Sinai, the divine glory issuing forth from the tent took the form of fire, a fire that consumed the burnt offerings and fat portions on the altar (Lev 9:24). This vision of divine glory elicited an ambiguous response: the people "shouted and fell on their faces" at the sight of the theophanic fire, whether from joy or terror we cannot be sure. What is certain, however, is that through the sacrificial liturgy, the people of Israel drew near to God in his holiness. That nearness may turn out to mean either life or death (as the story of Nadab and Abihu, which follows close behind this episode, proves). Ideally, however, the vision of divine holiness would be the joy and blessing of Israel; it is blessing, after all, and not curse that Aaron places on the people

---

[12]Kleinig, reasoning along these lines, calls Levitical sacrifice "a divine-human enactment." John Kleinig, *Leviticus* (St. Louis: Concordia, 2003), 3.

at the moment the LORD appears to Israel at the altar. The end of Levitical sacrifice, we can conclude, is a blessed sight of God's glory—beatific vision.

The plot of Levitical sacrifice thus moves by some kind of causal logic from God's gracious call to sinners to their blessed reception of the *visio Dei*. To say this much is already to make a significant statement about Levitical sacrifice, one that is capable of informing our interpretation of the cult in important ways.[13] What is most interesting, however, and most important for this study, is some account of *how* and *why* the plot moves from call to vision. If there really is some whole, complete, unified action by which this plot moves from beginning to end, then what is that action?

The mysterious middle. What we need, in other words, is some account of the "middle" of Levitical sacrifice, of that which brings the beginning to the end. It is here, in the middle, that we most squarely confront the mystery of the cult. Recalling Scheeben's words, to say *that* Levitical sacrifice moved from merciful call to blessed vision is one thing; to say *how* it did so is another. To be sure, on a Christian reading, it did so only symbolically (or, if one is feeling bold, it did so sacramentally). But to call that movement symbolic is not to deny it a causal logic. If God truly authored Levitical sacrifice, and if he did so as a witness to Christ, then it is reasonable to assume that there is a plot that moves from beginning to end by some action; or, better, by some character performing some action in some setting.

A shorthand way to refer to this action, I want to suggest here, is "atonement." In a broad sense, and in keeping with the concept of plot, *atonement* can be defined as the action by which the conflict introduced by sin is brought to resolution.[14] By means of atonement, sin is somehow overcome, and the purposes of God that stand behind his gracious call to fellowship are realized. Atonement, then, is at the heart of the action of Levitical sacrifice and holds a privileged and essential place in the mysterious middle of the cultic plot. So states Hartmut Gese: "In the Priestly theology,

---

[13]In short, this construal of the cult's plot allows for a positive reading of the cult: positive in the sense that God had a definite purpose for the cult that accounted for yet went beyond accommodation to Israel's weakness, and positive in the sense the cult aimed at the reception of some good and not only a negation of some evil.

[14]Recall that in the introduction I define *atonement* as an act of compensation and cleansing that qualifies a sinner for the presence and service of God. That definition, I believe, is consonant with the much looser definition of atonement I give here.

atonement is regarded as the basis of the cult. It was recognized that cult is possible only as an act of atonement, and therefore atonement must determine the nature of the cultic realm."[15]

To recapitulate: There is a *plot* to Levitical sacrifice, a unifying action that moves from some beginning through conflict and on to a fitting end. That beginning is God's gracious call to sinners, and the end is beatific vision. What, then, lies in the mysterious middle? How does the Levitical cult move from its beginning to its end? In what follows, I will argue that the plot of Levitical sacrifice moves from beginning to end by way of *return through death*.

Return

In multiple senses, the plot of Levitical sacrifice hinges on the act of return.[16] Return, for reasons I will detail shortly, might even be called the "essential act" of sacrifice—though this return is in truth a sequence, not a single act. It is return, in other words, that makes sacrifice what it is and gives it its God-ordained efficacy.[17]

Return to Eden. In the previous chapter, I followed Morales in arguing that Israel's approach to the tent of meeting symbolized a return of humanity to the Garden of Eden. Morales roots his account of this return in the cultic-mountain motif that runs through the Pentateuch. In his account, Eden was the original cultic mountain, the place where God dwelled among the people he had created for himself to receive their worship and give them his blessing. But that blessing, as we sadly know so well, was forfeited by Adam and Eve because of their disobedience, and they were subsequently exiled from the garden. As Genesis moves on, the problem of humanity's alienation from

---

[15] Hartmut Gese, "The Atonement," in *Essays on Biblical Theology*, trans. Keith Crim (repr., Eugene, OR: Wipf & Stock, 2018), 100.

[16] I hope that my choice of the concept of return will be vindicated by the exposition of Levitical sacrifice given below. As a brief initial justification, I will mention here that Levitical sacrifice involved giving something to God, who always gives first, and that it also involved a movement toward God's holy presence. Both senses of *return*, as both gift and pilgrimage, will be considered below.

[17] As noted in the introduction to this study, B. B. Warfield argued powerfully that the essential act of sacrifice was slaughter. While I have the deepest respect for Warfield and his account of sacrifice, and while I argue that the death of the victim does play a constitutive role in Levitical sacrifice (and that of Christ), I believe that the notion of return better accounts for the entirety of the Levitical movement from call to vision.

God only worsens. But God, who is rich in mercy and determined to bless his creatures, resolves to bring humanity back to himself. Thus, the book of Exodus recounts how YHWH rescues a people for himself and brings them to a new Eden, a new cultic mountain: Mount Sinai. As the nation of Israel enters into covenant with God and the mountain, humanity again comes to dwell on God's "holy hill" (see Ps 15:1). And in the tent of meeting, Morales continues, the experience of Sinai was "relived—recreated and re-experienced." Sinai itself being something of a new (postfall) Eden, the tent simultaneously served to symbolize that original "garden of God," a point highlighted by the cosmic imagery in the tent and its construction. Thus, in the erection of the tabernacle, Morales asserts, "The garden of Eden [was] planted, as it were, in the midst of Sinai's arid wilderness." To draw near to the tent, Morales concludes, was therefore to return symbolically to the Garden of Eden through the cult. Indeed, "the tabernacle cultus is presented as a mediated resolution to the crisis introduced in Genesis 3 with humanity's expulsion from Eden," Israel's sacrificial worship constituting a "journey into the Presence of God." Through the cult, a way was opened for humanity to draw near to God once again by way of what Morales calls the "Levitical way," a "cultic journey" of "ascent into the presence of God."[18]

Looking briefly at Leviticus 1:2-3, we can see that there is good reason to follow Morales's construal of sacrificial worship as a cultic journey. As Rolf Knierim comments, sacrificial worship would have begun with a literal journey, even a "pilgrimage." In Leviticus 1:2-3, the offeror is instructed to "bring" his offering to the LORD. This act of bringing, Knierim notes, is identified by the text as sacred, being the beginning of the worshiper's offering and so part of the "ritual proper."[19] Leviticus thus envisions the cultic activity that culminates at the altar beginning at the worshiper's home as he selects an appropriate offering and journeys with it to the sanctuary.

Knierim puts his finger on a legitimate assumption of the text here, one that puts what follows Leviticus 1:2 in a certain frame. Sacrifice begins with movement—the movement of a worshiper toward God, a movement that

---

[18]Michael L. Morales, *Who Shall Ascend the Mountain of the Lord? A Biblical Theology of the Book of Leviticus*, New Studies in Biblical Theology (Downers Grove, IL: InterVarsity Press, 2015), 106, 98, 111, 75, 124.

[19]Rolf P. Knierim, *Text and Concept in Leviticus 1:1-9: A Case in Exegetical Method* (repr., Eugene, OR: Wipf & Stock, 2010), 32.

answers God's own move into the tent with its subsequent invitation to his people.[20] A literal cultic journey to the tent of meeting would have thus been the norm for Israel's laypeople; those called by the LORD through Moses in Leviticus 1:1-2 are envisioned as living some distance from the tent. In sacrifice, Israel thus returns, literally and symbolically, to God's dwelling place, where they might "gaze upon the beauty of the LORD" (Ps 27:4). Grateful return, in response to God's grace, is central to the plot of Levitical sacrifice.

Returning obedience (repentance). The symbolic return to Eden is important, but it does not exhaust the sense in which return constitutes the plot of Levitical sacrifice. A second sense of return in Levitical sacrifice is the "return" of obedience to the divine command. Perhaps this return is better termed "response," or even "repentance." Regardless, the idea of obedience, and of *learning* obedience, is at the heart of the book of Leviticus, so much so that it is not unjustly called the "real heart" of sacrifice.[21]

As important as the narrative context of Leviticus is, it must not be forgotten that most of the book consists of divine commands. And, in the priestly perspective of Leviticus, obedience to divine command is a matter of life and death. Indeed, obedience often seems to be *the* issue in biblical accounts of sacrifice. Certainly, this is true when we think outside Leviticus. Israel's prophets, as we are so often reminded, proclaimed that God valued obedience more than sacrifice; see, for example, Jeremiah 7:22-23, which goes so far as to say God did not at first mention sacrifice when he rescued Israel out of Egypt but charged them with the words, "Obey my voice, and I will be your God." A similar perspective is found in 1 Samuel 15:22—"To obey is better than sacrifice, and to listen than the fat of rams." At other times, obedience is portrayed not as an alternative to sacrifice but its fulfillment. The sacrifice of Jesus is the prime example. According to Hebrews 10, it was the obedience of Jesus, an obedience unto death, that

---

[20]In Christian Eberhardt's description, "the entire process of sacrifice" is "a gradual movement toward and through the sacred space and an approach to God," a movement, he adds, that "commences at the house of the offerer." See Eberhardt, *The Sacrifice of Jesus: Understanding Atonement Biblically* (repr., Eugene, OR: Wipf & Stock, 2018), 71.

[21]Rowan Williams, *The Sign and the Sacrifice: The Meaning of the Cross and Resurrection* (Louisville, KY: Westminster John Knox, 2017), 29. Here we are reminded of the assertion of Heb 5:8 that Jesus "learned obedience through what he suffered."

constituted the offering of his body, fulfilled the cult, and sanctified his people. Similarly, one could say that it was the obedience of Abraham that constituted his sacrifice of Isaac (Gen 22). Abraham, being tested by God, obeys the divine voice even as it calls him to offer up Isaac as a burnt offering. In the end, Abraham offers the ram that God provides "instead of his son" (Gen 22:13). Still, the LORD seems the count the obedience that bound Isaac and placed him on the altar as something like a covenant sacrifice; after Abraham's offering, God confirms and even enriches his covenant promises to Abraham.[22] Without obedience, Scripture everywhere insists, there is no true sacrifice, for obedience is to some degree the very purpose and of sacrifice.[23]

Within Leviticus, obedience is equally important to sacrifice. This is evident, first of all, in that "the voice of the LORD fills the pages of Leviticus." Leviticus is "divine speech more obviously than any other book of the Bible, for every section begins with 'the LORD spoke to Moses.'"[24] Not only so, but when the LORD speaks in Leviticus, he is almost always issuing a command. John Kleinig emphasizes the gracious nature of these commands: they are creative, sanctifying, life-giving decrees.[25] They established rituals through which God intended to communicate his grace and holiness to Israel. But they are divine commands all the same and thus call for a response of total obedience. The LORD's claim on Israel and his demand that they keep his commandments was inherent in every sacrifice.[26]

Without obedience to these commands, Israel could not participate in God's holiness, for these commands "deal with the reception of God's holiness and ongoing participation in it."[27] In this way, obedience was integral

---

[22] Note how emphatic is God's language in Gen 22:16-18, and how it goes beyond the reach of previous blessings: "Because you have done this and have not withheld your son, your only son, I will *surely* bless you, and I will *surely* multiply your offspring as the *stars of the heaven* and the sand that is on the seashore. And your offspring shall *possess the gate of his enemies*, and in your offspring shall all the nations of the earth be blessed, because you have obeyed my voice." See Peter J. Gentry and Stephen W. Wellum, *Kingdom Through Covenant: A Biblical-Theological Understanding of the Covenants*, 2nd ed. (Wheaton, IL: Crossway, 2018), 323.

[23] As Augustine states, what is offered in sacrifice is ultimately love for God and love for neighbor, the commands that fulfill the Law (*City of God* 10.5).

[24] Kleinig, *Leviticus*, 1.

[25] Kleinig, *Leviticus*, 2-3.

[26] Gordon Wenham, "The Theology of Old Testament Sacrifice," in *Sacrifice in the Bible*, ed. Roger T. Beckwith and Martin J. Selman (repr., Eugene, OR: Wipf & Stock, 2004), 84.

[27] Kleinig, *Leviticus*, 408.

to the cultic journey of sacrificial worship. Only by obedience to God's life-giving prescription could Israel find healing and communion with God. And not only so, but only by obedience to the Levitical legislation could Israel fulfill its calling to be a blessing to the nations, a life-giving community through which all peoples return to God. As Sklar states in a passage that brings several themes of Levitical sacrifice (covenant, creation, and consecration) into view:

> By following the laws of Leviticus, the glorious vision of Eden would be realized, as the people of God fulfilled their mission of living out his justice, mercy, kindness and love throughout the earth. They would indeed be a covenant people, in close relationship with their holy covenant king, filling the earth with his holy, just and blessed kingdom. . . . [Leviticus] mapped out a way for humanity to experience the riches for which we have been created: close fellowship with our Creator and the spreading of his good kingdom in all the earth.[28]

Obedience was thus an essential component of the Levitical return to God. By Israel's obedience, they would return to God and even lead the nations back to God.[29]

In this respect, the Levitical legislation was both pedagogical and anagogical. Part and parcel with Israel's task was the demand that they unlearn the ways of the nations. The Levitical laws, including the laws for sacrifice, were intended to recall Israel from their idols to the service of the living God. In this repentance, Israel would find their way back to God and take the nations with them. Repentance, a return to obedience (and *of* obedience), thus lay at the heart of Levitical sacrifice, the institution of which was surprisingly relevant to their mission among the nations.

Returning gifts in gratitude. To the return to Eden and the return of obedience we can another return that belongs to the plot of Levitical sacrifice: the return of God's gifts in gratitude and adoration. If obedience is constitutive of sacrifice, then gratitude is equally so. The return of gratitude,

---

[28] Jay Sklar, *Leviticus*, Tyndale Old Testament Commentaries (Downers Grove, IL: IVP Academic, 2014), 55.

[29] Or so it was hoped. The OT is the story of how Israel fails to fulfill this calling. Still, it is helpful to see that this was indeed Israel's calling and that their fulfillment of this calling depended in part on their obedience to the Levitical law.

in fact, brings us more directly into contact with the action of Levitical sacrifice as it is described in the text. For, as we will see, when Israel comes to the altar, they offer only what they have first received from YHWH's hand, presenting to him "the things which are his own."[30] It is in and through this return of gratitude that Israel, hearkening to the divine voice, returns to their Lord and Maker.

Looking again at Leviticus 1:2, we can begin with an obvious but interesting observation. When YHWH invites Israel to bring an offering, he specifies that they may bring an "offering of livestock from the herd or from the flock." The herd and the flock, of course, consist of the animals Israel had at hand and therefore could reasonably be expected to offer. It should not be missed, however, that in inviting Israel to offer sheep and cattle, YHWH invites Israel to offer of what would have been essential to their livelihood. These were the animals that, among other things, Israel depended on for food.[31] And that they did so seems important to Levitical sacrifice.

Food offerings. As we read further into Leviticus 1, we encounter the curious assertion that Israel presented their sacrificial victims to the LORD as a "food offering" (Heb. אִשֶּׁה; Lev 1:9, 13, 17).[32] The term "food offering" is encountered repeatedly in Leviticus 1–7 and even seems to speak to the overall meaning of the cult; "an enormous amount of evidence . . . portrays Israelite sacrifice as food for YHWH."[33] Every offering mentioned in these chapters is spoken of in relation to YHWH's food offerings, and at least

---

[30] Irenaeus, *Against Heresies*, trans. John Keble (repr., Nashotah, WI: Nashotah House, 2012), 4.18.5. Irenaeus goes on to describe what we can call a gift cycle between God and obedient humanity. As the church receives from God and offers its return of gratitude, God then blesses the church, showing that our gifts are offered not because God needs them but because we need God, who intends to bless us through our obedience. "For God Who stands in need of nothing, takes to Himself our good works, in order that He may grant unto us a return of the good things which belong to Him" and thus perpetuate the gift cycle.

[31] Gese highlights that no inedible animals were allowed on Israel's altar ("Atonement," 101).

[32] So the ESV, a translation favored by Richard Averbeck. Averbeck rejects the RSV's translation of אִשֶּׁה as "fire offering," noting that the etymological case on which that translation depends is too uncertain. He prefers the more general translation "gift." See Averbeck, "אִשֶּׁה," in *New International Dictionary of Old Testament Theology and Exegesis*, ed. Willem A. VanGemeren (Grand Rapids, MI: Zondervan, 1997), 1:541. Milgrom likewise rejects that translation and proposes "food gift" in its place. See Jacob Milgrom, *Leviticus 1-16: A New Translation with Introduction and Commentary*, Anchor Yale Bible 3 (New Haven, CT: Yale University Press, 2009), 161.

[33] Gary A. Anderson, *Sacrifice and Offerings in Ancient Israel: Studies in Their Social and Political Importance*, Harvard Semitic Monographs 41 (Atlanta: Scholars Press, 1987), 15.

some portion of each offering is contributed thereunto. The burnt offering is wholly offered to the Lord as a food offering (Lev 1:9). A "memorial portion" of the grain is similarly presented as "a food offering with a pleasing aroma to the Lord" (Lev 2:2); likewise, the fat of the peace offering (Lev 3:3). The fat of the purification offering is not itself identified as a food offering, but its fat is nevertheless removed from the sin offering itself and burned "on top of the Lord's food offerings" (Lev 4:35). The fat of the guilt offering is treated the same and is in fact called a food offering (Lev 7:5). Indeed, all fat, from whatever offering, is claimed by the Lord (Lev 3:16) and designated as a food offering (Lev 7:25).

From Leviticus 1–7, one cannot escape the conclusion that the presentation of YHWH's food offering was a central concern of the Levitical cult. Add to these chapters the witness of Numbers 15, and the presentation of food offerings appears to be only more important to the cult; there, Israel is instructed to present wine along with its offerings when they come into the land, making the idea of a divine banquet all the more pronounced. Thus, as Richard Averbeck states, the term "food offering" can be used "in a general sense to refer to all the offerings that the sons of Israel presented to the Lord."[34]

That the offerings are considered food for YHWH is both perplexing and revealing. YHWH, of course, does not need this "food." Unlike the gods of Israel's neighbors, he does not "eat the flesh of bulls or drink the blood of goats"; even if he did, he is quite capable of taking care of himself, "for the world and its fullness" are his (Ps 50:12-13). "The whole tenor of ancient Israel's belief in Yahweh," Walther Eichrodt insists, "is irreconcilable with the idea that God is fed by the sacrifice."[35] Indeed, the cultic legislation itself discourages Israel from thinking of God with such gross anthropomorphisms; that YHWH has and gives life, without receiving life from anyone or anything else, is foundational to the priestly worldview.[36] Why, then, should Israel offer YHWH food, a practice that seems so out of sync with their theology? I offer three suggestions.

---

[34] Averbeck, "אִשֶּׁה," 542.
[35] Walther Eichrodt, *Theology of the Old Testament*, trans. J. A. Baker (London: SCM Press, 1961), 1:143. Eichrodt acknowledges that "the Israelite sacrifice *ultimately derives* from the conception of feeding the deity." He doubts, however, that this idea was still "a *living* reality in Israel" (emphases original).
[36] Morales, *Who Shall Ascend*, 31.

First, Averbeck states that such offerings would assure Israel that their God was actually dwelling in the temple; "the fact that food and drink were used as offerings suggests that active occupation of the tabernacle by the Lord."[37] The food offerings, as they were consumed in the divine fire, served as signs of God's covenantal presence. The devouring fire and ascending smoke of the altar represented YHWH's consumption of the offering and thereby testified to his commitment to dwell among Israel. It may not be too much to refer to the sacrifice as sacraments in this sense, as symbols that assured Israel God's grace to and pleasure in his people.[38] The food offerings were signs of YHWH's covenant promise and were given for Israel's assurance, not YHWH's sustenance.[39]

A second explanation for why Israel, despite their theology, should present food offerings to YHWH is that doing so is a fitting way to depict the goal or end of sacrifice: communion with God (which, as I have argued, culminates in beatific vision). Biblical authors, from both Old Testament and New Testament, appear to assume that sacrifice intends and achieves participation or communion (Gk. κοινωνία) with its divine (or demonic) recipient. This seems to be Paul's understanding of Israel's sacrificial system: those who eat the sacrifices are "participants [κοινωνοὶ] in the altar," just as those who eat "what pagans sacrifice" are participants with demons (1 Cor 10:18-20). Israel's prophets agree: sacrifice intends union (of some sort) with the deity, which is why offering sacrifice to any deity but YHWH was an act of such gross infidelity.[40] Again, there may well be more than a

---

[37] Richard E. Averbeck, "Sacrifices and Offerings," in *Dictionary of the Old Testament: Pentateuch*, ed. T. Desmond Alexander and David W. Baker (Downers Grove, IL: InterVarsity Press, 2003), 724.

[38] Such an understanding of Israel's sacrifices is not unlike Calvin's understanding of the function of the two sacraments of the Christian church, baptism and the Lord's Supper. "The sacraments," he explains, "are exercises that make us more certain of the trustworthiness of God's Word.... For by them he manifests himself to us ... as far as our dullness is given to perceive, and attests his good will and love toward us more expressly than by word." John Calvin, *Institutes of the Christian Religion*, ed. John T. McNeill, trans. Ford Lewis Battles (Louisville, KY: Westminster John Knox, 1960), 4.14.6. Similarly, Israel's sacrifices are signs of the covenant ratified by the meal partaken of by Israel's elders in Ex 24:11, when they ascended the mountain, "beheld God, and ate and drank."

[39] See Michael B. Hundley, *Keeping Heaven on Earth: Safeguarding the Divine Presence in the Priestly Tabernacle* (Tübingen: Mohr Siebeck, 2011), 100-103, 113-15, for the difference in ideology of divine meal between Israel and its ancient Near Eastern counterparts.

[40] In Jer 3:6, Israel's unfaithfulness is said to have taken place "on every high hill and under every green tree," that is, in places of sacrifice.

little hint of this idea in the background of Levitical sacrifice: insofar as God instituted Levitical sacrifice to curb Israel's idolatrous tendencies, sacrifice is assumed to aim at communion with the deity to whom it is offered. As a shared meal, food offerings would have been a fitting medium for κοινωνία between God and Israel, for to share one's table is to share one's life.

This aspect of Levitical sacrifice comes out most clearly in the peace offering, which was concluded with a shared meal among the priests, the offeror, and his friends/family.[41] Kleinig notes that this meal represented divine hospitality: "[YHWH] was their divine host. . . . God himself provided this meal. . . . The Israelites who were his guests enjoyed his divine hospitality." Kleinig adds that this meal "united the Israelites as a holy people with their holy God" and "confirmed their right to live on his land" (i.e., Canaan). Here Kleinig is reading the peace offering as something of a tribute; it is the gift that the chiefs of Israel were to bring to the LORD when they appeared before him (e.g., Ex 34:23-24) and that recognized his ownership of the land. Their honor was reciprocated by God's, as he "acknowledged their status and reaffirmed their privileged position" as he presided over the peace offering. Thus, by the meal of the peace offering, "the God of Israel, the land of Israel, and the people of Israel were all integrated harmoniously."[42] It is little, wonder, then, that upon crossing the Jordan, Israel (per Moses' instruction) was to "sacrifice peace offerings and . . . rejoice before the LORD" (Deut 27:7).

Milgrom reminds us that, contrary to what has sometimes been suggested, the idea of a "mystic union" with YHWH, in which Israel would somehow partake of the divine substance through the medium of the sacrifice, must be rejected.[43] Nevertheless, the idea of a *covenantal* union with the LORD is not altogether inappropriate here, for there is undeniably a strong sense of table fellowship in this sacrifice. The peace offering was "a sacrifice designed to sustain the covenant relationship," one in which the covenant fellowship between God and Israel was remembered and celebrated.[44] And so, I suggest, could we think of the idea of a food offering in general.

---

[41] Gordon Wenham, *The Book of Leviticus*, New International Commentary on the Old Testament (Grand Rapids, MI: Eerdmans, 1979), 83.
[42] Kleinig, *Leviticus*, 93-94.
[43] Milgrom, *Leviticus 1-16*, 221.
[44] Wenham, *Leviticus*, 77.

In this way, the concept of a food offering points to the covenant reciprocity that was ideally shared between YHWH and his people. There was in the symbolic sharing of food a cycle of give and take, reception and return, that attested to and nourished the covenant bond created by the grace of God. And this may be even more to the point. So, a third suggestion as to why Israel was invited to bring food offerings to the altar: when YHWH identifies Israel's sacrifices as food offerings, he declares his intention to enter into a *gift cycle* with Israel—that is, a sequence of giving and receiving that enacts covenantal communion.[45]

Reception and return. When Israel offers food to YHWH, Israel offers what they have first received from his hand. Food is perhaps the quintessential gift that YHWH presents to his people, one that often functions as "a symbolic concretization of divine grace," as Moberly says of the manna.[46] On numerous occasions throughout the canon, the LORD's gift of food accompanies his promise and manifests his mercy. Consider this brief survey. Upon creating Adam and Eve, God blesses them and gives them an abundance of food, the fruit of every tree in the Garden of Eden, which the LORD himself had planted for them (Gen 1:29). When YHWH brings Israel out of Egypt and to Mount Sinai, their elders ascend the mountain, where they "beheld God, and ate and drank" (Ex 24:11). As Israel wanders in the wilderness, YHWH feeds them, day by day, with a bread that falls from heaven. As they dwell in the land, they enjoy the fulfillment of his promise to give them "a good and broad land, a land flowing with milk and honey" (Ex 3:8). When they later prove unfaithful, YHWH reminds them that "it was I who gave her the grain, the wine, and the oil" (Hos 2:8).[47] While they languish in exile, God assures them that he will restore their fortunes, and they will once again "plant vineyards and drink their wine, and they shall make gardens and eat their fruit" (Amos 9:14). Most significantly of all, God's people are fed through Jesus Christ. "I am the bread of

---

[45]Moshe Halbertal, *On Sacrifice* (Princeton, NJ: Princeton University Press, 2012), 7-18.
[46]R. W. L. Moberly, *Old Testament Theology: Reading the Hebrew Bible as Christian Scripture* (Grand Rapids, MI: Baker Academic, 2013), 84.
[47]Of course, we could say much about the gift of food in the NT, too. Jesus Christ identifies himself as the bread of heaven (Jn 6:51). His body and blood are presented to us in bread and wine. The hope of the Christian is to eat and drink at Christ's table at the coming of his kingdom (Lk 22:30). These are not arbitrarily chosen images.

life; whoever comes to me shall not hunger. . . . I am the living bread that came down from heaven. If anyone eats of this bread, he will live forever" (Jn 6:35, 51). By bread and wine Christ is still remembered today in the sacrament of the Lord's Supper, a participation in his body and blood (1 Cor 10:16).

Thus, when Israel offers food to YHWH in the Levitical cult, they are returning a gift previously received from him, a gift that is charged with religious significance. By offering of the flock and the herd, Israel offers a portion of what God has provided for them in his steadfast love. YHWH gives to Israel as their Creator and covenant Lord to meet their creaturely needs and fulfill his covenant promise.[48] He also gives to them in the sacrificial meals, sharing his holiness with them as he allows them to eat from his altar—"God used this most holy food to communicate his holiness."[49] In every way, God's gift of food was a constant proclamation of his love, mercy, faithfulness, generosity—in a word, his grace. When Israel offers their sacrifices, they are therefore responding and appropriating God's grace. By returning to God a portion of what they have received, they acknowledge God as Creator, answer his pledge of covenant love and lordship with their own pledge of gratitude and submission, and participate in his holiness. To borrow from John Barclay's *Paul and the Gift*, we might say that when Israel presents their offerings to YHWH, YHWH's previous covenant gifts are "realized." The return that is offered in response to God's grace is not "instrumental"—that is, it is not a means of persuading God to continue to be gracious. Rather, the return offered is "integral to the gift itself," because what is being offered is holy covenant friendship with her Creator and Lord.[50] To return, in this case, is to rightly receive; faithful reception and return were bound up in a single, sacred act.

---

[48]See Ps 145:15-16: "The eyes of all look to you, and you give them their food in due season. You open your hand; you satisfy the desire of every living thing."
[49]Kleinig, *Leviticus*, 11.
[50]John M. G. Barclay, *Paul and the Gift* (Grand Rapids, MI: Eerdmans, 2015), 438, 518. To be sure, some commentators note that the burnt offering, for instance, might be offered along with prayer in order to underscore the offeror's prayers; such an act may appear instrumental. But if we may draw on the examples of the Psalms, prayers are underscored not by bribery but by appeal to God's covenant promise. The burnt offering, then, would not be offered to sweeten the deal but to acknowledge that one's prayer is offered with faith in God's steadfast love to Israel.

"The sacrificial act is therefore a symbolic recycling of the gift to its origin."[51] And, in that recycling, a bond of communion is formed. Sacrifice, says Eichrodt, "represents not only the gifts of man to God but also the gifts of God to man." And in this exchange, God and humanity "are united by the strongest possible bond. . . . By [the offeror] himself partaking of the gifts which have been dedicated to God and so now belong to him, man receives a share in the divine life."[52] In other words, we could say that the sacrificial act aimed at proper participation in a divinely initiated gift cycle and the fellowship created therein.

Gift cycle. Levitical sacrifice was therefore an act of return by which Israel participated in a sacred gift cycle with YHWH. According to Moshe Halbertal, the exchange of gifts between God and humans creates a "gift bond," a relationship of communion between giver and receiver. This, he argues, was the aim of sacrifice. Gift, Halbertal asserts, is the fundamental meaning of sacrifice in the Hebrew Bible. And, given the nature of God, "who is in the first place the provider of the good and in no need of it," any sacrificial gift offered to him "functions as a token of submission and gratitude." In turn, God's reception of the sacrificial gift "is not driven by need or interest but rather is an expression of welcoming and goodwill."[53] Halbertal highlights the potential for rejection created by God's disinterested reception; since God does not need our gifts, he is under no necessity to reciprocate them.[54] Biblical sacrifice is thus an offering in the modern sense of the word, something that may or may not be accepted.

As real as that possibility of rejection proves to be in Scripture, the more dominant note in Leviticus is God's delight to receive Israel's offerings. In Leviticus 1, God not only invites Israel to bring their gifts but attests to his pleasure in those gifts. The worshiper who offers rightly can expect that the burnt offering will be "accepted before the LORD," according to Leviticus 1:3. Moreover, the worshiper can expect that God will receive the gift as "a food offering with a pleasing aroma to the LORD" (Lev 1:9, 13, 17). According to Milgrom, the phrase "pleasing aroma" (Heb. רֵיחַ־נִיחוֹחַ) "connotes something

---

[51]Halbertal, *On Sacrifice*, 11.
[52]Eichrodt, *Theology of the Old Testament*, 1:154-55.
[53]Halbertal, *On Sacrifice*, 12, 15, 13.
[54]Halbertal's exhibit A: Cain and Abel's story as told in Gen 4 (*On Sacrifice*, 8-9).

pleasurable to the deity."[55] Even if the more negative idea of soothing or placation is present here as well, God's delight to receive the offering (and the one who presents it) seems the dominant note.[56] Indeed, it is worth noting that joy is perhaps the emotion most often associated with sacrifice in Scripture; YHWH's delight in receiving their gifts (ideally) found its counterpart in Israel's joy in presenting them. Deuteronomy speaks of the joy with which Israel is to keep its sacrificial feasts (Deut 16; 26); the Psalms time and again speak of the joy of appearing at the house of God and presenting offerings (e.g., Ps 43:4: "Then I will go to the altar of God, to God my exceeding joy"). At the altar, through the exchange of gifts, Israel delights in their LORD, and the LORD delights in his people.

God's freedom to reject the gift may come with the threat of rejection, but it likewise attests his grace in receiving it. For God to enter into a gift cycle is "an act of love rather than duty."[57] Humans might (perversely) attempt to treat offerings instrumentally and "strategically," as a means of getting something they want from God.[58] But a God who does not need our gifts cannot be manipulated by them. His participation in the gift cycle can only be for the sake of eliciting and enjoying a noninstrumental relationship of love with his people. The exchange of gifts between God and humanity is ultimately a form of attention—God's attention to creatures with their needs and desires, and humanity's attention to God in his provision and kindness.[59] Sacrificial gifts are "dialogical," says Terry Eagleton, allowing parties to "recognise one another through the back-and-forth circulation of presents."[60] In the happy exchange of grace and gratitude, the LORD calls, and his people respond. YHWH, by his gifts, recognizes Israel as his people; Israel, by their

---

[55] Milgrom, *Leviticus 1–16*, 162.
[56] That the idea of soothing or placation is also present is argued by many, e.g., Wenham, *Leviticus*, 56. Milgrom believes that translations such as "appeasing, placating, soothing," though commonly found, are misleading (*Leviticus 1–16*, 162).
[57] Halbertal, *On Sacrifice*, 11.
[58] In Habermas's vocabulary, *strategic* action is utilitarian and means using another for your own purposes. *Communicative* action, on the other hand, seeks to reach an agreement with another. See Jürgen Habermas, *The Theory of Communicative Action*, vol. 1, *Reason and the Rationalization of Society*, trans. Thomas McCarthy (Boston: Beacon, 1984).
[59] Halbertal, *On Sacrifice*, 22.
[60] Terry Eagleton, *Radical Sacrifice* (New York: Yale University Press, 2018), 116. The latter quote is attributed by Eagleton to Marcel Hénaff, *The Price of Truth: Gift, Money, and Philosophy* (Stanford, CA: Stanford University Press, 2010), 107.

reception of those gifts and fitting return, recognizes YHWH as their God. And so, the cultic gift cycle creates and maintains a bond of loving fellowship.[61]

Creation, covenant, consecration. By offering their returns in response to God's grace, Israel enacted the truths of creation, covenant, and consecration—three themes prominent in the narrative context of Levitical sacrifice.[62] The LORD alone, Levitical sacrifice proclaimed, was Israel's maker, covenant Lord, and consecrator. Sacrifice was a means by which Israel acknowledged these truths and allowed themselves to be formed by them.[63] If YHWH was not the true source of all they offered him at the altar, this would not be so; Israel's gifts would too easily be seen as attempts to bargain with God, to use their own resources to put him in their debt. But by offering what they have first received, Israel acknowledges God as their Creator and sustainer. Not only so, but by offering them as a means of returning to God himself, they acknowledge God as their true end as well. At the altar, YHWH is worshiped as Israel's origin and end.

The living sacrifice. To state briefly how this paradigm of reception and return could be applied to the sacrifice of Christ: the Catechism of the Catholic Church notes that the sacrifice of Christ is, first, "a gift from God the Father himself, for the Father handed his Son over to sinners in order to reconcile us

---

[61]The notion of a sacrificial gift cycle may sound suspect to ears alert to the postmodern critique; Jacques Derrida has famously denied that gifts can really be given, since they create an expectation of return. An exchange of gifts, in his account, is portrayed as a dreadfully burdensome affair, marked by crudely economic calculations instead of the spontaneity and self-forgetfulness of genuine love. See, e.g., Jacques Derrida, *Given Time: I. Counterfeit Money*, trans. Peggy Kamuf (Chicago: Chicago University Press, 1992). Derrida's assumption seems to be that true love can ask nothing of the beloved; it must be void of any and all *eros*, of the desire to *possess* the beloved in some sense. A true gift, therefore, would be one given with no desire for return or even gratitude. Derrida's account of the gift has a prima facie plausibility—gift giving *can* become burdensome, competitive, and manipulative. But a moment's reflection shows it to be much too cynical. Scripture portrays gift exchange in a manner much truer to life (as Eagleton quips, "One would not have wished to spend Christmas in the Derrida household" [*Radical Sacrifice*, 107]). As we have seen, manipulative gift giving is simply not possibly with the God of Scripture. And yet this God insists on gift giving, all the same. It is possible for gifts to be genuine acts of attention and goodwill that aim at the good of the other. And even if those gifts ask for reciprocity, that need not be unloving. The classical understanding of love as aiming at both union with and the good of the other is preferable to Derrida's exclusively altruistic and disinterested account.

[62]See Frank H. Gorman, *Divine Presence and Community: A Commentary on the Book of Leviticus*, International Theological Commentary (Grand Rapids, MI: Eerdmans, 1997), 4-14.

[63]The formative function of liturgy is widely attested. For a recent Christian account, see James K. A. Smith's Cultural Liturgies series.

with himself. At the same time, it is the offering of the Son of God made man, who in freedom and love offered his life to the Father through the Holy Spirit in reparation for our disobedience."[64] In other words, the sacrifice of Christ consists of the gift of both the incarnate Son from the Father to humanity, and from the incarnate Son back to the Father as a representative of his people. There is in the sacrifice of Christ, then, a gift cycle, a reception and return of the gift for the sake of covenant union and communion.

Along similar lines, Rowan Williams offers an interesting suggestion based on the language of John 5:19, where Jesus proclaims that the Son does "only what he sees the Father doing." "So Jesus' obedience," he reasons, "becomes the way in which the love of the eternal God shines in Jesus' life and death back to the Father: perfect harmony [between] the gift of God and the response from the earth." In Jesus, he explains, God both "pours out love and draws it back . . . the Father pouring out his love, the Son watching what the Father is doing and playing it back to him." In this way, the incarnate Son offers, on our behalf, "a gift to God that is worthy of God. What gift could be worthy of God except God's own love?"[65] The incarnate Son, who is God's gift to the world (so Jn 3:16), offers to the Father his own perfect love for God and neighbor, all for the sake of the world. The reception and return of true sacrifice thus finds its fulfillment in Jesus Christ.

It finds fulfillment, too, in the living sacrifice of the church. Romans 12:1 urges the church "by the mercies of God, to present your bodies as a living sacrifice, holy and acceptable to God." In context, this presentation seems to mean proper reception and return of God's gifts. The opening chapters of the epistle identify ingratitude, the failure to receive and return God's gifts properly, as the root of all our evils: "For although they knew God, they did not honor him as God or give thanks to him, but they became futile in their thinking, and their foolish hearts were darkened. . . . Therefore, God gave them up in the lusts of their hearts to impurity" (Rom 1:21, 24). But whereas the debased mind is marked by ingratitude, the renewed mind (Rom 12:2) propels the devotion of the entire self to God in gratitude for his mercies,

---

[64]*The Catechism of the Catholic Church, with Modifications from the* Editio Typica (New York: Doubleday, 1997), 614.
[65]Williams, *Sign and the Sacrifice*, 33-34.

recognizing that "from [God] and through him and to him are all things. To him be glory forever. Amen" (Rom 11:36).

Thus I propose that the act of reception and return lies at the heart of biblical sacrifice and the center of the Levitical plot. Even in the atoning offerings, in which the notion of grateful return might seem inappropriate or inadequate, the pattern holds; according to Leviticus 17:11, God has "given" blood on the altar to make atonement for the "souls" of Israel, who by their participation in the sacrificial ritual make a sort of return of that blood.[66] It is therefore by returning gifts that Israel returns to God in worship and obedience. By return, that is, Israel heeds the LORD's call and moves toward the promise of beatific vision.

However, here we do well to remember the conflict of the Levitical plot—the reality of sin, a reality that the LORD in his holiness is not willing to accept and, as Genesis 2:17 so famously reveals, has sentenced to death. Leviticus takes sin and its divine sentence with full seriousness. The return of sacrifice, therefore, is a return *through* death.

THROUGH DEATH

"The way to God," Morales writes, "is through a bloody knife and a burning altar."[67] Morales makes this statement in the context of analyzing the six rites of the "cultic journey" to God. Those rites include (usually in this order) the presentation of the offering, followed by the hand-leaning, slaughter, blood manipulation, burning, and communion rites—all of which were often followed by a benediction.[68] Morales is careful to note that the entire sequence is essential to Levitical sacrifice; no one moment or rite can be isolated from the others and put forth as the "real meaning" of sacrifice. Specifically, the slaughter of the victim should not be singled out as "the essential act of sacrifice"; it is an overstatement to assert that "sacrifice is inherently the destruction of the victim."[69] Leviticus presents the entire sacrificial sequence of rites as necessary to the journey.

---

[66]Kleinig emphasizes the point: "God grants to the people both the blood for atonement and atonement through the blood" (*Leviticus*, 357).
[67]Morales, *Who Shall Ascend*, 124.
[68]Morales, *Who Shall Ascend*, 125-41.
[69]Leon Morris, *The Apostolic Preaching of the Cross*, 3rd ed. (repr., Grand Rapids, MI: Eerdmans, 1976), 121. For "the essential act of sacrifice," see B. B. Warfield, "Christ Our Sacrifice," in *The*

Nevertheless, it is reasonable to give the slaughter rite a privileged place in our analysis of sacrifice.[70] The theological weight of death in the biblical canon is not easily forgotten when we turn to sacrificial ritual.[71] And the existential weight of death, and of putting a living being to death, is not easily shrugged off. That weight is easily felt in Levitical descriptions of slaughter, which depict the slaughter as personally involving the offeror in a number of ways.

Death in the cultic sequence. The (apparent) sequence of sacrificial worship is relevant here, especially its beginning stages. First, the offeror, having chosen his offering from herd or flock and led it to the tent, proceeds to present his animal to the priest. Here the personal cost involved in sacrifice is highlighted: the assumption is that the victim is either part of one's own livestock, and so raised at the offeror's own expense and toil, or else purchased by the offeror.[72] Next, the hand-leaning rite. Biblical scholars now generally agree that this act probably did not signify the transfer of sin and guilt from offeror to victim (except in the case of the scapegoat; but there the procedure differs).[73] More likely, it was meant to reiterate personal ownership and, more significantly, signify personal identification, even a

---

Person and Work of Christ, ed. Samuel G. Craig (Phillipsburg, NJ: Presbyterian & Reformed, 1950), 404.

[70] Not all biblical scholars agree here. Roy Gane, for instance, states that the slaughter "is a relatively low point in terms of sanctity: it involves no contact with the most holy altar and thus can be performed by a lay person." Gane, *Cult and Character: Purification Offerings, Day of Atonement, and Theodicy* (Winona Lake, IN: Eisenbrauns, 2005), 60. But even if slaughter is not necessarily the "defining element of Israelite sacrifice" (60), it is nevertheless a necessary element when the offering is an animal—which is often the case, by divine prescription. I would submit, however, that both Scripture and experience teach that any necessary death is highly significant.

[71] Though I believe Leon Morris overstates the case, I find his insistence that we not forget the significance of death and blood in the larger biblical story when interpreting to the Levitical cult to be sensible. To be sure, we must be sensitive to context and not rush to conclusion; Morris might risk "illegitimate totality transfer" in his argument that since blood signifies death (or "life poured out") in so many OT narratives, it must signify the same in all cultic ritual. Nevertheless, it is difficult to think for long about death in Levitical ritual without thinking of the deaths of Adam and Christ in all their theological significance.

[72] Morales, *Who Shall Ascend*, 125; Knierim, *Text and Concept*, 32.

[73] The hand-leaning rite in the scapegoat was performed with two hands instead of one, included the confession of sins during the hand-leaning, and resulted in the release of the sin-bearing goat into the wilderness, not in its presentation on the altar of God. See Morales, *Who Shall Ascend*, 128, for why the animal should be seen as a "vicarious substitute" for the worshiper but not a sin-bearing substitute. That this act signified the transfer of sin and guilt from offeror to victim is still commonly argued by some who are eager to defend a penal-substitutionary view of Levitical sacrifice. E.g., Michael S. Horton, *The Christian Faith: A Systematic Theology for Pilgrims on the Way* (Grand Rapids, MI: Zondervan, 2011), 493.

relationship of vicarious substitution.⁷⁴ This identification might mean different things—perhaps that the "benefits" of the sacrifice would be "credited" to the offeror.⁷⁵ But Wenham argues that this act forms a symbolic identification between offeror and offering, so that what the offeror "does to the animal, he does symbolically to himself." More specifically, "the death of the animal portrays the death of himself."⁷⁶ Knierim adds that this act, in all sacrifices, comes just before the act of slaughter, and concludes that "its meaning is specifically related to the act of killing."⁷⁷

The hand-leaning is therefore "an act of dedication to sacrificial death." At the same time, it is an act of transferring the animal to YHWH's ownership. The hand-leaning therefore marks out the victim for "death for the sake of its *transportation* . . . to Yahweh."⁷⁸ The hand-leaning rite is in this way ordered to the slaughter of the offering and likely establishes a relationship between the death of the offering and the death of the offeror. Thus, even if the hand-leaning rite does not represent the imputation of sins to a penal substitute, it nevertheless brings us face to face with the sentence of death hanging over the offeror and presses on us a sense of death's necessity for one's return to God; "God must be approached through death."⁷⁹

By the time we reach the slaughter of the animal, the offeror's involvement in that slaughter has already been established both literally (as it is *his* offering) and symbolically (as his offering represents himself). Our sense of that involvement grows only more acute when we read that the offeror himself slaughters the victim "before the Lord" (e.g., Lev 1:5, 11; 3:1; 4:24), a phrase Frank Gorman interprets as "in the realm of the sacred" and that seems to add significance to the moment of slaughter.⁸⁰ The offeror

---

⁷⁴Milgrom, *Leviticus 1–16*, 151–52.
⁷⁵Sklar, *Leviticus*, 90.
⁷⁶Wenham, "Theology of Old Testament Sacrifice," 77. In his larger commentary on Leviticus, Wenham argues that it is possible to see the laying on of hands as an imputation of sin from the offeror to the animal. The principal he insists on is substitution, but he believes it unnecessary to decide whether this meant receiving the death penalty on behalf of the sinful offeror (*Leviticus*, 62).
⁷⁷Knierim, *Text and Concept*, 38.
⁷⁸Knierim, *Text and Concept*, 38.
⁷⁹Morales, *Who Shall Ascend*, 129.
⁸⁰Gorman, *Divine Presence and Community*, 25. Other ritual acts are also said to take place "before the Lord." In each case, however, I would argue that this formula is meant to impresses the sacred significance of ritual action on the reader; even if it simply means "in the Lord's presence," it signifies action done with unusual awareness of the Lord's holy presence. And, more

then dismembers the animal and gives it to the priest to burn on the altar. The extent of the offeror's involvement in the animal's death is impressive and by itself instructive. The act of slaughter might symbolize the offeror's total surrender to the LORD and his sentence against him; it might demonstrate "a willingness to die to oneself, along with an acknowledgement and submission to the judgment of God."[81] It may even speak of the necessity of "dying to the old creation so as to live to the present one."[82] But undoubtedly, it testifies to an economy in which death—one's personal involvement in death—is for some reason necessary for one's return to God. It testifies, indeed, to an economy in which death precedes and even gives rise to life.

After the death of the offering, the cultic turn toward life begins. This "after" is not just *post hoc* but *propter hoc*. The slaughter of the offering (and the manner of the slaughter: slitting the throat) is important not least because it leads immediately to the blood-manipulation rite and eventually the consumption of the offering (i.e., the communion rite). Just what the blood manipulation means will be examined more fully when we turn to the details of the burnt offering. For now, it is enough to say that, according to Leviticus 17:11, sacrificial blood represents life. Here, we speak of atonement: the blood, with the life that it carries, is said to be given by YHWH for the sake of atonement.[83] According to Morales, the rationale of atonement through blood is that "life ransoms from death, and life wipes away the stain of death." Smearing sacrificial blood on the altar, for instance, "serves to wipe away and obliterate the pollution of death," for "life obliterates death."[84] Again, that thesis will be tested when we examine the details of the burnt offering. But even if it is too soon to say *how* blood expiates sin, the sacrificial sequence makes it plain *that* it does so: following the application of blood, Israel is granted access to God.

---

often than not in Lev 1–7, the formula "before the LORD" is used of either the slaughter rite or the blood-manipulation rite.

[81] Wenham, "Theology of Old Testament Sacrifice," 77; Morales, *Who Shall Ascend*, 129.

[82] Morales, *Who Shall Ascend*, 129. Interestingly, cf. Karl Barth, *Church Dogmatics*, vol. 4.1, *The Doctrine of Reconciliation*, ed. G. W. Bromiley and T. F. Torrance, trans. G. W. Bromiley (London: T&T Clark, 1956), 280.

[83] Kleinig refers to the Hebrew וַאֲנִי נְתַתִּיו לָכֶם as a "formula of divine assignment," emphasizing that the blood is given to Israel and given for this specific purpose (*Leviticus*, 357).

[84] Morales, *Who Shall Ascend*, 131.

The blood-manipulation rite is followed by the burning rite, which seems to signify YHWH's reception of the offeror's gift (and the offeror himself) as a "pleasing aroma" as it ascends heavenward. The potential significance of the burning rite should not be overlooked; according to Christian Eberhardt, it "aims at transforming the sacrificial substance and transporting it to God."[85] According to Stanislas Lyonnet and Léopold Sabourin, the offeror is transported, too: the offering, "transformed into the vapor of smoke (but not destroyed or reduced to nothing), could ascend unto God ... and thus represent in a visible manner, as it were, the return of man to God."[86] This return achieved, the communion rite naturally follows: "Upon ascending into the heavenly abode of God, the Israelite enjoys the hospitality of the house of God," a point highlighted when the offeror (with friends and family) was given his portion of the sacrificial meat.[87] The Israelite has now returned and received life in the presence of the Lord, and he can do so because he has somehow traveled *through* death.

Death as crisis. In this review of the sacrificial rites, the slaughter, it should be repeated, is not identified as the defining element or essential act of Levitical sacrifice. Nevertheless, the slaughter of the victim plays a pivotal role. To draw once more on a literary term, the death of the offering seems to be the *crisis* in the Levitical plot, the "decisive action" on which the plot turns. "*Crisis* is applied to the episode or incident wherein the situation of the protagonist [here, the offeror] is certain either to improve or worsen."[88] Crisis is distinct from climax, though they often occur together; climax is usually considered both a turning point and a moment of greatest emotional response, whereas crisis is strictly a structural element in narrative or drama. Thus, crisis is not necessarily the moment of greatest importance, but it is a decisive turning point, a point at which a decisive action is taken and the protagonist's fate is sealed.

The death of the sacrificial victim, I submit, is the *crisis* of the cultic plot, for it seals the fate of the one who would return to YHWH via the Levitical way. The actions that precede the slaughter—the presentation and

---

[85] Eberhardt, *Sacrifice of Jesus*, 71.
[86] Stanislas Lyonnet and Léopold Sabourin, *Sin, Redemption, and Sacrifice: A Biblical and Patristic Study* (Rome: Editrice Pontificio Intituto Biblico, 1998), 169. Cf. Morales, *Who Shall Ascend*, 135.
[87] Morales, *Who Shall Ascend*, 137-38.
[88] Holman and Harmon, *Handbook to Literature*, 112.

hand-leaning—are ordered to the slaughter, and in the slaughter their meaning is realized. The actions that follow the slaughter, on the other hand—most immediately the blood manipulation and the burning—not only require the slaughter but are each a fulfillment of the slaughter: sacrifices are slaughtered *so that* their blood might be applied on the altar; they are "slaughtered in flesh *in order* to rise in smoke."[89] The death of the offering is no more definitive of sacrifice than the manipulation of blood or the burning. Neither is it any more essential to the sacrificial act; there must be blood, and there must be burning. All the same, given its place in the Levitical plotline, the death of the victim appears as the *decisive* moment, the true turning point in the cultic plot.

The necessity of death. Plot, I said above, follows a rule of necessity—or, more precisely, a rule of *fittingness*.[90] A plot is a single, continuous action in which one event follows another naturally, by some logical and intelligible relation of cause and effect. If that is so, then we can and must ask about the necessity of sacrificial death, which I am calling the *crisis* of the cultic plot. If the slaughter is the turning point in the sacrificial return to God—the decisive act that gathers up what precedes and issues forth in all that follows—then why? Why, in the narrative enacted at the altar, must there be death?

Giving a full answer to this question, I believe, requires canonical context. The problem of death, in its dreadful significance and necessity, is *the* problem in the biblical narrative. Creatures made to receive life from God are now given over to death. Why should this be the case, and what can be done about it? Given the way the Levitical cult summarizes and enacts the pentateuchal narrative—and the way it forecasts the completion of that narrative in Christ—it is reasonable to treat the Levitical necessity of death in light of the canonical necessity of death, and vice versa. "Canon sense" is

---

[89] Peter J. Leithart, *Delivered from the Elements of the World: Atonement, Justification, Mission* (Downers Grove, IL: IVP Academic, 2016), 169, emphasis added; see Gane, *Cult and Character*, 62.

[90] I use the term *fittingness* to highlight the point that the logic of cause and effect in a narrative is not the same as that in mathematics. Narratives involve characters who act in freedom and may sometimes use that freedom to act irrationally. Cause and effect in narratives can therefore be unpredictable, in the sense of unforeseen. Still, a plot implies some organic relationship between the many different acts that make up a single narrative. That organic relationship is what I am trying to identify here.

therefore required to answer this question.[91] And, given the importance of death and its necessity in the biblical story line, that canon sense needs to be informed by mature theological voices from the church catholic. In reality, I will be addressing the question of the necessity of death for our return to God, either directly or indirectly, throughout the rest of this study. Here I will address the beginnings of an answer that is rooted in what can be considered a "narrative necessity," a necessity that is conceived as fitting action for a given character (in this case, primarily God) in a given situation (in this case, creation followed by sin).

Throughout the history of the church's reflection on the necessity of death in humanity's return to God, a great number of answers have been proposed. There may be various reasons death is necessary—we might speak of pedagogical necessity, redemptive necessity, a legal or penal necessity, a necessity of satisfaction, even a sacramental and ontological necessity. All of these ideas are interesting and important proposals, and each may have its contribution to make in our interpretation of the burnt offering. The strategy of this study, however, is to look at the cult with some help from the tools of narrative analysis. What follows, then, is a suggestion as to the narrative necessity or fittingness of death in Levitical sacrifice, and the larger biblical story of which it is symbolic. The necessity in question, I would argue, is not a strictly logical or physical necessity. It is, rather, a theological necessity—a necessity that seems required by the goodness of God's character and the shape of the narrative.

Athanasius on the necessity of death and the divine integrity. Consider this proposal of Athanasius. In his *On the Incarnation*, Athanasius explains the problem of sin and death as an issue of divine integrity. It is important to note that he does so by following the flow of the biblical narrative; "The biblical narrative is Athanasius' soteriological template."[92] What Athanasius does, in other words, is not to offer logical proofs for how the story of creation, sin, and salvation must go but to trace out the logic of Scripture's redemptive narrative as it attests the goodness of divine action.

---

[91] Kevin J. Vanhoozer, *The Drama of Doctrine: A Canonical Linguistic Approach to Christian Theology* (Louisville, KY: Westminster John Knox, 2005), 324.
[92] Thomas Weinandy, "Athanasius' Incarnational Soteriology," in *T&T Clark Companion to Atonement*, ed. Adam. J. Johnson (London: Bloomsbury T&T Clark, 2017), 135.

Given the character of God, the manner in which he has acted toward humanity from the beginning, and the subsequent rebellion of humanity against its Creator, death is the only fitting result. And yet, he states emphatically, death cannot be the end of the story. There must be a return of humanity to God. He begins his argument thus:

> For God has not only created us from nothing, but also granted us by the grace of the Word to live a life according to God. But human beings, turning away from things eternal and by the counsel of the devil turning us towards things of corruption, were themselves the cause of corruption in death, being, as we have already said, corruptible by nature but escaping their natural state by the grace of participation in the Word, had they remained good. . . . When this happened, human beings died and corruption thenceforth prevailed against them.[93]

Note how, for Athanasius, everything begins with the creative act of God, the *beginning* of the plot, so to speak: God created humanity so that they might have life through participation in the Word, the eternal Son of the Father. This appears in Athanasius's exposition as a beginning in the true sense: it is that which "does not itself follow anything by causal necessity, but after which something naturally occurs."[94] Nothing provokes God to this gracious creative action, and his creation of humanity is "from nothing." Only by participation in the Word do we truly have life.[95] The sentence of death that God issues against sin is therefore the necessary consequence of this beginning: having rejected the Word by whom they received life, death was the only possible outcome. One might wonder whether this "law of death," as Athanasius calls it, could be suspended. But Athanasius argues that this would be absurd.

> It was absurd, on the one hand, that, having spoken, God should prove to be lying: that is, having legislated that the human being would die by death if he transgressed the commandment, yet after the transgression he were not to die

---

[93] Athanasius, *On the Incarnation: Greek Original and English Translation*, trans. John Behr, Popular Patristics Series 44a (Yonkers, NY: St. Vladimir's Seminary Press, 2011), sec. 5.
[94] Holman and Harmon, *Handbook to Literature*, 360.
[95] According to Athanasius, "since the Father creates through the Word, the Word is the ontological and epistemological bond between the Father and humankind" (Weinandy, "Athanasius' Incarnational Soteriology," 136).

but rather this sentence dissolved. For God would not be true if, after saying we would die, the human being did not die.[96]

There is a legal necessity to the death of humanity here. God had sentenced sin to death; therefore it must be so. But note, too, the necessity of character: God must be true to himself, otherwise we land in absurdity. As he continues, Athanasius doubles down on this point and uses it to explain why repentance alone cannot save us from this sentence:

> For it was absurd that God, the Father of truth, should appear a liar for our profit and preservation. What then had to happen in this case or what should God do? Demand repentance from human beings for their transgression? One might say that this is worthy of God, claiming that just as they were set towards corruption by the transgression, so by repentance they might be set towards incorruptibility. But repentance would [not] have preserved the consistency of God, for he again would not have remained true if human beings were not held fast by death.[97]

This, in part, is the necessity of death for Athanasius: without death, the plot of the divine economy becomes absurd, and the divine character proves untrue. Given how God has created humanity and what God has said, death is the only possible outcome of humanity's disobedience.

But at this point, Athanasius asks another question. In response to humanity's plight, "What should God, being good, do?" For as much as it would be absurd for God to retract his sentence of death against sin, it would be equally unbecoming to neglect his creatures and allow them to be wholly destroyed. He states, "It was proper not to have come into being rather than to have come into being to be neglected and destroyed. The weakness, rather than the goodness, of God is made known by neglect if, after creating, he abandoned his work to be corrupted." So "once he made him and created him out of nothing," he adds, "it was most absurd that his works should be destroyed, and especially before the sight of the maker. It was therefore right not to permit human beings to be carried away by corruption, because this would be improper and unworthy of the goodness of God."[98]

---

[96] Athanasius, *On the Incarnation* 6.
[97] Athanasius, *On the Incarnation* 7.
[98] Athanasius, *On the Incarnation* 6.

In Athanasius's view, it is right that God should reclaim humanity by reuniting them to his Word; it is right, in other words, that there should be a return to God. It is only right, then, that God would send the Word into human flesh to bring humanity out of its corruption and death. But, again, there must be death, lest the law of death established by God be despised. "Since all were liable to the corruption of death," he argues, the incarnate Word had to go through death too. "For the Word, realizing that in no other way would the corruption of human beings be undone except, simply, by dying," took to himself "a body capable of death, in order that it . . . might be sufficient for death on behalf of all." Thus, he "fulfilled in death that which was required."[99] For Athanasius, the incarnation is proof that there must be a return to God; God will not have it any other way. But so too must there be death, for the integrity of God requires it. Had God not pronounced the sentence in the beginning of the story, perhaps it would not be so. But given the shape of the biblical narrative, a return to God through death is necessary. It is the right way for the story to come to its conclusion.

Athanasian resonances in Leviticus. The account of death's necessity that Athanasius gives finds resonance in the Levitical plot, for he roots its understanding of that necessity in the character of God, the law of God, and the shape of the biblical narrative—all of which, we saw in Leviticus 1:1, are highly significant to the setting of Leviticus. Consider, first, how Athanasius's emphasis on the law of God finds agreement in Leviticus. Recall that when Israel approaches YHWH, they do not circumvent his law but approach the law itself as it is housed in the ark of the covenant, the very footstool of God. Not only so, but as they approach that law, they approach *by* law—by the law uttered by God himself throughout the book of Leviticus. The sacrificial legislation is of one piece with the law that pronounces the covenant curse for sin; this law refuses to overlook sin and ignore its consequences. And as a covenantal act, Levitical sacrifice may have been about more than the law but never less. Athanasius's insistence that God remains true to his law, then, fits well with Leviticus. There must be death, in this perspective, because the law says so.

---

[99]Athanasius, *On the Incarnation* 9.

Next, as Athanasius rooted the necessity of death in the character of God, so too, it seems, does Leviticus. The holiness associated with the divine name, YHWH, is impressed on readers throughout the book of Leviticus. It is this holiness that marks the nature of Israel's relationship with God, that sanctifies Israel and their tabernacle, and that engulfs their offerings in flame. It is also this holiness that, when it is disrespected, consumes Nadab and Abihu. It is this holiness, finally, that Israel will be called to imitate in a life of justice, purity, and love. In the Levitical outlook, holiness ultimately has to do with life and death; to be holy is to be associated with God and the fullness of his life; to be unholy is to be excluded from that life.[100] Thus, as Athanasius associated life with God and death with sin, so too does Leviticus. To be corrupted by sin is to be as incompatible with God as life is with death. It is therefore to be under the curse or law of sin. For God simply to ignore that corruption, to welcome sinners back in their corruption, without first being rid of it, would require, as Athanasius suggests, that he become something other than

---

[100] The literature on the meaning of holiness in Leviticus, and the related concept of clean, is extensive. Mary Douglas, in her groundbreaking *Purity and Danger*, argues that the unclean, which is the antithesis of the holy, is fundamentally disordered or out of place. "Dirt," she reasons, "is matter out of place," and the same principle explains the categories of clean and unclean in Leviticus. Holiness, she goes on to reason, essentially means wholeness; to be holy is to be whole, to be one; holiness is unity, integrity, perfection of the individual and of the kind." Douglas, *Purity and Danger: An Analysis of Concepts of Pollution and Taboo* (New York: Routledge, 2002), 44, 67.

Jacob Milgrom, on the other hand, argues that to be unclean in the Levitical world is to be associated with death. Milgrom notes that there are in Leviticus only three sources of ritual impurity for persons: contact with a corpse, leprous disease, and genital discharge. Milgrom proposes that what these have in common is an association with death. In the case of contact with a corpse, the association is obvious. In genital discharge, he explains, there is a loss of "the life force," a loss that represents death even as it (ideally) brings about life. And leprosy (or "scale disease") made one unclean not because of the fear of spreading disease (though that may have been acknowledged by the law) but because of a resemblance to death; the one suffering from such a disease would have "been like a corpse." Standing against these "forces" of impurity, Milgrom continues, is holiness, which stands for life. In Israel's cult, "the forces pitted against each other in a cosmic struggle are no longer the benevolent and demonic deities who populate the mythologies of Israel's neighbors, but the forces of life and death," the latter being identified as forces that have been "set loose by man himself through his disobedience to or defiance of God's commandments." Milgrom, *Leviticus 1–16*, 46-47.

In the end, it seems that these two outlooks are complementary. Gorman has argued cogently that priestly rituals are therefore concerned with "creating life and maintaining order"; they function "to affirm life and maintain the very good order of creation" (*Divine Presence and Community*, 16). Life and order are inseparable, and both are relevant to the biblical concept of holiness.

himself, something other than holy. Consecration, like covenant, requires death for sin.

For Leviticus as for Athanasius, God's law and character are not available to us in abstraction. They are known to us, rather, within a narrative, the story of God's goodness to humanity that begins in the creation account of Genesis.[101] God, it seems, has purposes: namely, the sharing of his own life and glory with his creatures. And the realization of this purpose, by the law and character of God, requires putting sin to death. We know this simply because, time and again, it is what God does. In the narrative Leviticus recalls, God puts the sinful and corrupt to death for the sake of guarding the goodness of creation, and he faithfully brings his people *through* death. After Adam and Eve's disobedience and corruption, they are banished from the garden. The reason, it seems, is that access to the tree of life while in their corrupted state would be somehow ruinous. God therefore removes them from the garden and puts cherubim armed with flaming swords in place to guard the way. The point: the life that the tree gives would somehow be spoiled by sin. If Adam and Eve are to return to it, it will have to be through death—death, presumably, to their sin-corrupted nature.

The point is similar in the story of the flood. The earth lies corrupted by sin and filled with violence, so much that the LORD is grieved and resolves to put an end to humanity. But God, faithful to his creation, does not simply destroy it. Rather, he remakes it, as we see when Noah is constituted a new Adam. Noah and his family survive. But they survive as those brought through death—through the chaotic, uninhabitable waters, into the renewed earth that the flood creates.[102] A similar narrative is seen in the exodus. Pharaoh's rebellion against YHHW leads to the undoing of Egypt and eventually their death; Israel, on the other hand, is brought through death as they are spared from the death of the firstborn and brought through the deadly waters of the Red Sea. Sin, personified by Egypt, is put to death, and yet God brings for himself a people out of this death.

---

[101]To speak here of the goodness of God reminds us that the whole biblical story is not necessary in a strict sense. Rather, what I am arguing for throughout is what has often been called the fittingness of the biblical narrative, and the divine economy it reveals, given the character of God.

[102]Morales, *Who Shall Ascend*, 57-58.

The necessity of coming through death by means of sacrifice in Israel's return to God therefore makes good narrative sense by the time we reach Leviticus, for it is a well-established pattern, a pattern that agrees with both the purposes and the character of the Lord as revealed in the story to this point. It is a necessity that comes from God's commitment to his creation—which, being rooted in God's grace, is not a strict logical necessity but what I am calling a narrative necessity. By putting sin to death and yet bringing his people through death, God stays the course, we might say; he sticks to the plot and remains true to character.

Recapitulation. Before concluding this chapter, a brief word should be said about how this construal of the Levitical plot might inform a Christian account of atonement.

In the previous chapter, I noted that the notion of recapitulation may have an important role to play in sacrificial atonement. For Irenaeus, with whom the concept of recapitulation is often associated, recapitulation is a rhetorical or literary device in which the events of a given narrative are briefly repeated, in summary fashion, so that the significance of a series of events may be more clearly recognized; think of a lawyer's closing argument.[103] Following this definition, the present work reads the Levitical cult as a kind of ritualized recapitulation, as a gathering up of the preceding pentateuchal narrative of creation and covenant.

As we analyze the plot of Levitical sacrifice in this chapter, we are led to the same conclusion. The plot of Levitical sacrifice, if the preceding account has merit, *just is* the plot of the biblical story. Sacrifice seems like something intended to be a summary of the whole story—a succinct, precise statement of what is achieved for our salvation. Even a brief glimpse of the imagery of death followed by ascension (as the smoke rises from the altar) suggests that Levitical sacrifice foretold not only the death of Christ but his resurrection and ascension as well. Indeed, the sacrifice appears to be something like the divine economy *in nuce*: here, God's creative intentions, the sin of humanity with its fatal consequences, and the divine plan of salvation all seem to be concentrated in what we call the sacrifice of Christ.

---

[103]John Behr, *Irenaeus of Lyons: Identifying Christianity*, Christian Theology in Context (Oxford: Oxford University Press, 2013), 137.

If we are to see the work of Christ in Leviticus, then we are to see that Jesus' death (which on this reasoning would be considered the *crisis* of the biblical plot), by a narrative necessity or fittingness, issued forth in his resurrection and ascension—*propter hoc*, not merely *post hoc*. Or, to use an important term from the epistle to the Hebrews, it issued forth in his perfection: the resurrected and ascended Christ "has been made perfect forever" (Heb 7:28). And his resurrection, ascension, and perfection secure that of the church: "For by a single offering he has perfected for all time those who are being sanctified" (Heb 10:14). In his sacrifice, Jesus has risen to heaven and in doing so has opened a "new and living way" for us to follow (Heb 10:20). If sacrifice means a return to God through death, issuing ultimately in the beatific vision, then to speak of Jesus' sacrifice is to speak of his completion of the human task and the fulfillment of the human destiny—that is, communion with God. By offering himself in obedience, journeying through death on humanity's behalf, being raised to new life, and then ascending into heaven, Christ has fulfilled not only the plot of the Levitical cult but also what seems to be the purpose of God: the praise of God's glory in the redemption and perfection of all things (Eph 1:3-14).

Thus, in Christ's journey to God through death, the beginning is brought to the end. The conflict is overcome, and God's good purposes are brought to realization by the one sacrifice of the incarnate Son of God. To speak of Jesus' sacrifice, I tentatively conclude, is to speak of recapitulation.

The Levitical Way

This chapter has argued that Levitical sacrifice has a plot, a unified course of action that binds together the various episodes or moments of Levitical sacrifice in a single, purposeful, and intelligible movement. That plot, which begins with the Lord's gracious call to Israel and ends in beatific vision, is one of return through death. In repentance, obedience, and gratitude, Israel returns to the Lord and his glory by the means he has provided them: the sacrifices of the Levitical cult. The way is hard; it is a journey of repentance and bloodshed that takes the offeror through death. Yet it is the way God has graciously provided, the way that brings Israel back to himself, and the way God the Son traveled for himself—not symbolically, as in the Levitical cult, but really, in his life, death, resurrection, and ascension.

That, at least, is what this study is claiming. The Levitical way of return to God through blood and fire prophetically disclosed the mission of Jesus Christ, who fulfilled the cult's promise through his own blood and in the fire of his resurrection and ascension. By his sacrifice, a "new and living way" has been opened for our return to God (Heb 10:20). This is our salvation and the fulfillment of God's purposes for us. Somehow, in Christ, we move through death into the newness of life, even fellowship in the divine life.

To recall Scheeben's remarks: this movement to life or beatific vision is the cult's way of identifying the *that* of our salvation. To say that this movement has taken place by return (which I characterized by obedience and gift) and through death—through, that is, an act of recapitulation—may give us an outline of the *how* of salvation. But to say more about the *how*, it will be necessary first to say something more about the *who*. It will be necessary, that is, to say something about the identity of the Levitical offeror.

Hero

Sacrifice and Sonship

AN OFT-CITED MAXIM IN LITERARY STUDIES states that "character is plot." Plot, as noted in the previous chapter, gives a story coherence, so that an analysis of plot gives some account of what happens, how it happens, and why. That analysis, however, is incomplete until due attention is given to the question of *who*. What moves a plot forward is not simply events but action, not just happenings but doings. A plot therefore implies an agent. And the better we understand the identity and moral character of that agent—of the central *who* in a story—the better we understand *why* and *how* the *what* comes about. The more we come to understand who Dostoevsky's Raskolnikov really is, for example, the more we come to understand why he murdered the old woman and Lizaveta and what the story is really about.[1]

For Levitical sacrifice, too, character is plot. This applies, of course, to the character of Israel's God; as we have seen already, the holiness and grace of God stand at the origin of the Levitical cult as the reason for its existence. This maxim applies also to the character of Israel as God's people. Their mixed character—their identity as God's chosen people joined to their sin-corrupted moral condition—goes far in explaining why the cultic plot is what it is (i.e., return to God through death).

In this chapter, however, I will focus on character in the Levitical cult in a more specific sense. Here I will consider the identity and character of the *hero* of the Levitical story—that is, of the central agent, whose fate

---

[1] The reference is to *Crime and Punishment* by Fyodor Dostoevsky.

constitutes the focus of the narrative. Who, we can ask, stands at the center of things in Leviticus 1? In what follows, I will be arguing that the central character of the story of the burnt offering is the offeror. It is the offeror who has set out on the Levitical journey and is performing most of the action. This offeror, however, is nameless, known to us only as a son of Israel (Lev 1:2). He therefore stands in the text as a type. And I believe he stands as a type not only of any given Israelite but of the true Israelite, Jesus Christ.[2]

This identification of Jesus Christ as the hero or protagonist of the Levitical story may be expected; this is, after all, a study that intends to contribute to Christian doctrine. Nevertheless, it requires arguing, for the question of how an Old Testament text such as Leviticus refers to Christ is far from settled. It will be therefore necessary to say something about typology and the distinction between its prospective and retrospective modes. That discussion, applied to the text of Leviticus 1, will allow me to identify the hero of the cult as the son of God, a title that gives clarity to the type-antitype that exists between the nameless offeror of Leviticus and Jesus Christ and that may even allow us to ponder the possibility of an eternal archetype of Levitical sacrifice within God's own triune life.

This chapter will therefore consist of three sections. In the first, I will argue that the offeror is the hero of the Levitical story and a filial figure. The Levitical offeror played the role of the son of God, a conclusion already nodded to earlier in the study. In playing this role, the Levitical offeror anticipated the coming of a greater Son of God, one who would fulfill the pattern set by the offeror and thereby take hold of the reality the cult foreshadowed.[3] In the second section, I will briefly argue that Jesus Christ is the one who fulfills this pattern. I will give attention here to the relationship between sacrifice and sonship, especially as that relationship is highlighted in the epistle to the Hebrews and its reading of the Levitical cult. In the third and final section, I will ask whether this connection between sonship and sacrifice can be further extended. Specifically, is there a relationship between the act of sacrifice as Leviticus depicts it and the eternal act of divine

---

[2]This may strike some readers as odd, since Jesus is also typified by the offering. But, as I will show below, this is a reading invited by the NT, especially Hebrews. Moreover, in an adequate Christian theory of sacrifice, the offeror's gift is an extension of the offeror's self.

[3]I will capitalize "Son of God" when referring to Jesus Christ, since "Son" functions then both as a title that is roughly equivalent to Messiah and as a reference to his divine sonship.

sonship? Anglican theologian E. L. Mascall believed there was, and his argument will be considered in detail. The motivation behind this question is that of searching out the fittingness of the divine economy. Why was it fitting that the Son, not the Father or Spirit, become incarnate and offer himself for our salvation? Saying something about that fittingness will yield insight into the story of sacrifice and the mechanism of atonement.

THE OFFEROR AS FILIAL FIGURE

The offeror, the hero. The argument of this chapter begins by identifying the offeror as the hero of the Levitical story. What does this mean?

The hero (or heroine) of a work of literature is simply defined as the "central character" of the work—the "focus of interest." The hero is the "protagonist," a term that was used for the "first" or chief player in a Greek drama whose "fortunes are the chief interest" of the story. The hero and his character—his identity, origins, qualities, aspirations, and so on—are therefore essential to the plot.[4] The plot depends "(1) on the general estimate we are induced to form . . . of the moral character and deserts of the hero . . . (2) the judgments similarly we are led to make about the nature of the events that actually befall the hero . . . and (3) the opinions we are made to entertain concerning the degree and kind of his responsibility for what happens to him."[5] In other words, the character of the hero, what happens to him in the course of the story, his responsibility in it all—these are central, pressing questions in the analysis of a story and its meaning. The hero is, in short, the primary focus, primary actor, and primary sufferer. Who he is, what he faces, what he does, and what he comes to in the end are the audience's foremost concerns.

When we look to the text of Leviticus, we find the offeror playing the part of the hero. This is evident for a number of reasons. When the curtains open on Leviticus's ritual stage, it is the offeror who stands in the spotlight as the "first" actor. To refer again to Leviticus 1:2, there we read the LORD's command that Moses "speak to the people of Israel and say to them, When any of you

---

[4]Hugh Holman and William Harmon, *A Handbook to Literature*, 6th ed. (New York: Macmillan, 1992), 225, 380. Throughout Lev 1, the offeror is grammatically masculine, and this grammatical custom may carry theological weight. I will therefore be using masculine pronouns to refer to the offeror throughout this chapter.

[5]R. S. Crane, cited in Holman and Harmon, *Handbook to Literature,* 361.

brings an offering to the LORD, you shall bring your offering of livestock."
The LORD, of course, is the first speaker of Leviticus, and this is an important
point, a reminder that the whole of Levitical ritual is founded by the LORD's
gracious initiative. The first act in the ritual itself, however, belongs to the
offeror when he brings near his offering to YHWH. As Rolf Knierim was
quoted as saying earlier, the "ritual proper" begins with the offeror selecting
his offering, presumably at his home, from his own herd or flock.[6] Note here
too that though the LORD commands Moses to issue this summons "to the
people of Israel" (Heb. אֶל־בְּנֵי יִשְׂרָאֵל), the ritual instructions themselves
depict the offeror as singular; as the ESV has it, "when any one of you brings
an offering to the LORD" (Heb. אָדָם כִּי־יַקְרִיב מִכֶּם קָרְבָּן לַיהוָה). Though the
LORD and his election of Israel as a corporate covenant people are of great
importance to the setting of Leviticus, it is an individual offeror at center
stage when the ritual begins.

As the ritual instructions continue, we find that the offeror is not only the
first actor in a temporal sense but the chief actor throughout: "The main
person involved in this ritual enactment was the Israelite layperson."[7] It is
the offeror who, in the instructions for the burnt offering, brings his gift to
the tent, seeks acceptance from the LORD, lays his hand on the head of the
animal, and puts it to death. It is then the offeror who flays and butchers the
offering and washes the pieces in water. The priests play their part, to be
sure—they sprinkle and pour out the blood of the offering, and they arrange
the butchered pieces on the altar. Their mediation between the offeror and
the altar is essential to the ritual. Still, it is the offeror who is doing most of
the work.

It is the offeror, too, whose fate is in question throughout the ritual. In
the burnt offering, the offeror, it seems, has come seeking acceptance
(Lev 1:3). In the grain offering of Leviticus 2, it would seem he is seeking the
pleasure of the LORD. In the peace offering, he seeks fellowship. In the purification and reparation offerings, he seeks, in one way or another, an
atonement that will free him from the guilt and corruption of a particular
transgression. And in all these offerings, he seeks God, whose presence is

---

[6] Rolf P. Knierim, *Text and Concept in Leviticus 1:1-9: A Case in Exegetical Method* (repr., Eugene, OR: Wipf & Stock, 2010), 32.
[7] John Kleinig, *Leviticus* (St. Louis: Concordia, 2003), 60.

the goal of the Levitical cult. In each case, then, the offeror comes to the altar seeking, and readers of the ritual are most interested in what he will find. The instructions for the rituals often include promises of success for the offeror, should he offer faithfully. In Leviticus 1, when he comes to be "accepted," his offering "shall be accepted for him to make atonement for him" (Lev 1:4). YHWH will receive his sacrifice as a "food offering with a pleasing aroma to the LORD" (Lev 1:13), a sign of God's delight in gift and giver. But as so much of the biblical witness to God's response to sacrifice makes plain, acceptance and favor were not automatic at the altar. An offering was a plea for acceptance, fellowship, atonement, or whatever else, but not a guarantee. The LORD reserves the right to refuse the offering, and thus the offeror's fate hangs in the balance.[8] Indeed, the presentation of offerings in Scripture is sometimes portrayed as a test, and procedural adherence alone was no guarantee of passing.[9] And so, the question of the offeror's acceptance before God occupies the reader's interest.

For these reasons, I submit, the offeror is the hero of the Levitical story of sacrifice (at least in the story of Lev 1).[10] But what more can we say about the Levitical offeror and his character? Here I will argue that the offeror is a filial figure. That is, he is both a figure *who is filial* and a figure *of the filial*. The Levitical offeror is *a* son of God, and he is also a type of *the* Son of God.

The offeror as filial. First, a figure who is filial. Recall that, in the narrative context of Leviticus, Israel is identified as the son of God. In Exodus 4:22-23, YHWH says to Pharaoh, "Israel is my firstborn son, and I say to you, 'Let

---

[8]Halbertal highlights this point while considering the story of Nadab and Abihu. He refers to ritual as a "protocol that protects from the risk of rejection." Moshe Halbertal, *On Sacrifice* (Princeton, NJ: Princeton University Press, 2012), 15-17.

[9]Cain and Abel's famous story is an example here. The theme of testing plays an important role in this story, and while we read there that the LORD did not have regard for Cain and his offering, we do not learn why. There is no obvious procedural or ritual fault on Cain's part mentioned in the text. For further reflection, see R. W. L. Moberly, *The God of the Old Testament: Encountering the Divine in Christian Scripture* (Grand Rapids, MI: Baker Academic, 2020), 124-64.

[10]An objection to this identification may insist that God is the hero of the Levitical cult, as his being and act are always primary in the Bible. This is true and a reasonable point to make in Leviticus—the cult, as I have said, was first and foremost something God did for Israel and only secondarily something Israel did for God. However, though the offeror's act is always enabled and elicited by a prior act of God, it is nevertheless the offeror's act that the text is focused on, and the offeror's fate that is the text's main concern. Another objection might posit the high priest as the hero of Levitical sacrifice. And, if I were reading the instructions for the Day of Atonement, I would in that case agree. But in Lev 1, this is not so. The offeror, again, is the primary (human) actor here.

my son go that he may serve me.'" Note that there seems to be a link here between sonship and sacrifice—the service Israel was to offer was cultic, a sacrificial feast (Ex 5:1; 8:25-27; 10:9). Israel's sonship was both relational and functional. Israel enjoyed a covenant relationship with the LORD that grounded their cultic calling. "It is only in discharging this calling," Nicholas Perrin tells us, "that Israel becomes the son of God in the fullest sense."[11] It would seem, then, that the Israelite offeror was taking up a filial task at the altar, enacting his identity as a son of God.

Much the same impression is given when we recall the Adamic nature of Israel's identity and calling. I argued earlier that the cult was meant to symbolize a return to Eden. The tent of meeting was a representation of that original cultic mountain, the "holy hill" (Ps 15:1) where God dwelled among his creatures and blessed them with life in the fullest sense.[12] G. K. Beale has argued that the blessing and command of the original Adamic commission was passed from Adam to Noah and then to Abraham and his descendants, and that this commission was to be fulfilled in and through the tabernacle. At the temple, Israel reprised Adam's role, receiving the mandate God had originally given to Adam to represent God to the nations and extend his blessing to the rest of creation.[13] This too suggests the offeror should be seen as a filial figure. In Adam, the filial and the priestly coincided. Perrin notes that Adam was both the original priest and the original son of God.[14] These two privileges did not simply coexist in one person but were thoroughly integrated: Adam was to offer all things in praise to God just as he had received all things from God's fatherly hand. To play Adam's role, then, was to play the role of priestly son of God.

A final reason for seeing the offeror as a filial figure is that, as I argued earlier, sacrifice was a filial act. The Levitical cult was a covenantal

---

[11]Nicholas Perrin, *Jesus the Priest* (Grand Rapids, MI: Baker Academic, 2018), 37.

[12]Michael L. Morales, *Who Shall Ascend the Mountain of the Lord? A Biblical Theology of the Book of Leviticus*, New Studies in Biblical Theology (Downers Grove, IL: InterVarsity Press, 2015), 52. For his reading of Eden as the original cultic mountain, Morales cites Ezek 28:13-14: "You were in Eden, the garden of God.... You were on the *holy mountain* of God" (emphasis added). For a fuller account of the significance of mountain imagery in the Pentateuch, see Michael L. Morales, *The Tabernacle Pre-figured: Cosmic Mountain Ideology in Genesis and Exodus*, Biblical Tools and Studies 15 (Leuven: Peeters, 2012).

[13]G. K. Beale, *The Temple and the Church's Mission: A Biblical Theology of the Dwelling Place of God*, New Studies in Biblical Theology 17 (Downers Grove, IL: InterVarsity Press, 2004), 95-96.

[14]Perrin, *Jesus the Priest*, 85.

institution, designed to illustrate and celebrate the covenant relationship between YHWH and Israel; "covenant principles" were "expressed visually in sacrifice."[15] Sacrifice was therefore a matter of kinship, since covenant was a means of establishing and maintaining a relationship of kinship between two previously unrelated parties.[16] We can even say that sacrifice was meant to enact the bond of kinship between Israel and YHWH, to make it manifest in action. Often this kinship relation was put in terms of husband and wife, so that Israel commits adultery when she sacrifices to other gods. Other times, however, the bond enacted in sacrifice is thought of in filial terms: Israel dishonors YHWH as Father by offering "polluted food" at the altar (Mal 1:7). Judging by Malachi's critique, we can say that the altar was the place where the offeror was to present not only his gift but his filial homage and obedience to the LORD.

Thus, to appear before YHWH as an offeror was to appear before him as son. And for this reason, the hero of the sacrificial story can be identified as the son of God—a point to which I will be returning.

The offeror as figure. But the offeror of Leviticus 1 was not only filial but also a figure, or type. In literature, a type is "a character who is representative of a class or kind of person."[17] The offeror of Leviticus fits this description well. Again, the offeror is nameless, and he is envisioned to be any one of the sons of Israel. The "he" we encounter again and again in Leviticus 1–7 is representative in this sense; "he" stands for any Israelite worshiper who, as son, would approach God at the altar.

But there is good reason to think of the Levitical offeror as a type in a more specific sense, just as there is good reason to read all of Levitical sacrifice figuratively. Throughout this study, I have been arguing that Levitical sacrifice gathered up, in a sense, all the preceding narrative we find in the Pentateuch.[18]

---

[15] Gordon Wenham, "The Theology of Old Testament Sacrifice," in *Sacrifice in the Bible*, ed. Roger T. Beckwith and Martin J. Selman (repr., Eugene, OR: Wipf & Stock, 2004), 84.

[16] Frank Moore Cross, "Kinship and Covenant in Ancient Israel," in *From Epic to Canon: History and Literature in Ancient Israel* (Baltimore: Johns Hopkins University Press, 1998), 7.

[17] Holman and Harmon, *Handbook to Literature*, 486.

[18] The readings of Leviticus offered by Gorman and Morales have been the most helpful in explaining how Leviticus recalls and "enacts" (Gorman's term) the history and theology of God's works of creation, exodus, and covenant recorded in Genesis–Exodus. See Frank H. Gorman, *Divine Presence and Community: A Commentary on the Book of Leviticus*, International Theological Commentary (Grand Rapids, MI: Eerdmans, 1997); Morales, *Who Shall Ascend*.

The tent of meeting recalled Eden and Sinai and figuratively reenacted the stories of those places.[19] The fire on the altar recalled the fiery presence of the LORD that fascinated Moses in the burning bush, led Israel out of Egypt and through the wilderness, and terrified them at Sinai.[20] The priests, again, carried on the original Adamic commission and were thus figures in some sense of obedient humanity.[21] Levitical ritual is heavy with symbolism that reaches back into Israel's past and brings all its significance to the altar so that the history of God's covenant with Israel is recapitulated there.

A central claim of this study, however, is that Leviticus looked not just to the past but the future. Levitical sacrifice reached forward to events yet to come, bringing the significance of those events to the altar so that the hope of what God would do for Israel was in some way manifested in the blood, fire, and smoke of sacrifice. In other words, Levitical sacrifice was prophetic. This claim has long marked Christian readings of Leviticus, and for good reason.[22] Jesus himself invites a prophetic reading of the cult, claiming that, as with the Prophets and the Psalms, the things written in the Law were ultimately about himself (Lk 24:44). Revelation transposes cultic scenery into the heavenly sphere, suggesting an eschatological fulfillment of the cult in the reign of the ascended Christ and his church.[23] And, most explicitly of all, the epistle to the Hebrews reads the cult prophetically, as a witness to the sacrifice of Christ and the perfection of his church, suggesting that the Levitical cult spoke to realities both above (i.e., in the heavenly sanctuary) and beyond (i.e., eschatologically, as the church is gathered to the eternal city of God) its original historical context, whatever that might have been.[24]

---

[19] Again, Morales sees the tabernacle as both "Eden regained" (*Who Shall Ascend*, 106) and a perpetuation of "the Sinai experience of engagement with God" (96).

[20] Milgrom, among others, notes that God "transferred to the Tabernacle his earthly presence in the form of the fire-encased cloud" and thereby made Sinai the model for the "meetings" that would take place there. Jacob Milgrom, *Leviticus 1–16: A New Translation with Introduction and Commentary*, Anchor Yale Bible 3 (New Haven, CT: Yale University Press, 2009), 142.

[21] Beale, *Temple and the Church's Mission*, 75.

[22] I would argue that this stretches back at least to the writers of the NT. Even if one may argue with that assessment, a prophetic reading of the cult is at least as old as Justin Martyr's *Dialogue with Trypho*.

[23] For example, Rev 8:3-4 pictures an altar in heaven on which the prayers of the saints are offered up to God (interestingly, by the priestly mediation of an angel).

[24] Benjamin J. Ribbens, *Levitical Sacrifice and Heavenly Cult in Hebrews* (Boston: de Gruyter, 2016), 15.

In light of this New Testament reading of the cult, I do not believe it to be too much to suggest that Jesus Christ is the true hero of the sacrificial story. The most important sense in which the offeror of Leviticus is a figure is the sense in which he prefigured Christ. The offeror was a symbol not only of every Israelite offeror but of the true Israelite, the final offeror who would fulfill the cult and all its promises. And, of course, on a Christian reading of the cult, this final offeror can be none other than the incarnate Son of God.[25]

Retrospective and prospective typology. As merely Christian as this reading may appear, some might consider it irresponsible. Did Leviticus, in its original historical context, really intend to say anything about Jesus Christ? And if the human author(s) of Leviticus did not intend it, then how are we doing justice to the text when we name Jesus as the hero of the Levitical story? The proposal presented in this study depends on a prospective, forward-looking relationship between figure and fulfillment, that is, between the cult and the Christ. But can that be defended?

This question is important, for the answer determines how far we are able to go in a theological reading of the cult. Can I really read the details of the cult and its various sacrifices as prophetic witnesses to the work of Christ, to the point that I am able to make claims about the mechanism of atonement in Christ's death and resurrection on that basis? Or is the cult's witness less precise, providing an image to give us an entryway for understanding the death and resurrection of Christ but incapable of serving as a prophetic explication of Christ's work?

To answer this question, it is necessary to attend to the distinction between retrospective and prospective typology. Retrospectively, typological (or figurative) reading is, in the words of Richard Hays, an exercise in

---

[25] And, we could add, his body, who offers itself to God through him. See an example of this reading in Augustine, *City of God* 10.6: "the whole redeemed community, that is to say, congregation and fellowship of the saints, is offered to God as a universal sacrifice, through the Great Priest who offered himself in his suffering for us." Augustine, *Concerning the City of God Against the Pagans*, trans. Henry Bettenson (London: Penguin Books, 1972). Also interesting is the argument of Gunton that the sacrifice of Christ "is the basis and enabler of sacrifices" made by the church. See Colin Gunton, "The Sacrifice and the Sacrifices: From Metaphor to Transcendental?," in *Trinity, Incarnation, and Atonement: Philosophical and Theological Essays*, ed. Ronald J. Feenstra and Cornelius Plantinga Jr. (South Bend, IN: University of Notre Dame Press, 1989), 225.

"reading backwards." Hays distinguishes between prediction and prefiguration, and believes the latter best describes the way figuration works in Scripture. We cannot assume, he states, that the Old Testament authors were conscious of predicting or anticipating Christ. It follows that we should understand figuration more as an act of "retrospective recognition" than prospective prediction. The correspondence between type and antitype, figure and fulfillment, "can be discerned only after the second event has occurred and imparted a *new pattern of significance to the first*."[26] Hays allows that "once the pattern of correspondence has been discerned, the semantic force of the figure works both ways, as the second event receives deeper significance from the first." Still, figurative reading on this view is much more an act of "reception" than "production," to the point that "it would be a hermeneutical blunder to read the Law and the Prophets as deliberately *predicting* events in the life of Jesus," though there may be in the Old Testament "an unexpected *foreshadowing* of the later story."[27]

Hays is a wonderfully intelligent reader of Scripture, and he is right about the retrospective *recognition* of figurative relationships—the christological meaning of the Old Testament Scripture was most fully discerned after the fact of Jesus' life and ministry.[28] And, to be clear, Hays is careful to state at points that it is the *comprehension* of the figural relationship that "must be retrospective."[29] Nevertheless, Hays's proposal in *Reading Backwards* leaves something to be desired for a theological reading of a text such as Leviticus. Hays's emphasis on the retrospective aspect of typology, with very little said about any prospective aspect of typology, may leave us questioning the integrity of the Old Testament's witness to Christ. If the Old Testament's witness to Christ is more a result of apostolic exegesis than Old Testament intentionality—if it is always more retrospective than prospective—then we may have reason to worry that the we have lost the Old

---

[26] Richard B. Hays, *Reading Backwards: Figural Christology and the Fourfold Gospel Witness* (Waco, TX: Baylor University Press, 2014), 2-3, emphasis added.
[27] Hays, *Reading Backwards*, 3, 2, 94, emphasis original.
[28] There may have been recognized types of the one to come before the advent of Christ; Israel awaited a prophet like Moses and the Son of David. But Hays's point is that the kind of detailed figurative reading we see through the church's history, and even in the NT, wherein OT events are read as corresponding to specific events in the life of Christ, is possible only after the life and ministry of Christ.
[29] Hays, *Reading Backwards*, 93.

Testament as a meaningful source for Christian doctrine. Brevard Childs, reflecting on Hays's *Echoes of Scripture in the Letters of Paul*, questions the wisdom of an approach that looks at how the apostles read the Old Testament and says, "Go and read likewise." Childs fears that such an approach comes too close to "identifying the Old Testament with the New," threatening to reduce the Old Testament's witness to the New Testament's use of the Old Testament. The Old Testament, Childs insists, "bears its true witness as the Old which remains distinct from the New."[30] But if the typological relationship is determined by apostolic reception alone, then how can we confidently read the Old Testament as a discrete witness to Christ today? We are not apostles.

To be fair, Hays does not say the typological relationship is created or constituted by the apostles' reception of the Old Testament. However, he also says little about what does create that relationship. In my judgment, if we are to confidently read the Old Testament christologically, we need some account of the *cause* of the typological relationship. And the best account of that cause, I believe, is one that grounds the typological relation in the divine economy, so that the relation between figure and fulfillment is providentially (and prospectively) ordered.

In his *Against Heresies*, Irenaeus reflects on Jesus' assertion to the Jews, "You search the scriptures because you think that in them you have eternal life; and it is they that bear witness about me," for "[Moses] wrote of me" (Jn 5:46; see Jn 5:39). Irenaeus remarks that, indeed, "the Son of God is as seed scattered everywhere in His Scriptures." "Neither," he adds, "can one count the instances wherein the Son of God is set forth by Moses: and the very day of His Passion he was not ignorant of, but in figure foretold Him." For an example, Irenaeus points to the Passover, which he believes "announced" the suffering of Christ beforehand. For Irenaeus, then, the type-antitype relation is strongly prospective. The figures of Christ revealed in the Law and Prophets, of which there are too many to count, foretold not only the *that* of our salvation but also the *how* and the *who*. And this point must be insisted on, for it is a hermeneutical implication of a fundamental claim of Christian theology: "that there is one God Almighty, Who created all

---

[30]Brevard S. Childs, *Biblical Theology of the Old and New Testaments: Theological Reflection on the Christian Bible* (Minneapolis: Fortress, 1992), 84, 77.

things by His Word . . . both by His Word and His Spirit making and ordering and guiding and giving being to all."[31]

This is the theological claim famously identified by Irenaeus as the "rule of faith." Important to note here is that this rule is a statement about both the identity of God and his providential ordering of all things. The Father of our Lord Jesus Christ, Irenaeus insists, is the same God and Creator of all things who gave the law to Moses and spoke through the prophets. This God has always spoken through his one Word, God the Son. Since by his Word the Father made all things, "by the creature itself doth the Word reveal God the Creator, and by the world, the Framer of the World." "By the Law and the Prophets," he continues, "did the Word preach both Himself and the Father. . . . And by the same Word, made visible and tangible, the Father was declared." Thus the Father always acts and reveals himself by the Son, and "from the beginning the Son . . . reveals the Father unto all, whom the Father wills, and when He wills, and as He wills." Or, as he states elsewhere, "there is therefore one God the Father, as we have declared; and one Christ Jesus our Lord, coming throughout the Economy, and gathering up all things into Himself."[32]

By his use of the word *economy*, Irenaeus introduces a crucial concept for a figurative reading of the Old Testament. John O'Keefe and R. R. Reno note that this term "denotes good order and arrangement of affairs." An economy, they add, is something like a plot; it is a carefully arranged sequence of events held together by some intelligible purpose or meaning.[33] John Behr similarly notes that the term refers to "an administration or arrangement, more generally, and, in rhetorical and literary theory, it was used to refer to the arrangement of a poem." For Irenaeus, the works of creation, providence, and redemption constitute a single divine economy—"one all-embracing and singular divine plan." That plan is revealed to us in the Scriptures as they describe how "the Hands of God, that is, Christ and the Holy Spirit, effect the one all-embracing economy, or arrangement, of God, which begins with his stated intention to create a human being in his own image and likeness

---

[31] Irenaeus, *Against Heresies*, trans. John Keble (repr., Nashotah, WI: Nashotah House, 2012), 4.10.1; 1.12.1.
[32] Irenaeus, *Against Heresies* 1.12.1; 4.6.6; 4.6.7; 3.16.6.
[33] John J. O'Keefe and R. R. Reno, *Sanctified Vision: An Introduction to Early Christian Interpretation of the Bible* (Baltimore: Johns Hopkins University Press, 2005), 37.

and is completed at the end in Christ himself." For Irenaeus, Behr notes, Christ is both "the beginning and end of the economy." Just as through the Word Adam is formed, so by the Word incarnate Adam is fulfilled or perfected.[34] One might add that, for Irenaeus, Christ is the "middle" of the economy too, as all the story of Israel is likewise summed up and completed in Christ. In other words, Christ is "the logic or purpose in and through which the whole divine economy is conceived and implemented."[35] Christ is not simply the conclusion of the biblical story; he is the *hypothesis* of the whole. Jesus Christ is the principle of arrangement in God's dealings with the world, the Logos of the Father by which he carries out his single plan.

For Irenaeus, there is thus a providential ordering of all things that is revealed in Scripture and summed up in Christ. And this, Behr notes, is why Irenaeus can read Scripture the way he does. Scripture, for Irenaeus, is a "compendium or 'thesaurus,' that is, a 'treasury,' of images, words, and reports, which gives flesh to the Christ proclaimed by the apostles, who in turn reveals the work of God deployed throughout the whole economy described in Scripture."[36] That is, the persons, events, institutions, and words of the Old Testament can reveal Christ to us, can "give flesh to" or fill out our picture of who Christ is and what he has accomplished, because Christ was the meaning of them all from the beginning.

I believe that something like Irenaeus's account of the divine economy and its revelation in Scripture is necessary for confidently reading the Old Testament as a witness to Christ. By God's providence, the events, persons, and even places of the Old Testament speak prophetically, and thus *literally*, of Christ.[37] That is, they are intended as disclosures of his person and work.[38] Of course, this need not mean that the human authors of the Old Testament were always conscious of predicting events in the life of Christ, as Hays

---

[34]John Behr, *Irenaeus of Lyons: Identifying Christianity*, Christian Theology in Context (Oxford: Oxford University Press, 2013), 125, 121-23.
[35]O'Keefe and Reno, *Sanctified Vision*, 39.
[36]Behr, *Irenaeus of Lyons*, 128.
[37]Commenting on the exegesis of Nicholas of Lyra, David Steinmetz, "The Superiority of Precritical Exegesis," *Ex auditu* 1 (1985): 77, notes a distinction in the "literal sense" of Scripture (which can be defined as "the meaning intended by the author") between "literal-historical" and "literal-prophetic" senses. The literal-prophetic sense would be an intentional reference to Christ by the author, who is ultimately God.
[38]Don C. Collet, *Figural Reading and the Old Testament: Theology and Practice* (Grand Rapids, MI: Baker Academic, 2020), 3.

warns against. However, the larger concern of Irenaeus (shared in this study) is with *divine* authorial intention. And as wrongheaded and arrogant—even blasphemous—as we can sometimes be when claiming insight into the divine intentions, I believe we are safe in claiming that, as Jesus himself claimed, God intends for the Law and Prophets to speak to us of Christ. The Old Testament should not be reduced and flattened so that its witness is equated with that of the New Testament; the two Testaments speak of Christ with "two very different voices."[39] Yet each testament speaks of Christ by divine intention.

Typology in Leviticus. On this understanding of typology, the offeror of Leviticus can serve as a prophetic figure of Christ. For, as stated above, there is good reason to see the entire cult as prophetic, as speaking to and promising an even greater reality than what Israel enjoyed at the tent. This is the conclusion drawn by the book of Hebrews, of course; earthly priests "serve a copy and shadow of the heavenly things," and Moses built the tabernacle according to the "pattern" he saw on the mountain (Heb 8:5). The tent, and all its cultic rituals, were types of things heavenly realities, things that would one day be realized on earth.

But the typological function of the cult is not a claim of the New Testament alone. It is not simply a result of early Christians retrospectively fitting Jesus into their Jewish worldview. The same conclusion is also discernible within the pages of the Old Testament. The Old Testament, as noted earlier, seems to view the tent itself as a renewal of Eden and therefore as holding out the promise of Eden's fulfillment. In Geerhardus Vos's words, the tabernacle pointed to "the renewal of the paradise-condition . . . a full future paradise . . . the new world."[40] According to Beale, this is the view of the prophets. Isaiah and Ezekiel alike spoke of "a worldwide eschatological temple that perfectly reflects God's glory."[41] They thus speak of a *new* temple, one that will encompass all heaven and earth, the "building" of which will constitute a new heavens and new earth.[42] Beale even sees this eschatological outlook in

---

[39]Childs, *Biblical Theology*, 78.
[40]Geerhardus Vos, *Eschatology of the Old Testament*; quoted in Beale, *Temple and the Church's Mission*, 98.
[41]Beale, *Temple and the Church's Mission*, 26.
[42]See especially Beale's chapter "The Temple in Ezekiel 40–48 and Its Relationship to the New Testament," in *Temple and the Church's Mission*, 335-64.

Leviticus itself. In Leviticus 26:3-12, the LORD promises that if Israel walks in his statutes, then he will walk with them. That is, he will bless them with rain, produce, peace, abundance, and, best of all, his own presence: "I will make my dwelling among you" (Lev 26:11; Heb. וְנָתַתִּי מִשְׁכָּנִי בְּתוֹכְכֶם). Beale sees this promise as a reference to a future, eschatological presence among his people, one merely symbolized by the Levitical tent of meeting: "The Levitical promise of God's 'walking among' the people likely expresses a more ultimate personal and intense relationship than his present dwelling with them in an encased structure."[43]

If this is sound, then the tent and the entire cult with it served a figurative function that was known from its beginning. And if the whole served a figurative function, then so too, it would seem, did the parts, the offeror included. Like the priests, the sacrifices, the altar, the holy of holies, and everything else on the temple grounds, the offeror was a figure of a greater, eschatological reality.[44] The offeror may be figurative of more than one eschatological reality.[45] But as a filial figure, who by his offering returns to God, there is one candidate who is most obviously fit to play the role of offeror, who seems most clearly to be the reality that the offeror "spoke" of: Jesus Christ, the divine Son incarnate.

ANTITYPE: JESUS CHRIST AS FILIAL FULFILLMENT

Christ as offeror. Christ the priest, yes; Christ the sacrifice, undoubtedly. But Christ the offeror? Here I answer yes.

In the Levitical plot, the offeror stands center stage, before the altar of YHWH, seeking entrance into the divine favor and presence by enacting his filial identity through sacrifice. In doing so, he depicts and typifies the sacrificial work of Christ whereby he reconciles us to God. The New Testament affirms that while Christ is the true priest, and his body the sacrifice, he is also the one who brings the offering. Jesus' identity as offeror may be hinted

---

[43]Beale, *Temple and the Church's Mission*, 111.
[44]Biblical typology, I believe, works on a logic that is more eschatological than Platonic. That is, it points forward to future realities, not just to nonmaterial realities thought to be above or beyond or underlying the material (though there is an element of that present, especially in the typology of the Levitical cult).
[45]Specifically, the role seems ascribable both to Christ, the incarnate Son, and to the many sons he brings to glory (Heb 2:10), on behalf of whom he was offered.

at in the Gospels, as they tell of Jesus making pilgrimage to Jerusalem for the Passover in the days leading up to his death. As the Levitical ritual began with the offeror's journey to the tent, so Jesus' sacrifice begins when he sets his face to go to Jerusalem. Ephesians 5:2 more explicitly identifies Christ as offeror. There we read that "Christ loved us and gave himself up for us, a fragrant offering and sacrifice to God." This seems to imagine Christ as the offeror of Leviticus 1 as he presents a burnt offering (in Christ's case, of himself) for "a pleasing aroma to the Lord" (Lev 1:9).

It is the epistle to the Hebrews, however, that most consistently identifies Christ as offeror. Hebrews, of course, identifies Christ as playing the role of high priest and primarily follows the logic of the Day of Atonement as it does so. Nevertheless, the Christ of Hebrews simultaneously plays the part of the offeror of Leviticus 1. Like the Levitical offeror, Christ is the one who has drawn near (Heb 10:1) to bring his offering—that is, his own body—to God. Like the Levitical offeror, Christ receives the benefits of his sacrifice; through his self-offering he was "made perfect" (Heb 5:8-9). And so, like the Levitical offeror, Christ by his sacrifice is granted access to the divine presence, and indeed opened a "new and living way" of return to God, that we too may draw near (Heb 10:20). For Hebrews, Jesus Christ not only stands above us as intercessor but also stands beside us as brother (Heb 2:11-12), as one who is leading us in return to God and glory as he makes his own return. Christ thus brings to fulfillment the sacrificial movement toward God that the Levitical cult symbolized. By the offering of the incarnate Son, the Levitical offeror has returned to God through death and now shares in the glory of the divine presence.

Much of what the New Testament says about the work of Christ presupposes his fulfillment of the role of offeror. And, for this reason, the same is presupposed in much of the church's theological reasoning. To cite one famous example, Anselm took it on himself to search out the logic of Christ's fulfillment of the offeror. On the logic of the *Cur Deus Homo*, it is fitting that Christ, the God-man, be the one to present the redemptive offering to God. Humanity owes to God a great debt of obedience and worship. The God-man makes satisfaction precisely by taking onto himself the role of offeror and giving God the obedience he deserves—that is, the subjection of the will to God by which God is rightly honored in the creature. The Son, by his death, did precisely this: "He gave his life, so precious; no, his very self; he gave his person—think of it—in all its greatness, in an act of his own, supremely great, volition." This was the Son's "voluntary gift" offered to God; "Christ gave himself up to death for the sake of God's honour."[46] Christ offered of his own, at his own cost—from his own "herd" or "flock" (Lev 1:2), so to speak—to compensate for humanity's debt of obedience and honor. And so he redeemed humanity by playing the offeror.

Jesus Christ thus plays the role of offeror, and in doing so fulfills and completes that role. His act—his giving of his own in filial obedience—is the fulfillment of the offeror's act. His movement—return to God through death—fulfills the offeror's movement. And his destiny—life in God's presence—fulfills the cult's promise as to the offeror's destiny. So, in what we can call the literal-prophetic meaning of Leviticus, Jesus Christ is the hero of the Levitical story. He is the chief actor, the one with whom we are most immediately concerned as we read, since, as the fulfillment of the cult, it is ultimately his offering of which we are reading. By divine inspiration and appointment, Leviticus speaks prophetically of Jesus Christ's self-offering by presenting the offeror—his action, movement, reception—as a figure, type, and pattern to be fulfilled in Christ.

Sacrifice and sonship. We should add to this, however, that as with the Levitical offeror, the offering of Jesus was a filial act. In the Gospel of John, Jesus speaks of going to the Father through his death (Jn 14:12, 16:10). It is as Son returning to his Father that Jesus fulfills the cultic plot. And, interestingly, one could argue from John that this return is simply a matter of Jesus doing what comes naturally; as the incarnate Word, who is eternally with (and perhaps "toward") the Father (Jn 1:1), Jesus' return to the Father is an enactment of his eternal identity.[47] Since he is the one who is always with the Father, it is only natural that the life of Jesus, the incarnate Son, would culminate in a sacrificial movement toward the Father. The same point can be made from Hebrews. There we read that Christ's self-offering was an act of the Son and for the sons—one by which God brought "many sons to glory"

---

[46]Anselm, *Why God Became Man*, in *Anselm of Canterbury: The Major Works*, ed. Brian Davies and G. R. Evans (Oxford: Oxford University Press, 1998), 1.11; 2.18.

[47]ὁ λόγος ἦν πρὸς τὸν θεόν can possibly be translated as "the Word was toward God" or even "the Word was facing God." Scott R. Swain, *The Trinity: An Introduction*, Short Studies in Systematic Theology (Wheaton, IL: Crossway, 2020), 44.

(Heb 2:10). Gareth Lee Cockerill comments that, according to the epistle, Christ's self-offering and high priesthood are "the fulfillment of his sonship," even his divine sonship.[48] Torrance sees a similar connection in Hebrews: what Christ offered to God according to the epistle was a sacrifice of "filial obedience," of "faith, trust, love, worship, prayer, and praise."[49]

Similarly, Thomas Weinandy highlights the relationship between sacrifice and sonship by speaking of Jesus' "filial loving sacrificial death on the cross" as an enactment of the "Our Father" or Lord's Prayer. On the cross, he notes, Jesus names God "my God" and "Father." As he dies, he prays, "Into your hands, I commit my spirit." Jesus thus died and gave up his life in faith; "he gave over and so entrusted his spirit to his 'heavenly' Father." In this way, he hallowed the Father's name in a sacrificial death. "When Jesus lovingly placed his spirit in the hands of the Father, when he breathed his last, he who bears the name 'Son' perfectly hallowed him who bears the name 'Father,' and in doing so made reparation or satisfaction for humankind's sinful un-hallowing acts, which desecrated and violated his Father's holy name." In his sacrifice, Weinandy concludes, we see Jesus "reestablishing humankind's holy relationship to his all-holy Father, restoring humankind's holiness."[50]

Weinandy's words remind us of a point mentioned earlier in this study, that it is by his obedient sonship, manifested in his offering, that Jesus satisfies the demands of covenant, creation, and consecration. In his sacrifice, Jesus enacts his filial identity and so fulfills the kinship demands of covenant, he brings to realization God's purposes for creation by fulfilling Adam's priestly and filial commission by proving himself to be the true Son of God, and he satisfies the demands of consecration by hallowing the Father's name and giving those who share in his sonship by faith his Holy Spirit, by which they are claimed as God's own possession. Christ's fulfillment of the role of offeror is therefore a filial fulfillment. This is not to say that enacting his filial identity is all Jesus did on the cross or that this is all there is to say about it.

---

[48] Gareth Lee Cockerill, *The Epistle to the Hebrews*, New International Commentary on the New Testament (Grand Rapids, MI: Eerdmans, 2012), 62, 70.
[49] Thomas F. Torrance, *Atonement: The Person and Work of Christ*, ed. Robert T. Walker (Downers Grove, IL: IVP Academic, 2009), 274.
[50] Thomas Weinandy, *Jesus Becoming Jesus: A Theological Interpretation of the Synoptic Gospels* (Washington, DC: Catholic University of America Press, 2018), 203, 404.

It is to say, however, that *what* Jesus did on the cross and *how* he did it are rooted in *who* he is. Jesus completes the story of sacrifice by acting as the true Son of God in his obedience unto death.[51] The *who* of atonement is therefore the ground of the *how*.

These arguments for Jesus' filial fulfillment of the Levitical offeror suggest a deep correlation between the person and work of Christ. They also open up an interesting avenue for theological reflection. All of the authors surveyed just now suggest that Jesus Christ fulfills the Levitical cult by enacting his divine identity as Son from within his humanity. By living out his eternal relation to the Father in his human nature, the Son offers himself in all obedience to his Father. Thus the idea of Christ's sacrifice, we are led to think, "thrusts its roots deep into the abyss of the Trinity. . . . The sacrificial surrender of the God-man was to be the most perfect expression of that divine love which, as God, He shows forth in the spiration and effusion of the Holy Spirit."[52] In other words, the suggestion is made that the sacrifice of the incarnate Son corresponds to something that belongs to the eternal life of God as Father, Son, and Holy Spirit.

But is this sound? Can we see in the Trinity some analogue—or archetype—of the Son's incarnate sacrifice?

Archetype: The Eternal Filiation of The Son

E. L. Mascall's "Sonship and Sacrifice." In a short essay titled "Sonship and Sacrifice," first published in 1962, Anglican theologian E. L. Mascall argues that the "essence" of all true sacrifice has its "prototype in the Holy Trinity." That is, in Mascall's thinking, the movement and character of biblical sacrifice corresponds in some measure to the movement within the triune life of God, the eternal generation of the Son from the Father and his return to the Father in the procession of the Spirit. "The Father," Mascall states, "eternally begets the Son by an act of complete self-communication." And, in "filial response," the Son "eternally responds to the Father in an act of filial

---

[51]In Mark's Gospel, as a centurion watches Jesus die, he exclaims, "Truly this man was the Son of God!" (Mk 15:39). This is the first time in that Gospel that this identification is made by someone other than the narrator or a demon. It is in his death that Jesus is recognized as Son of God for Mark.

[52]Matthias Joseph Scheeben, *The Mysteries of Christianity*, trans. Cyril Vollert, SJ (New York: Herder & Herder, 1946), 446.

self-giving. . . . The Son, eternally recognizing the Father as the source of his personal distinction, offers himself back to the Father as the Father's loving Son." This claim, as Mascall acknowledges, had little precedent in the Christian tradition at the time.[53] So how did he arrive at it?

In developing his argument, Mascall hits some of the same notes as those heard in this study: the centrality of sacrifice in biblical religion, a conviction that sacrifice means more than death or destruction, an assertion that proper creatureliness is implicit in the sacrificial act.[54] Mascall insists that, on the biblical understanding, what is being offered to God is the offeror himself, not simply the victim. And, in so offering himself, the offeror rightly recognizes God as Creator—that is, the origin and end of all things. In an important statement, Mascall claims that "in being offered to God, a creature is simply fulfilling the law of its being as a creature. God is both its efficient and final cause, its alpha and omega, its beginning and end. The creature is made by God and for God; its *esse* is both *esse ab Deo* and *esse ad Deum*. The sacrificing of a creature to God is the ritual expression of its ontological status."[55]

Mascall adds to this that the offering (or the offeror *via* the offering) is presented to God that it may be "accepted and transformed by his acceptance."[56] To be received by God is, for Mascall, to be filled with his Spirit. Thus, for him, there is a certain kind of gift cycle at work in sacrifice: the offeror, receiving his being from God, offers himself to God in creaturely honor and obedience, that he may find even greater life in God, life transformed by the Holy Spirit. There is a definite pattern of reception and return here, similar to the one sketched out in the previous chapter of this study. And that cyclical understanding of the sacrificial act is key to Mascall's argument, for it is this that allows us to see what he calls the prototype of sacrifice in the eternal generation of the Son.

---

[53] E. L. Mascall, "Sonship and Sacrifice," *Canadian Journal of Theology* 8, no. 2 (April 1962): 92. If Mascall has read Bulgakov's *Lamb of God* (an important influence on von Balthasar's account of a "primal kenosis" within God in the generation of the Son, as well as other accounts of intratrinitarian "suffering"), he does not acknowledge his debt. Of course, it has become common to propose an element of *sacrificial* love within God. Often, *sacrificial* in this case has been equated with *suffering*, or at least a potential for suffering. That is not the case with Mascall, however, who maintains a Thomistic doctrine of divine attributes while arguing for a prototype for sacrifice within the divine processions.

[54] Mascall, "Sonship and Sacrifice," 89.

[55] Mascall, "Sonship and Sacrifice," 91-92.

[56] Mascall, "Sonship and Sacrifice," 91.

As noted above, Mascall argues that as the Son receives his personal distinction from the Father by the Father's eternal communication of the divine essence, so he eternally offers his "filial response" to the Father and "offers himself back to the Father as the Father's loving Son." He appeals here to John 1: "'In the beginning' the Word was not only *theos* but *pros ton theon*, leaning, as it were, towards the Father." The concept of the Son's eternal filial response is key to Mascall's argument, and he is careful to qualify how it is and is not like the creaturely act of sacrifice. In fact, it would be wrong to label the Son's response to the Father as an act of "homage," "worship," or "sacrifice," for these terms do not do justice to the equality of Father and Son. What we see in this response, he explains, is not sacrifice itself but the "uncreated prototype of the homage, worship, and sacrifice that a rational creature is bound to offer." These rational creatures, Mascall explains, are created sons made in the image of the eternal Son. And so he can say that "man, then, created by God and for God, was meant to achieve his fulfillment and beatitude by offering himself to the Father in a life of joyful and loving filial obedience which would have been an analogous reflection on the created level of the eternal act of filial response made by the Son on the uncreated level in the life of the Trinity."[57] True sonship, Mascall is saying, has a sacrificial shape; sonship is an act of reception and return. Humanity's sacrificial acts therefore imitate, in their creaturely way, the act of the eternal Son.

Mascall's argument presents difficulties, which he anticipates. The most obvious question to ask concerns the place of death in sacrifice. If sacrifice, as this study has argued, is a return to God through death, then must we allege that there is a death (or an analogue to death, or perhaps the possibility of death) in the Son's eternal act?[58] Drawing on the work of Eugene Masure, Mascall answers no. He quotes Masure's assertion that

> the substance of sacrifice . . . is the final meeting of the creature with the Creator, the return of the creature to Him who has made it for Himself so that it may find its end and therefore its happiness in Him and for His glory. . . . Sacrifice is the movement or action by which we try to bring ourselves to God,

---

[57]Mascall, "Sonship and Sacrifice," 92-93.
[58]Hans Urs von Balthasar proposes that there is the possibility of death in *Theo-Drama: Theological Dramatic Theory*, vol. 4, *The Action*, trans. Graham Harrison (San Francisco: Ignatius, 1994).

our end, to find true beatitude in our union with Him. *To sacrifice a thing is to lead it to its end.*[59]

The making of a return to God, of recognizing our origin as our end, is therefore essential to sacrifice for Mascall (and Masure). Death, however, is not. It is only because of sin that humanity must suffer death to gain true life. Because of sin, there must be blood, for "without the shedding of blood there is no remission. But in the beginning, it was not so."[60] Mascall more precisely locates the necessity of death after sin in humanity's divided will, reasoning that a person "divided in himself [as we all are in our sin] can only present a gift to God by removing it entirely from his own possession, and therefore he slays or burns his offering so that it may wholly pass into the presence of God." The suffering and death of the Son, he asserts, are therefore "essential and inevitable when a perfect offering of a human life was made in a fallen world." "Nevertheless," he adds, "the death was the offering of life and not its destruction."[61] Mascall can reason, then, that some analogue or archetype of sacrifice can belong to the divine life, even while that life remains immutably and impassibly blessed.

Mascall's argument is appealing for a number of reasons, not least of which is its effort to speak of something like sacrifice in the eternal generation of the Son without deviating from his commitment to a fully Thomistic understanding of the divine attributes and trinitarian relations.[62] Of even greater value for this study, however, is the answer it suggests to the essential question for the doctrine of atonement: Why the God-man? In fact, Mascall pushes us to improve this question and state it more precisely: Why the Son of God incarnate? For Mascall, the incarnational question seems to focus on the shape of eternal sonship and the way it is savingly communicated to the human creature. This, in itself, is instructive. As Fred Sanders notes, "what the apostles want to show is that Jesus was the Son: He came, lived, taught, acted, died, and rose again like the Son of God: the Son in particular, in person." Jesus Christ saves not by incarnating undifferentiated

---

[59]Eugene Masure, *The Christian Sacrifice: The Sacrifice of Christ Our Head* (London: Burns, Oates & Washbourne, 1944), 41; quoted in Mascall, "Sonship and Sacrifice," 93, emphasis original.
[60]Masure, *Christian Sacrifice*, 38; Mascall, "Sonship and Sacrifice," 93.
[61]Mascall, "Sonship and Sacrifice," 94, 98.
[62]For more on his understanding of divine attributes, see E. L. Mascall, *He Who Is: A Study in Traditional Theism* (London: Longmans, Green, 1943).

(or unappropriated) divine attributes so much as by "living out in his human life the exact same sonship that makes him who he is from all eternity as the second person of the Trinity."[63] Or, as Webster puts it, "Jesus' human history is exhausted in the fact that it is the . . . acting out in time (but not, as it were, constituting for the first time) the eternal relation of Father and Son."[64] Or again, in T. A. Noble's words, "The crucifixion of anyone else (even had that person been innocent and sinless) would not be gospel at all. Everything depends on *who* was crucified. The key to the Work of Christ is the Person of Christ. The key to the atonement is the incarnation. The necessary undergirding for soteriology is Christology."[65] Mascall's identification of a prototype of sacrifice in the eternal filiation of the Son, if it can be maintained, can illumine our understanding of Christ's sacrifice by grounding its *what* and *how* more squarely in the *who*.

Eternal generation and the esse of the Son. But can Mascall's argument be maintained? I believe that, even if we cannot be fully certain of Mascall's proposal, we can at least say that it is consonant with classical trinitarian theology, especially that of a Thomist stripe. Consider, first, its consonance with Thomas's doctrine of eternal generation and the way it gives rise to what is sometimes called the Son's personal mode of subsistence or *esse*.

We can begin with Thomas's insistence that the generation of the Son is an internal act of God: "The very Son begotten by the Father is not outside the Father, but in him."[66] In *Summa Contra Gentiles*, Aquinas is concerned that the generation of the Son be properly distinguished from creaturely generation. He makes this distinction by noting that the Son's generation is an intellectual and not bodily act, as is necessary given God's immaterial nature. Generation in God is an intellectual act, the act that expresses his knowledge of himself. And as the understanding of the intellect remains in the subject who understands, the procession of the Word in God takes place wholly within the divine being. The generation of the Word is therefore not

---

[63]Fred Sanders, *Fountain of Salvation: Trinity and Soteriology* (Grand Rapids, MI: Eerdmans, 2021), 22.

[64]John Webster, "'It Was the Will of the Lord to Bruise Him': Soteriology and the Doctrine of God," in *God Without Measure*, vol. 1, *God and the Works of God* (London: T&T Clark, 2016), 156.

[65]T. A. Noble, *Holy Trinity, Holy People: The Historic Doctrine of Christian Perfecting*, Didsbury Lecture Series (Eugene, OR: Cascade Books, 2013), 159.

[66]Thomas Aquinas, *Summa Contra Gentiles*, book 4, *Salvation*, trans. Charles J. O'Neil (Notre Dame, IN: University of Notre Dame Press, 1975), 11.7.

an act of the divine will with an external terminus.[67] Rather, the Son is the "interior Word" of the Father.[68] It follows, then, that when the Father communicates his essence to the Son, there is no movement outside himself; when he gives himself, he is not giving himself away. In Aquinas's account, eternal generation belongs to the self-existent, self-contained perfection of God. It gives testimony not to any sort of loss or potential for loss in God but to the fullness of the divine life.

Second, the Father's act of eternal generation gives shape to the modes of subsistence—the personal properties—of both the Father and the Son. Rowan Williams helpfully expounds Thomas's conception of the Son's personal mode of subsistence in his book *Christ the Heart of Creation*. He begins by explaining Thomas's language of the *esse* of the Son. For Aquinas, the *esse* of a thing is its distinctive act of being or mode of existence. An *esse* is not to be confused with an essence, the set of properties or qualities constitutive of a certain kind of subsistent. Rather, "*Esse* means active existence, and so denotes all that is involved in being the particular kind of substance a thing is."[69] Again, according to Thomas, a distinct *esse* or mode of existence can be posited of each divine person: "Though the same Nature is in Father and Son, it is in each by a different mode of existence, that is to say, with a different relation."[70] And the *esse* of each is dependent on, or a realization of, that person's relations to the others. The *esse* of the Son is therefore his distinctive act of being the Son, an act that, Williams notes, "is what it is in virtue of its eternal relation to God the Father."[71] Here, we come close to the Thomistic understanding as a divine person as a subsistent relation. The Son, on this account, just is his relation to the Father; "filiation" in God "is the Son."[72]

Significantly, Williams believes that Son's distinctive act of being includes a return of sorts to the Father. He describes the Son's distinctive act of being

---

[67]Thomas Aquinas correctly saw such an understanding of eternal generation as constitutive of Arianism (*Summa Theologica* 1.27.1). Cf. Lewis Ayres, *Nicaea and Its Legacy: An Approach to Fourth-Century Trinitarian Theology* (Oxford: Oxford University Press, 2004), 41-61.
[68]Thomas Aquinas, *Summa Contra Gentiles* 4.11.7.
[69]Rowan Williams, *Christ the Heart of Creation* (London: Bloomsbury Continuum, 2018), 26.
[70]Thomas Aquinas, *De potentia*, q. 2, a. 1, ad 13, quoted in Gilles Emery, OP, *Trinity, Church, and the Human Person: Thomistic Essays* (Naples, FL: Sapientia, 2007), 134.
[71]Williams, *Christ the Heart of Creation*, 29.
[72]Thomas Aquinas, *Summa Theologiae* 1.40.1.

as "an eternal living-out of divine life in the mode of 'filiation.' . . . The divine life receiving divine life as eternal gift and eternally giving it in return." The Son is "distinct within the divine life simply in virtue of the relation of having-been-generated by the Father so as to reflect and return to the Father what has been bestowed on it in its eternal generation." Indeed, Williams goes so far as the speak of the Son, by way of his generation of the Father, as the "eternal form of dependence." Dependence need not mean inferiority or subordination, as Nicene orthodoxy vigorously insists; the word in this case marks a distinct mode of possessing the divine nature (i.e., "from the Father"), not an inferiority of substance (which is strongly denied by the creed's *homoousion*) or a subordination of will (of which there is one in God). The "form of living the divine life in the mode of reception and response," he therefore insists, "is no less truly divine . . . than its source." Nevertheless, Williams argues that the Son's act of being can be recognized as an "analogue of 'createdness' within the divine life—that is, a form of living the divine life in the mode of reception and response."[73]

Williams's language of *return* to describe the Son's personal mode of subsistence does not, I admit, enjoy widely established precedent. But similar statements about the Son's personal mode of subsistence are made by other admirers of Thomas. According to Gilles Emery, "the Son is turned to the Father who begets him," as his existence "is always relative to the Father."[74] Thus the Son, in some sense, exists both *from* and *to* the Father. For Weinandy, the Son just is "the act of giving himself to the Father as Son in the Spirit of love."[75] In both time and eternity, he argues, the act of the Son of God is wholly "focused on" the Father.[76] In the words of Joseph Ratzinger, "the Son by his essence is the gift and giving back of himself: this is what is meant by 'being Son.'"[77] And according to Norris Clarke, the Second Person of the

---

[73] Williams, *Christ the Heart of Creation*, 29, 89, 221, 220.
[74] Gilles Emery, OP, *The Trinity: An Introduction to Catholic Doctrine on the Triune God*, trans. Matthew Levering (Washington, DC: Catholic University of America Press, 2011), 27.
[75] Thomas Weinandy, "Trinitarian Theology: The Eternal Son," in *The Oxford Handbook of the Trinity*, ed. Gilles Emery, OP, and Matthew Levering (Oxford: Oxford University Press, 2011), 389.
[76] Thomas Weinandy, *The Father's Spirit of Sonship: Reconceiving the Trinity* (repr., Eugene, OR: Wipf & Stock, 2010), 30n11.
[77] Joseph Ratzinger, *Journey Towards Easter: Retreat Given in the Vatican in the Presence of Pope John Paul II*, trans. Dame Mary Groves (New York: Crossroad, 1987), 69.

Trinity is "pure subsistent Receptivity and Gratitude."[78] For all these thinkers, the Son's personal mode of subsistence seems to mirror what this study has identified the act of sacrifice, being marked by a *receiving from* in his generation and a turning or giving back to the Father in love. Perhaps, then, we see an eternal analogue of the human vocation as offeror in the Son's *esse*.

The Son's return and mutual glorification. However, it should still be asked whether this language of *return* is really appropriate. If there is a return in the Son, what kind of return would that be? It is important to be careful with this concept. The eternal return of the Son cannot consist in the overcoming of any distance, obstacle, or enmity within God. Whatever this return is, it should be conceptualized in a way that honors the eternal and immutable fullness of the divine life, as I believe we are required to do by Scripture.

One way of honorably conceptualizing of the Son's return is put it in terms of the mutual glorification of Father and Son. Care is still needed; Khaled Anatolios notes that a "major challenge to our efforts to construct a theology of intra-trinitarian mutual glorification is the seeming paucity of its presence in the tradition." He adds, however, that "this paucity is not reducible to complete absence." Anatolios points to the anti-Arian writings of Athanasius, whom he describes as speaking of the Father and Son as "knowing, loving, and honoring each other" in a relation of "fully personal, intersubjective communion."[79]

Athanasius believed that a relation of mutual glorification between Father and Son was implied by Proverbs 8:30, wherein divine wisdom, identified by Athanasius as the eternal Son or Word, says, "I was beside him, his delight. Day by day I rejoiced in his presence." Thus comments Athanasius, "The Father rejoices in the Son and in this same joy, the Son delights in the Father." Importantly for the current argument, this mutual delight is grounded in the Son's eternal generation. Proverbs 8, he argues, "proves that the Son is not foreign, but proper to the Father's Essence," for "the words denote what is His own and like." Athanasius explains that the Father did not delight in the Son "by acquiring delight in addition to himself" but "by

---

[78]W. Norris Clarke, *Person and Being* (Milwaukee: Marquette University Press, 1993), 21.
[79]Khaled Anatolios, *Deification Through the Cross: An Eastern Christian Theology of Salvation* (Grand Rapids, MI: Eerdmans, 2020), 232180.

seeing himself" in the Son, his eternal image. So, too, the Son delights in the Father as he "sees himself" in the Father.[80] The communication of the divine nature is therefore the basis of this mutual glorification.

Athanasius offered further argument for intratrinitarian mutual glorification and again grounded it in the Son's eternal generation by reflecting on the divine will. Opposing Arius, Athanasius insisted that the Son's existence is "by nature and not by will" (or intention).[81] That is, the Son's existence did not arise from the Father's will or decision but belongs to the divine nature; God is not triune by choice. Nevertheless, Athanasius goes on to say, the Son's existence is in fact willed by the Father in the sense that the Son's subsistence is "not without [the Father's] pleasure." Indeed, the Son is the object of the Father's pleasure and love. So, the Son being from the Father, and the divine will being one, the Son therefore returns this affection: "By that good pleasure wherewith the Son is the object of the Father's pleasure, is the Father the object of the Son's love, pleasure, and honor; and one is the good pleasure which is from Father in Son, so that here too we may contemplate the Son in the Father and the Father in the Son."[82] As they share the one divine will, the Father and Son mutually delight in the triune nature of God, which entails delight of the Father in the Son and the Son in the Father. And since the Son is eternally from the Father, his delight in the Father comes by way of receiving and returning the divine love. There may be more to say about intratrinitarian glorification than what Athanasius gives us in this reflection. But, as Anatolios justly concludes, we at least see the "foundation for our construction a conception of trinitarian mutual glorification" here, and, significantly, we see that the Son's eternal generation may well be the cornerstone of that foundation.[83]

Because he is eternally from the Father, the Son eternally offers a return to the Father of the love and glory he receives from the Father. Being

---

[80]Athanasius, *Against the Arians*, trans. John Henry Newman, in *A Select Library of Nicene and Post-Nicene Fathers of the Christian Church*, Second Series, ed. Philip Schaff and Henry Wace, vol. 4, *St. Athanasius: Select Works and Letters*, ed. Archibald Robertson (Buffalo, NY: Christian Literature, 1892), 2.82, rev. and ed. for New Advent by Kevin Knight, www.newadvent.org/fathers/28162.htm.

[81]Athanasius, *Against the Arians* 3.66. Intention is Anatolios's preferred translation (*Deification Through the Cross*, 183).

[82]Athanasius, *Against the Arians* 3.66.

[83]Anatolios, *Deification Through the Cross*, 184.

uncreated, this filial reception and return refer to an eternal relation, not to a sequence of actions, as it is with human offerors. Nevertheless, the Son's eternal glorification of the Father, in my judgment, can justly be thought of as a correlate of the creaturely glorification of God by means of a sacrificial gift from what he has first received from his hand.

The Son's return and the procession of the Spirit. Perhaps Mascall would have approved of conceiving of the Son's return in this manner. His own suggestion for speaking of that return, however, was to put it in terms of the procession of the Spirit. This, too, I believe, is a helpful way of thinking of the Son's return to the Father.

It is helpful here to consider Thomas Aquinas's account of the Spirit's procession. In his *Summa Theologiae*, Aquinas takes up Augustine's argument that "the Holy Ghost is He whereby the Begotten is loved by the one begetting and loves his Begetter."[84] Aquinas clarifies that the Spirit is not the cause or principle of the mutual love between Father and Son; speaking of that principle, it is more proper to say that "the Father and Son love each other not by the Holy Ghost, but by their essence." The Spirit is, however, the *procession* of that love; he is divine "Love proceeding" from Father and Spirit together.[85] On this ground, the Holy Spirit is properly named Love and Gift. Here again, Aquinas cites Augustine, specifically his statement that "as 'to be born' is, for the Son, to be from the Father, so, for the Holy Ghost, 'to be the Gift of God' is to be from the Father and the Son."[86] To understand this, Aquinas insists, we "must know that a gift is properly an unreturnable giving," as Aristotle says, and "thus contains the idea of a gratuitous donation." When we give anyone a true gift, he goes on to explain, what we give in the first place is "the love whereby we wish him well." Love, in this sense, is a "first gift, through which all gifts are given. So since the Holy Spirit proceeds as love . . . He proceeds as the first gift."[87]

Importantly, for Aquinas, the Spirit proceeds as "first gift" from both the Father and the Son. Relevant here is Thomas's conception of the *filioque*. Gilles Emery remarks that, in Thomas's view, "the Holy Spirit proceeds from

---

[84] Aquinas, *Summa Theologiae* 1.37.2. Thomas is quoting Augustine's *On the Trinity* 6.5.
[85] Aquinas, *Summa Theologiae* 1.37.2.
[86] Aquinas, *Summa Theologiae* 1.38.2, citing Augustine, *On the Trinity* 4.20.
[87] Aquinas, *Summa Theologiae* 1.38.2.

the Son insofar as the Son is begotten by the Father." The Son receives from the Father "the 'virtue' of breathing the Spirit and thus being 'Spirator' of the Holy Spirit along with the Father."[88] Interestingly, Thomas reasoned that this implies an "attachment" or inclusion of the procession of the Spirit in the generation of the Son; because of the Son's eternal generation, the Spirit proceeds both *a Filio* (from the Son) and *per Filium* (through the Son).[89] What the Son receives from the Father is what Thomas calls the "virtue" of breathing forth the Spirit. "The 'virtue' of breathing the Holy Spirit is thus *included* in the generation through which the Son receives his being as principle of the Holy Spirit."[90]

Of most immediate interest for this study is what Thomas thought the procession of the Spirit from the Father *through* the Son meant for the Son's personal mode of subsistence. Since the Holy Spirit is Love, it follows that the Son or Word from and through whom he proceeds "is not any sort of word, but one Who breathes forth Love."[91] Having received Love from the Father, the Son, in his eternal relation to the Father, subsists as one who eternally breathes forth that same Love. "It is the same love whereby the Father loves and whereby the Son loves, yet this love, the Son takes from the Father, but the Father has from no one else."[92]

The language of reception and return may be a legitimate means of speaking of the ordered procession of Spirit from the Father through the Son. To be sure, that language cannot be pressed too far. As Emery warns and as was said above in reference to mutual glorification, we are endeavoring to speak here of uncreated realities. We therefore must not imagine any kind of reception and return within God as a sequence of events or taking place in time (as arguments for an orthodox understanding of eternal generation have always insisted).[93] Nor should the Holy Spirit be thought of as something less than personal. The Spirit is not an object exchanged by Father and Son, and our language should guard against the

---

[88] Gilles Emery, OP, *The Trinitarian Theology of St. Thomas Aquinas*, trans. Francesca Aran Murphy (Oxford: Oxford University Press, 2007), 294.
[89] Aquinas, *Summa Theologiae* 1.36.3.
[90] Emery, *Trinitarian Theology of St. Thomas*, 293, emphasis original.
[91] Aquinas, *Summa Theologiae* 1.34.5 ad 2.
[92] Aquinas, *De potentia*, q. 10, a. 4, ad. 8, quoted in Emery, *Trinitarian Theology of St. Thomas*, 293.
[93] Ayres, *Nicaea and Its Legacy*, 41-61.

suggestion.⁹⁴ Nevertheless, a measured and responsible use of the language of reception and return can, I believe, do justice to the concept of the Spirit proceeding as Love and Gift from the Father through the Son. The Son makes a return to the Father by the procession of the Spirit, because in that procession the Son is known to be the Word who breathes forth Love in response to his eternal generation.

Something like sacrifice. In speaking of the Son's return in terms of the mutual glorification of the Father and Son and of the procession of the Spirit from the Father through the Son, I have not used the word *sacrifice*. It may seem to some readers that I have therefore done little to support my suggestion that the eternal Son is the archetype of the Levitical offeror. But the argument of this chapter is not that there is an actual sacrifice in God's inner life but that there is something analogous to it or that corresponds to it. If the creaturely act of sacrifice was intended to be an act of covenant love and creaturely honor offered to God, as I have claimed it is, then it seems this argument can be sustained. The Son's eternal generation from the Father allows us to conceive of an eternal return of love and glory from the Son to the Father. This return is by no means identical to creaturely acts of sacrifice—or obedience, or gratitude or anything else. Nor is it identical to the Son's incarnate sacrifice or obedience; "Mission necessarily includes procession," Bruce Marshall instructs us, "but procession does not at all include mission."⁹⁵ Nevertheless, in my judgment, it can justly be thought of as a divine correlate of creaturely sacrifice, which serves to reveal both why it is fitting to offer sacrifice to God and why it is right that the Son's incarnate life culminated in the supreme sacrificial act. The eternal Son, with these qualifications, can be identified as the archetype of the Levitical offeror.

THE SON AS HERO OF THE LEVITICAL STORY

This account of the Son's *esse* adds depth and clarity to Mascall's argument. And in doing so it lends further support to the argument pursued here: that the *what* and *how* of sacrifice ultimately arise from the *who* of sacrifice, and

---

⁹⁴For how Thomas guarded against such depersonalization of the Spirit, see Matthew Levering, *Engaging the Doctrine of the Holy Spirit: Love and Gift in the Trinity and the Church* (Grand Rapids, MI: Baker Academic, 2016), 101-2.

⁹⁵Bruce Marshall, "The Unity of the Triune God: Reviving an Ancient Question," *The Thomist* 74, no. 1 (January 2010): 23.

that the *who* of sacrifice finds its archetype in the eternal Son of God. The incarnation of this *who* is therefore the fulfillment of sacrifice and of everything promised to us in the Levitical cult. It is therefore Jesus Christ, the eternal Son of God incarnate, who is the hero, in the truest sense, of the Levitical story.

This claim is important as I finally turn to consider the action of the burnt offering. For if the sacrifice we read of here is a prophetic sign of the sacrifice of the Son, all being fulfilled in the one sacrificial act of the Son, then to some degree we should expect the burnt offering's atoning efficacy to issue from the filial *esse* of the Son. Somehow, it would seem, the burnt offering witnesses to the Son reconciling us to the Father by an act of perfect, incarnate sonship. Insofar as the burnt offering grounds a doctrine of satisfaction, that doctrine, we should expect, will speak of satisfaction through faithful sonship. But this, of course, cannot simply be posited; if it holds value for Christian theology, it must be demonstrated from the text.

To the text, then, we go, to see what we can of the mechanism of atonement in the ritual of the burnt offering, carefully considering the particulars of the ritual action of that offering.

FOUR

Action

Atonement Through the Obedience, Death, and Ascension of the Son

THE WAGER OF THIS STUDY is that Levitical sacrifice, the burnt offering in particular, prefigures and so proclaims the atonement of Christ, and that this proclamation is intelligible. The burnt offering, I believe, was a typological figure of the offering of Christ, meaning that it represented both the material elements of that offering (at minimum, a bloody death in devotion to God) and its significance (at minimum, atonement). To discern the logic of the burnt offering is therefore to discern (at least *something* of) the logic of Christ's saving life, death, and resurrection. By attending to the Levitical shadow, we learn something of the christological reality. This is one way the book of Leviticus witnesses to Christ.

In this chapter, we will begin to see whether this wager will pay out, whether these claims will actually bear any fruit. I will now focus full attention on the עֹלָה, which I have been translating as "burnt offering," and I will make an effort to discern what, exactly, this offering reveals about the atoning work of Christ.[1]

---

[1] The translation "ascension offering" may in some ways be better. It corresponds well to what happens in this offering: the entire victim ascends to the altar, and the smoke of its burning ascends into heaven. See Roland de Vaux, *Studies in Old Testament Sacrifice* (Cardiff, UK: University of Wales Press, 1964), 27. It also appears to be true to the Hebrew term for this offering, which probably means "ascending." See Gordon Wenham, *The Book of Leviticus*, New International Commentary on the Old Testament (Grand Rapids, MI: Eerdmans, 1979), 52. I have chosen, however, to stick with the translation "burnt offering" in most instances, since this translation also highlights what, as we will see, is an essential element of the offering (turning the offering into smoke) and is more customary.

That effort might strike some as naive. Leviticus does not in plain terms tell us how the עֹלָה itself was thought to make atonement, much less how its significance might be applied to Christ. Nor does the New Testament have much to say about how Christ acts as a burnt offering, nor is such reflection well-developed in the Christian tradition. One might therefore suspect that any attempt to state in precise terms how the burnt offering prefigures Christ's atoning work could only be the result of a subjective reading that sees in this offering what it already believes about atonement. The concern is legitimate. I have already stated my belief that too many readings of the Levitical offerings have made this error. Why should the reading offered in this chapter fare any better?

A completely objective reading is impossible, and I will not pretend to offer one. But I will try to keep my reading from being *merely* subjective, merely a projection of my own ideas onto the text. In other words, I will try to offer an honest reading of the text. And an honest reading, I believe, is a close and canonical reading that interacts with the Christian tradition. That kind of reading does justice to what Scripture is and is for—it does justice, in other words, to what we can discern of divine authorial intention—and it seeks to avoid the deceptive allure of a novel reading.[2]

But while the reading I offer below is not, I hope, novel, I do believe it makes a contribution to the doctrine of atonement. The burnt offering is rarely taken seriously as an atoning offering.[3] Consequently, it has seldom been taken seriously as a type of Christ's atoning offering and has therefore not been allowed to inform the Christian doctrine of atonement as much as it might. This offering, so important—even central—to the Levitical cult, has something to teach us about how atonement is made, and we should listen carefully.

In this chapter, I treat the עֹלָה under the rubric of "action" in the cultic story line laid out for us in Leviticus. By close attention to Leviticus 1:3-9,

---

[2]On the notion of doing justice to an author, see Kevin J. Vanhoozer, *Is There a Meaning in This Text?* (Grand Rapids, MI: Zondervan, 1998).

[3]Wenham notes the tendency among scholars to "play down the atoning value of the burnt offering" (*Leviticus*, 57). Klawans, for example, notes that at least for descriptive texts such as Ex 29:38-45, the burnt offering seems to be "completely devoid of any concern with expiation." Jonathan Klawans, *Purity, Sacrifice, and the Temple: Symbolism and Supersessionism in the Study of Ancient Judaism* (Oxford: Oxford University Press, 2006), 72.

I will consider the beginning, middle, and end of the burnt offering in an effort to discern the mechanism or logic of atonement at work therein. I intend to stick very close to the text indeed, considering it line by line from Leviticus 1:3-9.[4] What emerges as I do so will be an argument that the burnt offering proclaims atonement as satisfaction by recapitulation through the substitutionary obedience, death, and ascension of the son—in short, filial satisfaction.[5]

Ready for Action: A Brief Introduction to the Burnt Offering

In Leviticus 1:1-2, the sacrificial stage was set. All the narrative context of Leviticus was brought to mind, key themes were noted, an overview of the cultic plot was given, and the hero of the story was introduced. In Leviticus 1:3, the beginning of the action of the cult, the stage is set by the words, "if his offering is a burnt offering" (Heb. אִם־עֹלָה קָרְבָּנוֹ). A few comments on this introduction are in order.

Action. First, an explanation of what I mean by *action*. Action, in the sense that I use it here, is simply "the series of events that constitute the plot."[6] The action is how exactly the plot unfolds. If the plot of Levitical sacrifice is "return to God through death," then the action we are speaking of would be the steps by which that return is achieved. Given this simplistic definition, there may seem to be little promise in my use of "action" as a category for interpreting the burnt offering. But there are at least two advantages, I believe, in thinking of the ritual as this sort of action.

First, the definition of action as a sequence of events helps us remember that Levitical sacrifice is indeed a sequence, not a single isolated event.

---

[4] While the prescriptions for the burnt offering run from Lev 1:3-17, the bulk of the details is found in Lev 1:3-9, in which the offered animal is a bull. In the remaining verses, the same basic instructions are given for presenting an offering from the flock or of birds.

[5] It will be evident that the recapitulation I have in mind has a strong element of re-creation. The "correction and perfection" of the offeror comes about in an act of re-creation, wherein the offeror dies and rises with his offering.

[6] Hugh Holman and William Harmon, *A Handbook to Literature*, 6th ed. (New York: Macmillan, 1992), 4. Understood in this way, the burnt offering constitutes only part of the action in the Levitical plot. In other words, the burnt offering is not the whole story of how the offeror returns to God through death; it is not that whole series of events. The burnt offering might be thought of as something like an episode in the Levitical plot, a distinct and coherent unit of action that advances the plot without exhausting it.

Jonathan Klawans insists that we speak of a sacrificial process, and he points to the inadequacies of the theories of René Girard, Walter Burkert, and others who seem bent on reducing sacrifice to some single essential act.[7] Similarly, David Moffitt insists that much misunderstanding of Scripture, the book of Hebrews in particular, and of Christ's sacrifice has been generated by forgetting that sacrifice is a "multistep process" or "sequence."[8] To define action as a series of events reminds us that Levitical sacrifice is a sequence and that the entire sequence matters. Further, to think of Levitical sacrifice as a series of events that constitute a plot reminds us that sacrifice is a *meaningful* sequence of events. The action of Levitical sacrifice is not merely episodic but ordered, aiming at a certain goal: the return of the offeror to God through death.[9]

Second, to speak of action is to raise the question of actors, and that turns out to be an important one in Levitical sacrifice. Most obviously, the actors in the Levitical cult are the offeror and the priests. It is essential, however, that we remember God as a primary actor in the cult. Kleinig argues that as "the voice of the Lord fills the pages of Leviticus," an allusion to the fact that most of Leviticus consists of divine speech, so God is the primary actor or ritual agent in Levitical sacrifice. Nothing was accomplished in sacrificial rites, including that of the burnt offering, apart from God's "Word of promise and his gracious involvement."[10] Kleinig's statement is more than a bit of pious rhetoric but comes from a good reading of the text. There is the fact, first, that Leviticus does indeed consist largely of divine speech and begins with a divine address or invitation offered to Israel through Moses. God is therefore active in and through this ritual by his Word, as Kleinig insists. There is also the fact that the priests act as divinely empowered agents. As Kleinig notes, "Only the priests may dispose of blood and present the sacrificial portions on the altar." Surely

---

[7] Klawans, *Purity, Sacrifice, and the Temple*, 22-27.
[8] David M. Moffitt, *Rethinking the Atonement: New Perspectives on Jesus' Death, Resurrection, and Ascension* (Grand Rapids, MI: Baker Academic, 2022), 34, 124.
[9] Holman and Harmon, *Handbook to Literature*, 4. Similarly, Paul Ricoeur identifies two dimensions of narrative plots: an episodic dimension and a configurative dimension. The episodic is simply what happens, and the configurative is what unites the episodic in a single meaningful course of action. See Kevin J. Vanhoozer, *Biblical Narrative in the Philosophy of Paul Ricoeur: A Study in Hermeneutics and Theology* (Cambridge: Cambridge University Press, 1990), 93.
[10] John Kleinig, *Leviticus* (St. Louis: Concordia, 2003), 1, 60.

this is because only the priests were consecrated for such a task. But there is also a sense in which the priests, and the high priest in particular, acted as representatives of God and agents of divine blessing; see, for example, Aaron's blessing from the altar in Leviticus 9:22. Kleinig seems right in saying, then, that only the priests disposed of blood and presented offerings on the altar "because the Lord [was] at work in those enactments."[11] Finally, it is important to note that God acted in Levitical sacrifice through the fire on the altar, a fire that Exodus 40:34-38 identifies as the very presence and glory of the LORD. It is especially important for the burnt offering that God acted in this ritual by consuming and transforming the offering through the flame.

It therefore seems right to identify God as the "main actor" in this ritual, as Kleinig does.[12] Through this sequence of action, God was at work in Israel. Specifically, as the rest of this chapter will argue, God was at work to bring the offeror back to himself through the work of atonement.

The primacy of the burnt offering. That the עֹלָה is treated first in the prescriptions of Leviticus 1–7 may be significant. Most likely, this offering was not the first offering presented by the offeror as he approached YHWH; the "didactic order" of Leviticus 1:3–6:7 did not correspond to the "procedural order" of sacrifice at the tent.[13] Leviticus 9, in which "the system is seen in operation," describes the cultic service as beginning with a sin offering that was followed by a burnt offering that was followed by peace offerings (Lev 9:8-21).[14] Why, then, should the burnt offering be treated first in the didactic order? The answer, I believe, has to do with the primacy of the burnt offering for the Levitical cult.

---

[11] Kleinig, *Leviticus*, 60.

[12] Kleinig, *Leviticus*, 60. This identification should not undermine my identification of the offeror as the hero of Levitical ritual. God, in and through the agency of the offeror, the priests, and perhaps even the blood, is the one who makes the action happen, and in this sense is the main actor, i.e., the primary causal agent. The offeror is the one whom the action concerns, the main character or protagonist, and that is what I mean by hero.

[13] A. F. Rainey, "The Order of Sacrifices in Old Testament Ritual Texts," *Biblica* 51, no. 4 (1970): 485-98. Rainey bases his argument on the evidence of Lev 14–15 and Num 6, along with Ezek 43–45, and, like Morales, argues that the procedural order of sacrifice began with the sin offering, which was followed by the עֹלָה and concluded with the peace offering.

[14] William J. Dumbrell, *The Faith of Israel: A Theological Survey of the Old Testament*, 2nd ed. (Grand Rapids, MI: Baker, 2002), 43. See Michael L. Morales, *Who Shall Ascend the Mountain of the Lord? A Biblical Theology of the Book of Leviticus*, New Studies in Biblical Theology (Downers Grove, IL: InterVarsity Press, 2015), 122-23.

Morales claims that the burnt offering "may have represented the core, and perhaps even the summation, of the entire sacrificial system."[15] That claim may seem outlandish, but there is good reason to believe it is true. The burnt offering was definitive of the Levitical cult in multiple senses. First, there is the simple fact that the altar took its name from this offering; it is commonly referred to as "the altar of burnt offering."[16] Second, Exodus seems to suggest that the burnt offering would be central to Israel's covenant with YHWH. Morales notes that the blood of the covenant (Ex 24:8) was "collected" from burnt offerings; something about this offering, perhaps, makes its blood an appropriate symbol of Israel's covenant union with YHWH.[17] Exodus 29:38-46 seems to point in the same direction when it prescribes that burnt offerings be presented day and night. Israel, by prescription of the LORD, is to offer two lambs every day, one in the morning and the other at twilight. The LORD promises that as they do so, he will meet with Israel as their God: "It shall be a regular burnt offering throughout all your generations at the entrance of the tent of meeting before the LORD, where I will meet with you, to speak to you there. . . . I will dwell among the people Israel and will be their God" (Ex 29:42, 45). Morales comments that the daily burnt offering thereby fulfills the purpose of the altar; as the smoke of the burnt offering continually ascends, the altar serves its purpose as the meeting place between God and Israel.[18]

Third, there is the fact that every other offering mentioned in Leviticus is somehow enfolded into the burnt offering. Kleinig notes that, according to the prescriptions, the other offerings of Leviticus were in one way or another added on to the burnt offering, which was always the first to be placed on the altar.[19] The grain offering, for example, seems to be a

---

[15]Morales, *Who Shall Ascend*, 123.
[16]Michael L. Morales, "Atonement in Ancient Israel: The Whole Burnt Offering as Central to Israel's Cult," in *So Great a Salvation: A Dialogue on the Atonement in Hebrews*, ed. Jon C. Laansma, George H. Guthrie, and Cynthia Long Westfall, Library of New Testament Studies 516 (London: T&T Clark, 2019), 28. Morales notes that it is "so designated seven times in Exodus (30:28; 31:9; 35:16; 38:1; 40:6, 10, 29), seven times in Leviticus 4 (vv. 7, 10, 18, 25 [x2], 30, 34), and four [it appears to be five] times in Chronicles (1 Chron. 6:34; 16:40; 21:26, 29; 2 Chron. 29:18)."
[17]Morales, "Atonement in Ancient Israel," 61.
[18]Morales, "Atonement in Ancient Israel," 60.
[19]Kleinig, *Leviticus*, 40. Kleinig's understanding of the ritual order may seem to conflict with that of Rainey and Morales, mentioned above, and more importantly with the evidence of Lev 9. But that is not necessarily the case. The sin offering was enacted mainly by applying blood to the

vegetable accompaniment of the burnt offering as a "food gift."[20] The fatty portions of the peace offering were to be burned atop the burnt offering. So, too, it seems, was a fat portion of the sin offering (at least in the case of the sin offering for the common people; Lev 4:31) and the guilt offering (which apparently followed the same procedure as the sin offering; Lev 7:7). On this basis, Morales sees the expiatory sacrifices (i.e., the sin and guilt offerings) as being "pre-fixed" to the burnt offering and the peace offering as being "suffixed" to it.[21] The burnt offering is therefore the "fundamental sacrifice," since "all the other sacrifices are placed on it and so are virtually incorporated into it."[22]

Finally, and relatedly, the primacy of the burnt offering is apparent in the way the burnt offering seems to "encompass the whole ritual movement in itself."[23] Earlier in this study, I spoke of that movement as a return to God through death. This idea of return to God through death is visibly represented by the burnt offering as the smoke from the altar ascends to heaven. According to Kleinig, the Hebrew term (וְהִקְטִיר; from the root קָטַר) used to speak of the burning of the burnt offering (and, with it, all the offerings placed on the altar) means not simply "to burn" but "to make smoke."[24] The emphasis is not that the offering is being consumed by the flame but that it is being transformed into a sweet-smelling aroma that rises to heaven and is gladly accepted by God. Indeed, it is ascension and not obliteration that is the main idea of this offering, as etymology suggests: "The name of [the] holocaust, 'olāh, is ordinarily explained by the root 'ālāh, 'to ascend.' It is the sacrifice in which the victim 'ascends' to the altar, or, perhaps better, the smoke of which 'ascends' to God."[25] With its emphasis on ascension, the עֹלָה represents the movement and goal of the Levitical cult: reception into the presence of God.

---

horns of the altar, and only a small part of the animal was burned; the rest of the carcass was discarded in a clean place outside the camp (Lev 4:11-12). While the blood of the sin offering was applied first, then, the body of the burnt offering could still be the first thing placed on the altar. Moreover, if a burnt offering was really continually burning, then anything placed on the altar could be understood to be adding on to the continual burnt offering.

[20]Numbers 15:1-10 gives that impression when it prescribes the grain offering and a drink offering to accompany the burnt offering, leading us to picture a banquet presented to God.
[21]Morales, "Atonement in Ancient Israel," 65.
[22]Kleinig, *Leviticus*, 40.
[23]Morales, "Atonement in Ancient Israel," 65.
[24]Kleinig, *Leviticus*, 56.
[25]De Vaux, *Studies in Old Testament Sacrifice*, 27.

For these reasons, we can say that the burnt offering was "the paradigmatic offering in the Hebrew Bible" and the offering that "represents the purest form of divine service."[26] The עֹלָה was the most fundamental sacrifice, "the main sacrifice of the Israelite cult."[27] It was also "the perfect type of sacrifice" or the "sacrifice par excellence."[28] This is important to note. If the עֹלָה really is fundamental to the cult and paradigmatic, then its significance must shape that of the other atoning offerings. The sin and guilt offerings, in other words, must be somehow understood in light of the meaning and movement of the burnt offering. Each offering, of course, is distinct, and in my judgment has its own contribution to make to our understanding of atonement. However, if the burnt offering really represented a summation of the entire cult, then we should suspect that it provides a framework for understanding the sin and guilt offerings. We might even say that the sin and guilt offerings find their meaning as they are understood from within the meaning and movement of the burnt offering.

This might be surprising. Again, oftentimes, not much is made of the burnt offering when we think of sacrificial atonement; the sin offering is usually given pride of place. But why should that be the case? If the burnt offering is so central to the cult, ought it not be central to our understanding of how Jesus fulfills the cult and the promise of atonement it held out to Israel?

The burnt offering as gift. In addition to highlighting the primacy of the burnt offering, this opening phrase seems to speak to its character as well. The burnt offering is categorized here as קָרְבָּן. In one sense, קָרְבָּן is simply the Hebrew word for "offering." According to Leviticus 1:2, it seems that all that Israel will bring to the altar seems to wear this label. Whatever the offeror brings from either herd or flock will be קָרְבָּן.

It is nevertheless instructive to think more about this word. Eberhardt, noting that the word is derived from the Hebrew root קָרַב, which usually

---

[26] James W. Watts, "Olah: The Rhetoric of Burnt Offerings," *Vetus Testamentum* 66, no. 1 (2006): 125, 132.

[27] John E. Hartley, *Leviticus*, Word Biblical Commentary 4 (Grand Rapids, MI: Zondervan, 2015), 17. See Jacob Milgrom, *Leviticus 1–16: A New Translation with Introduction and Commentary*, Anchor Yale Bible 3 (New Haven, CT: Yale University Press, 2009), 176.

[28] De Vaux, *Studies in Old Testament Sacrifice*, 37; Philip Peter Jenson, *Graded Holiness: A Key to the Priestly Conception of the World*, Journal for the Study of the Old Testament Supplement Series 106 (repr., London: T&T Clark, 2021), 155.

means "to come near" or "to bring near," states that the "literal meaning" of קָרְבָּן is "that which is brought near to YHWH."[29] Milgrom notes that what is "brought near" as קָרְבָּן is not always placed on the altar. Sanctuary gifts, "such as draft animals and carts (Num. 7:3)" were also denominated קָרְבָּן.[30] A קָרְבָּן is therefore a gift, something presented to the LORD, a reality that is rightly reflected in the LXX translation of the term as δῶρον.[31] The characterization of the burnt offering as a gift is only strengthened as we keep reading. In Leviticus 1:9, as we have seen, it is identified as an אִשֶּׁה, often translated "food offering" or "food gift."[32] Averbeck affirms that this term means "gift or present" and states that it testifies to the gift aspect of all Levitical sacrifice.[33]

The terminology used of this offering agrees with its distinguishing characteristic. Unlike the other animal sacrifice, the entirety of the עֹלָה was placed on the altar and turned into smoke to be transported to YHWH. For this reason, it has often been thought of as an offering that expresses the "total and unreserved making over of a gift." Roland de Vaux adds that the burnt offering was "above all an act of homage, expressed by a gift."[34] This act of homage was, ideally, the concentrated ritual enactment of "a life yielded entirely unto YHWH, in full submission to his will and complete obedience to his law."[35]

Whatever else the burnt offering might prove to be, it is being introduced to us as a gift. And this gift carries within it the worship, devotion, and obedience of the offeror. We can express this idea with the words of Augustine: what the offeror of the burnt offering most truly presented to God was himself, offered unto God in humility and praise and consumed in "the burning fire of charity."[36] This too is a significant observation. Especially among Protestants, it has been typical to make a fairly sharp distinction

---

[29] Christian A. Eberhardt, *The Sacrifice of Jesus: Understanding Atonement Biblically* (repr., Eugene, OR: Wipf & Stock, 2018), 71.
[30] Milgrom, *Leviticus 1–16*, 145.
[31] Richard E. Averbeck, "Offerings and Sacrifices," in *New International Dictionary of Old Testament Theology and Exegesis*, ed. Willem A. VanGemeren (Grand Rapids, MI: Zondervan, 1997), 4:998.
[32] Milgrom, *Leviticus 1–16*, 145; Kleinig, *Leviticus*, 57.
[33] Averbeck, "Offerings and Sacrifices," 4:998–99.
[34] De Vaux, *Studies in Old Testament Sacrifice*, 37.
[35] Morales, "Atonement in Ancient Israel," 66.
[36] Augustine, *Concerning the City of God Against the Pagans*, trans. Henry Bettenson (London: Penguin Books, 1972), 10.3.

between expiatory and eucharistic sacrifice. Expiatory sacrifices are those that deal with sin by making atonement through blood; eucharistic sacrifices are those we offer with praise and gratitude in response to God's grace. However, the burnt offering may call into question a hard distinction between these two classes of sacrifice. For the burnt offering is to all appearances an offering of gratitude and homage, as Scripture so often attests. And yet it is also said to make atonement, both here in Leviticus 1:4 and, interestingly, later in Leviticus 16:24. Somehow, this one offering, presented as a gift, both represents the devotion of the offeror and makes atonement.

THE ACT OF SUBSTITUTION

תָּמִים—*Searching for a clean creature.* Turning at last to the details of the text, we see that the first stipulation given for the burnt offering is that it must be a male without blemish. It is customary to ask why this must be the case; why male, and why unblemished? As to the maleness, it could be that males were to be offered simply because they were more expendable.[37] A thriving herd or flock requires many healthy females but comparatively very few healthy males. Since the burnt offering was so commonly offered, it would make sense to offer the less necessary males. Readers of Leviticus have sometimes looked for a symbolic explanation. Philo said that the male was preferred because it is "more complete, more dominant than the female." Kleinig suggests that "the male was the head of the entire herd or flock and so was a representative of it."[38] It is difficult to be certain about any of these interpretations; the instructions for the peace offering allow females to be offered, while those of the sin offering in some instances stipulate that a female be offered, and it is hard to discern any reason these offerings would be more suitably female.

But what seems more important, and not quite so impenetrable, is that the offering be "without blemish" (Heb. תָּמִים). Milgrom derives this adjective from a verb meaning "be complete."[39] Kleinig understands it to mean "'complete,' 'intact,' or 'perfect.'" The animal is to be a perfect specimen of its

---

[37] Milgrom, *Leviticus 1–16*, 147; Kleinig, *Leviticus*, 61. Wenham, by contrast, argues that males were actually considered more valuable than females. His evidence: for a sin offering, a ruler had to offer a male goat, but a common person could offer a female (Lev 4:22-31; *Leviticus*, 55).
[38] Kleinig, *Leviticus*, 61.
[39] Milgrom, *Leviticus 1–16*, 147.

species."⁴⁰ This seems to fit with the evidence of Leviticus 22:17-25, where the requirement that offerings be without blemish is expounded. Blemished offerings, the Lord assures Israel, will not be accepted. Offerings must not be blind or mutilated in any way. They must not have a discharge or be scabbed, and no part should be irregular (e.g., having a part too long or too short; Lev 22:23). The animal, in short, must be perfectly healthy and must conform to the typical features of its species. This requirement, Kleinig notes, is frequently repeated in Leviticus.⁴¹

Why should Leviticus put so much stress on this point? One answer is that the offering of an unblemished animal fits the requirements of good gift giving. In Malachi 1, the Lord charges the priests of Israel with putting "polluted food" on the altar (Mal 1:7). The priests offer animals that are blind, lame, and sick. The Lord counts this as evil and asks the rhetorical question, "Present that to your governor; will he accept you or show you favor?" (Mal 1:8). When they come to the Lord with such a gift, why should they expect it to be acceptable and effective? (Mal 1:9). The dynamic at work here is that of gift giving.⁴² A blemished gift fails to honor its recipient. The gift character of the burnt offering therefore requires that it be unblemished.

There is, however, more to say on this point. The insistence that the burnt offering be תָּמִים seems to have a deeper theological significance. According to Leviticus, only the clean can be received by the holy; when the holy and the unclean come into contact, the holy is under threat of being profaned. And this the Lord will not allow. To desecrate any of his holy things is to put oneself in grave danger.⁴³ Leviticus considers an animal clean when it clearly fits in the order of creation as established in Genesis 1. The unclean is that which in some manner "violate[s] the order and categories of creation."⁴⁴ This ultimately is because violating the order of creation violates

---

⁴⁰Kleinig, *Leviticus*, 52.
⁴¹According to Kleinig's list, the adjective תָּמִים also occurs in Lev 1:10; 3:1, 6, 9; 4:3, 23, 28, 32; 5:15, 18, 25 (ET: Lev 6:6); 9:2, 3; 14:10; 22:19, 21; 23:12, 18 (*Leviticus*, 52).
⁴²Recent decades have seen a great deal of interest in the dynamics of gift giving. Barclay gives a good introduction to the most relevant literature and applies it to his interpretation of the Pauline epistles in *Paul and the Gift*, chap. 1, "The Anthropology and History of the Gift."
⁴³Jay Sklar, *Sin, Impurity, Sacrifice, Atonement: The Priestly Conceptions*, Hebrew Bible Monographs 2 (Sheffield, UK: Sheffield University Press, 2005), 154.
⁴⁴Mary Douglas, *Purity and Danger: An Analysis of Concepts of Pollution and Taboo* (New York: Routledge, 2002), 67.

the principle of life. God, the creation account demonstrates, has ordered all things for the sake of full and flourishing life. To violate that order is to embrace or embody chaos and death. God intends his world to be filled with images of his own life and vitality. Anything, then, that is associated with a lack or loss of life is unclean.[45]

Leviticus, I believe, requires us to be concerned with something like the philosophical notion of *form*. According to Knierim, "that the offeror must bring a 'male, perfect' presupposes not only that he knows the difference between male and female, and perfect and imperfect exemplars of cattle, but also that he selects from among his cattle . . . one exemplar." The idea of an exemplar is closely related to that of form; to be an exemplar is to be true to form.[46] A clean animal, then, one that embodies the life and fertility with which God has blessed his creation, is one that adheres to the form God intends for its species or class.[47]

There is some sense, Leviticus seems to be saying, in which there is a right way of being the particular kind of creature God has given one to be. There is a sense of wholeness that was ideal for sacrificial victims and that implied a normative way of being a bull or goat or lamb. To be suitable for sacrifice, we might say, was to adhere to the law of one's nature, the law written by God at the creation of the world.[48] This, of course, would apply to humanity

---

[45] Perhaps this explains why Lev 12 would find it necessary to say that an offering may not have damaged testicles or be castrated. Such a condition would mean a lack of "creativity, reproductive energy, and fertility" with which God blessed his creation in Gen 1. Frank H. Gorman, *Divine Presence and Community: A Commentary on the Book of Leviticus*, International Theological Commentary (Grand Rapids, MI: Eerdmans, 1997), 15.

[46] "That the offerer must bring a 'male, perfect' presupposes not only that he knows the difference between male and female, and perfect and imperfect exemplars of cattle, but also that he selects from among his cattle . . . one exemplar." Rolf P. Knierim, *Text and Concept in Leviticus 1:1-9: A Case in Exegetical Method* (repr., Eugene, OR: Wipf & Stock, 2010), 31. The idea of exemplar is closely related to that of form; "exemplar cause" can be another name for "formal cause." To be an exemplar is to be true to form.

[47] Douglas, *Purity and Danger*, 69. We should remember, of course, that conformity to class certainly did not mean for the ancient Hebrews what it means today. Our world and theirs have very different ways of classifying creatures.

[48] P. M. Venter, "Atonement Through Blood in Leviticus," *Verbum et Ecclesia* 26, no. 1 (October 2005): 279, argues that in the outlook of Leviticus, "Within the cosmic order holy primarily means whole." He adds that "to remain in the place allocated to you and to hold everything in equilibrium, is to keep God's order intact." God's law serves the cosmic order by keeping humanity in its place and in proper relationship to God and all else. Thus, "to be disobedient to God's law means to transgress these borders and disturb the order." Disobedience therefore makes the disobedient agent unclean and can make one's environment unclean.

as well. There is some sense in which Leviticus is concerned with *the proper way of being human*. There is a way of being human that is unclean, that violates the order established by God at creation. This way is demonstrated by the transgression of Adam and Eve: instead of ruling over creation by obedience to the word of God, they heed the voice of the serpent. The result is what Scripture calls humanity's corrupt "way" on the earth (see Gen 6:12). This way is obviously ethical; human beings following Adam break God's law. But there is also something ontological about this corruption. The corruption of human beings means that they have in some manner been separated from their form, the exemplar cause of humanity that determines their proper manner of existence.[49] Alternatively, we might speak of the *logos* of human being, the divine Word that specifies humanity's place and function in the created order.[50] Or, again, we might think of what Bonaventure called the "command of nature," a command that orders humanity to its proper end, by following which one would adhere to and preserve the good that God intends for humanity.[51] Whatever the terms we choose, the basic idea is that according to the Levitical ontology, there is a proper way to be human, just as there is a proper way to be a bull or ram. And that way is prescribed by the Word of God.

Made clean by the Word of God. This interpretation is supported by the biblical notion of being cleansed by the Word. The idea is explicit in the New Testament. In John 15:3, Jesus tells his disciples, "Already you are clean because of the word that I have spoken to you." As clean, they will be fruitful, if they abide in Christ and his word (Jn 15:4-7). The Word incarnate, and the word he speaks, make one clean and fruitful, filled with life and vitality. Similarly, in Philippians 2:15-16, Paul associates being "blameless and innocent . . . without blemish" with "holding fast to the word of life." In

---

[49]Here I am applying the thought of Thomas Aquinas, who spoke of corruption in terms of separation from form. Thomas Aquinas, *Light of Faith: The Compendium of Theology*, trans. Cyril Vollert (Manchester, NH: Sophia Institute, 1993), 69.

[50]Paul M. Blowers, *Maximus the Confessor: Jesus Christ and the Transfiguration of the World* (Oxford: Oxford University Press, 2016), 109-14, explains that according to Maximus the Confessor, "each individual creature has its unique status and vocation, its 'natural principle' and 'mode of existence'" establishes an "intrinsic interconnectedness" between that creature and all others. Maximus refers to the diverse natural principles of the different creatures as *logoi*, all of which participate in the Eternal Logos, by which all creatures are related to God as their Creator.

[51]Bonaventure, *Breviloquium*, trans. Dominic V. Monti, OFM, Works of St. Bonaventure 9 (Saint Bonaventure, NY: Franciscan Institute, 2005), 2.11.2.

Ephesians 5:25-27, we read that "Christ loved the church and gave himself up for her, that he might sanctify her, having cleansed her by washing of water with the word"—all to the end that he might present her to himself "without blemish." This statement seems to reflect the Levitical logic: an offering must be clean before it is consecrated. Christ gave himself to consecrate or sanctify the church. And he could do so because he had first cleansed the church by his word. This word acts like water, washing away that which is unclean and unable to participate in the divine holiness. In all these New Testament passages, it is the Word of God that makes clean.

The same teaching is implicit in Leviticus. To be unclean is to be out of accord, in some way, with the Word of God that has both spoken the world into being and defined right and wrong for moral agents. Leviticus 18 seems to make this point. Here we find a list of prohibitions in sexual relations: one may not sleep with a close relative, his neighbor's wife, an animal, and so on. To do so would be to commit an "abomination" (Lev 18:22, 27, 29) and make oneself "unclean" (Lev 18:20, 24, 30). Instead, Israel must walk in line with YHWH's words, follow his rules, and keep his statutes (Lev 18:4). It is only as Israel conforms to the word of the Lord that they will be clean and therefore be allowed to dwell in his land.

To be "without blemish" therefore implies conformity to the Word of God. Morales notes that when תָּמִים is used to describe humans, it means "blameless" or "whole-hearted." An important example of this usage is found in Psalm 15:1-2: Who shall dwell on God's holy hill? The one who walks תָּמִים, "blamelessly." Judging by the rest of that psalm, we can conclude that walking תָּמִים means moral conduct in conformity with the word and will of God. This obedience is what makes one clean, without blemish, blameless. But, again, this obedience is not merely ethical; it also has an ontological element. The truth of the Word of God is meant to reach down to the very heart of the human being, the core of the person's being, so that the person's mode of existence is according to the divine prescription. This becomes more evident as we consider the overall movement of the ritual for the burnt offering.

Return and judgment. יַקְרִיבֶנּוּ אֶל־פֶּתַח אֹהֶל מוֹעֵד—"He shall bring it to the door of the tent of meeting." After choosing a proper offering, the offeror brought his offering to the entrance of the tent of meeting (אֶל־פֶּתַח אֹהֶל מוֹעֵד).

Kleinig notes that this phrase was "a technical term for the eastern courtyard of the tabernacle in front of the altar for burnt offering. It extended from the altar to the entrance of the courtyard."[52] This suggests a parallel with the Garden of Eden. When God banishes Adam and Eve from the garden, he places the cherubim at what appears to be an eastern entrance into the garden to "guard the way to the tree of life" (Gen 3:24). Later in the Genesis narrative, an eastward movement is indicative of alienation from God; Cain is banished to a land "east of Eden" (Gen 4:16); "Lot journeyed east" when he separated from Abram and eventually settled in Sodom (Gen 13:11).

Given the symbolism of the east, when the offeror comes from the east to the altar with offering in hand, it is suggestive of unclean and alienated humanity returning to God's holy dwelling. At the altar, Adam seeks reentry into the garden.[53] To gain that reentry, he will have to face the flaming sword of the cherubim, which seems to be represented by the altar. The cultic journey back to God, as previously argued, is a return *through* death.

יַקְרִיב אֹתוֹ לִרְצֹנוֹ לִפְנֵי יְהוָה—"He shall bring it for his acceptance before YHWH." What happens when the offeror returns to the fiery gate of Eden, represented by the altar at the entrance of the tent? In a word: judgment. As he approaches the altar, the offeror is tested by the fiery glory of God dwelling therein.

The offeror comes to the altar and presents his offering "for acceptance." Knierim believes this translation insufficient: "The Hebrew word highlights pleasure, agreement, and favor."[54] But this quibble is unnecessary since to seek acceptance from the LORD just is to seek his favor, to be received by him with pleasure. What the offeror is seeking, Wenham states, is "peace with God."[55] The peace depicted by Leviticus 1 is more than mere coexistence. The LORD signals his delight in this offering, and its offeror, when he says it has a "pleasing aroma [Heb. רֵיחַ־נִיחוֹחַ] to the LORD" (Lev 1:9, 13, 17). Whatever else the phrase "pleasing aroma" might mean in this context, it seems to denote "something pleasurable to the deity."[56] And indeed, YHWH appears to take an almost sensual delight in this offering. As the offering is burned and the

---

[52]Kleinig, *Leviticus*, 53.
[53]Morales, *Who Shall Ascend*, 75-107.
[54]Knierim, *Text and Concept*, 35n26.
[55]Wenham, *Leviticus*, 56.
[56]Milgrom, *Leviticus 1-16*, 162.

smoke ascends to heaven, the LORD "smells" the savor of this food offering and receives pleasure from it. This delight in the offering is transferred to the offeror. In receiving the offering, the LORD joyfully received the offeror. What the offeror received from the burnt offering was therefore something akin to the justification signaled by the words, "Well done, good and faithful servant. . . . Enter into the joy of your master" (Mt 25:21).

But as Scripture so often attests, the offeror's acceptance was not automatic. The offerings had to meet certain physical criteria—in this case, a male without blemish—and follow the proper procedure to be accepted. But what seems most important to Scripture is not the technical qualifications of the offering but the spiritual disposition of the offeror. This is the implication of Malachi 1:7-8: by bringing blind and lame animals to the altar, Israel despises YHWH's name and thus commits evil. The quality of the offering reflects the quality of the offeror. Even when there was nothing to complain about in the offering itself, the offeror could still disqualify himself by presumption or hypocrisy. When the Israel of Isaiah's day, "laden with iniquity" (Is 1:4), presented their offerings to YHWH, he refused them: "What to me is the multitude of your sacrifices? . . . I do not delight in the blood of bulls, or of lambs, or of goats. . . . Bring no more vain offerings" (Is 1:11, 13). The acceptable sacrifice, on the other hand, was one offered in humility, repentance, and sincere faith. The God who is not pleased with burnt offerings, Psalm 51 tells us, will "delight in right sacrifices," those offered from a broken and contrite heart (Ps 51:17-19).

The burnt offering as test. The point here is that at the altar, the offeror was being tested. The refrain "before the LORD," so often repeated in the ritual instructions, may carry this implication. When the offeror approaches the tent, he approaches the symbolic throne of YHWH, from which he executes justice. Psalm 11:4 makes this connection: "The LORD is in his holy temple; the LORD's throne is in heaven; his eyes see, his eyelids test the children of man." Recall that the "footstool" of YHWH, the ark of the covenant, housed the Ten Commandments, the word of YHWH by which he administered his covenant with Israel. To approach YHWH's throne is to be tested by that word. Is the offeror in conformity to the word of God?

The consistent link between the burnt offering and testing outside Leviticus makes the association more certain. The burnt offering appears as a test in the story of Saul's rise and fall. In 1 Samuel 13, Saul fails by offering the burnt offering before Samuel's arrival, a violation of the LORD's command. In 1 Samuel 15, he fails by reserving the best of the Amalekite sheep and oxen for burnt offerings instead of devoting them to destruction. Whether sincere or a lame excuse, the burnt offering is the occasion of his failure in this instance too. Saul, Samuel therefore decrees, cannot be allowed to serve as the LORD's king. By failing the cultic test, he disqualifies himself.

Saul's failed burnt offerings stand in sharp contrast to the offering of Abraham, by which he passed the test and on the basis of which the covenant promises were confirmed and extended. In Genesis 22, God tests Abraham by commanding him, "Take your son, your only son Isaac, whom you love, and go to the land of Moriah, and offer him there as a burnt offering" (Gen 22:2). The identification of Abraham's sacrifice as a burnt offering is repeated throughout the episode (Gen 22:3, 6-8, 13). Abraham is a model of obedience throughout this episode. Whereas he previously has had the nerve to negotiate with the LORD, he now quietly obeys in faith (Heb 11:17). His faith is vindicated. The angel intervenes before the plunge of the knife, and a substitute is provided; Abraham finds a ram and "offered it up as a burnt offering instead of his son" (Gen 22:13). The LORD then promises his blessing: "Because you have done this and have not withheld your son, your only son, I will surely bless you, and I will surely multiply your offspring as the stars of the heaven and as the sand that is on the seashore. And your offspring shall possess the gates of his enemies, and in your offspring shall all the nations of the earth be blessed, because you have obeyed my voice" (Gen 22:16-18). This episode has often been seen as foundational for the Levitical cult, as "the original sacrifice to which all sacrifice points."[57] According to 2 Chronicles 3:1, Solomon built the temple on Mount Moriah, making the Jerusalem cult a memorial of the Akedah. Abraham's burnt offering thus "probably served to prefigure the entire cultic economy."[58]

Interestingly, Genesis 22's account of that offering may also present Abraham as a "new Adam." For "whereas Adam and Eve took upon

---

[57] Michael Wyschogrod, *The Body of Faith: Judaism as Corporeal Election*, 19; quoted in Matthew Pattillo, "Creation and *Akedah*: Blessing and Sacrifice in the Hebrew Scriptures," in *Sacrifice, Scripture, and Substitution: Readings in Ancient Judaism and Christianity*, ed. Ann W. Astell and Sandor Goodhart (Notre Dame, IN: University of Notre Dame Press, 2011), 250.
[58] Morales, *Who Shall Ascend*, 73.

themselves the right to decide good and evil, right and wrong, Abraham demonstrates in his binding of Isaac a sole and radical obedience to the commandments of God. While Adam and Eve are evicted from the garden, Abraham and his descendants are invited by God to take up residence in 'the land that I will show you' (Gen. 12:3)."[59] This association would reinforce the notion of the burnt offering as a test. Whereas Adam failed at the tree, Abraham obediently bound Isaac and placed him on the wood of the altar (Gen 22:9).

As the LORD appeared in fire on Sinai to test Israel (Ex 20:20), so he tested them at the tent of meeting, which was an extension of Sinai. The connection between testing and fire suggests that the point of the test is not examination as much as it is something like refining or perfecting. God seeks by testing "to draw out his people into fuller obedience and righteousness."[60] Or perhaps, borrowing language from Hebrews, we might say that the point of the test was that the offeror might learn obedience and be perfected (Heb 5:8-9). Then he might be accepted by God, even into the "inner place behind the curtain" (Heb 6:19).

That, at least, may have been the promise of the burnt offering. In the Levitical cult, this hope was prefigured only by the acceptance of the offering on the offeror's behalf, which was signaled in the next step of the ritual.

Substitution. וְסָמַךְ יָדוֹ עַל רֹאשׁ הָעֹלָה וְנִרְצָה לוֹ—"And he shall lay his hand on the head of the burnt offering, and it shall be accepted for him." If the burnt offering was indeed a test, we are struck by the offeror's apparent inadequacy for that test as we keep reading. The offeror cannot be accepted on his own. While the gift he brings is meant to represent his piety, it must actually become his replacement if he is to be accepted. It must stand as his substitute.

The meaning of the "hand-leaning" rite has been much debated.[61] Those who hold to a penal-substitutionary reading of sacrifice have long held this rite to be an illustration of the imputation of sins. The claim is

---

[59] Pattillo, "Creation and *Akedah*," 247-48.
[60] R. W. L. Moberly, "The Earliest Commentary on the Akedah," *Vetus Testamentum* 38, no. 3 (1988): 305.
[61] English translations often render וְסָמַךְ יָדוֹ as "lay his hand" on the head of the offering. But many translators agree that this phrase actually denotes a forceful leaning or pressing down on the head. See, e.g., Jay Sklar, *Leviticus*, Tyndale Old Testament Commentaries (Downers Grove, IL: IVP Academic, 2014), 90.

straightforward: "Guilt would be transferred from the worshipper to the sacrifice by the laying on of hands."[62] Most biblical scholars, however, disagree. The problem, they complain, is that the hand-leaning rite of Leviticus 1 is being confused with the scapegoat rite of the Day of Atonement. When the priest pressed his hands on the head of the scapegoat, it undeniably symbolized a transference or imputation of sin. Pressing both hands on the head of the scapegoat, and confessing Israel's iniquities, Aaron "shall put them on the head of the goat and send it away.... The goat shall bear all their iniquities on itself to a remote area" (Lev 16:21-22). The scapegoat rite differs, however, from the rite of the burnt offering. In this rite, no confession of sin is made; only one hand is laid on the head of the animal; that hand belongs to the offeror, not the priest; and the entire offering is then accepted by the LORD on the altar, not rejected and sent away, like the scapegoat.[63] It seems most likely, then, that the hand-leaning rite does not indicate a transfer of sin or guilt.[64]

What, then, would this rite signify? Milgrom thinks it simply denotes ownership.[65] Kleinig agrees and adds that because the animal belongs to the offeror, it "could therefore be used vicariously on his behalf to secure God's approval and acceptance."[66] Knierim argues that it is an act by which the animal is dedicated to sacrificial death and that serves to symbolize, simultaneously, the legality of the slaughter and the transfer of the victim as "property" to YHWH.[67] Wenham's opinion is that the act denotes an identification of the offering with the offeror, so that "what he does to the animal, he does symbolically to himself." The death of the animal therefore "portrays the death of himself. In the animal's immolation on the altar, his own

---

[62]Michael S. Horton, *Lord and Servant: A Covenant Christology* (Louisville, KY: Westminster John Knox, 2005), 233.

[63]Gordon Wenham, "The Theology of Old Testament Sacrifice," in *Sacrifice in the Bible*, ed. Roger T. Beckwith and Martin J. Selman (repr., Eugene, OR: Wipf & Stock, 2004), 79; Kleinig, *Leviticus*, 53; de Vaux, *Studies in Old Testament Sacrifice*, 28.

[64]To be sure, there are continuities in the hand-placement rites in the rituals for the scapegoat and the burnt offering in the simple fact that in both cases, hands are placed on the head of the animal/substitute. In my judgment, the continuity lies in the shared function of mediation. Both the scapegoat and the burnt offering were rituals of mediation, but the manner of mediation differed.

[65]Milgrom, *Leviticus 1-16*, 152.

[66]Kleinig, *Leviticus*, 53.

[67]Knierim, *Text and Concept*, 39-40.

surrender to God is portrayed." What the death of the sacrifice signifies, because of the substitutionary hand-leaning rite, is the absolute surrender of the worship to God and his just sentence of death.[68]

These proposals all have their merits. Wenham's, in particular, provides the neatest fit with what I have identified as the plot of Levitical sacrifice, the offeror's return to God through death. Perhaps there is in this rite an indication that the offeror himself will somehow be put to death and raised again through his offering—perhaps.

More confidently, we can say that the hand-leaning rite simply highlights the substitutionary nature of this offering, which seems to be implied by Leviticus 1:3-4: the offeror comes seeking acceptance from God, and, after leaning his hand on the offering, the offering is "accepted for him." The hand-leaning rite thus signifies (or even effects) a relationship between offeror and offering that allows for substitution. And it is for this reason that the hand-leaning rite is so significant. For good reason, readers of Leviticus have often perceived that whatever was happening in this particular act was of fundamental importance for understanding what this offering meant. The substitution that took place in the hand-leaning is a *mechanism*, a reality that links the action of the offering with its effect.[69]

What is substitution? Here it is important to give attention to the concept of substitution. In an essay on atonement in the Pauline epistles, Simon Gathercole distinguishes between exclusive and inclusive place-taking, the latter being his name for Hartmut Gese's construal of the relationship between offeror and offering in cultic atonement.[70] On the logic of exclusive place-taking, Gathercole explains, the substitute displaces and replaces the

---

[68] Wenham, "Theology of Old Testament Sacrifice," 77, 79. Interestingly, this interpretation calls to mind Augustine's argument that the sacrificial death of Christ's body was a sacrament of the death of our inner man, a reading he thought was suggested by Rom 6 and Eph 4. Augustine, *On the Trinity*, ed. John E. Rotelle, trans. Edmund Hill (Hyde Park, NY: New City Press, 1991), 4.1.

[69] See above, where I define a mechanism of atonement as that which explains why certain actions have atoning effects.

[70] Simon Gathercole, *Defending Substitution: An Essay on Atonement in Paul* (Grand Rapids, MI: Baker, 2015), explicates this distinction. Exclusive place-taking, in this case, would mean that Christ dies for us, and therefore we do not die—at least not the (penal) death he died. Inclusive place-taking would mean that Christ dies for us, and we therefore die with him. The latter position was developed by Gese in his interpretation of Levitical sacrifice, specifically the sin offering.

subject; the substitute does or suffers what the subject does not.[71] This is the logic, notably, of a penal-substitutionary view of the Levitical offering's slaughter: the offering dies so that the offeror does not. By contrast, the logic of inclusive place-taking includes a strong element of representation. For Gese, to whom Gathercole attributes this view, while the substitute replaces the subject, it does not displace the subject. Instead, there is "a continuation of the subject in a delegated succession." "In cultic atonement," Gese states, "the sacrifice of the victim's life is a substitution that includes the one bringing the sacrifice." This construal of substitution is used by Gese to argue against a penal-substitutionary reading of sacrifice. There is no transfer of sin in the hand-leaning rite, he asserts. Instead, there is an identification or delegation that allows the offering to take the offeror's place without excluding the offeror from the action. Atonement for Gese, therefore, comes by vicarious "contact with holiness." As the offering makes contact with the holy on the altar and even gains "incorporation into the holy," so too does the offeror. And in this way, the offeror is led through death as his "damaged being is reconsecrated and healed."[72]

In short, for Gese, the offeror somehow participates in the offering while being replaced by the offering. Without intending a wholesale endorsement of Gese's position on cultic atonement, I admit that his account of substitution contains a valid insight into the workings of the Levitical cult, particularly the burnt offering. There is an element of exclusivity in the substitution of the offering for the offeror—and that, I will argue below, is due to the offeror's absolute disqualification for the divine presence. The offering therefore does what the offeror could not do for himself, that is, gain acceptance into YHWH's presence. Nevertheless, the offeror seems to participate in the offering's movement toward God. Certainly, the offeror participates in the *outcome* of this offering; just as the offering, being placed on the altar of God, is thereby received by God, so the offeror is (symbolically) received into the life and joy of the divine presence. The language of imputation seems warranted here: the reward the offering is granted by passing

---

[71]I am also indebted to Fleming Rutledge for my terminology here; see her chapter "The Substitution" in Fleming Rutledge, *The Crucifixion: Understanding the Death of Jesus Christ* (Grand Rapids, MI: Eerdmans, 2015), 462-532.

[72]Hartmut Gese, "The Atonement," in *Essays on Biblical Theology*, trans. Keith Crim (repr., Eugene, OR: Wipf & Stock, 2018), 105-7, 110.

the test is shared with the offeror, without the offeror having to pass it himself. But it seems too that the offeror somehow shares in the *conditions* of that reception, the cleanness and the sanctity of the offering as it is received by God. This would mean a kind of transfer to the offeror of the offering's "without blemish" condition, or even a reconstitution of the offeror in the image of the offering—that is, in its conformity to the Word of God—and this would take us beyond the language of imputation and might suggest the language of impartation. However we formulate it, in my judgment we are warranted in saying that there must be some union between the offeror and his offering that grounds his participation in his offering's acceptance and condition.

But here we have nearly skipped a step, the crucial step. What has happened in this offering that allows for divine acceptance? How exactly does the offering open the way for the offeror's acceptance? The answer begins to be given in the next clause: atonement.

Atonement. לְכַפֵּר עָלָיו—"to make atonement for him." The burnt offering is accepted by YHWH so that it might make atonement for the offeror. Earlier in this study, I defined *atonement* as that which qualifies one for the presence and service of the LORD. In Leviticus, it includes both compensation and cleansing—or, in Sklar's terms, both a ransom and a purgation.[73] Again, it is not always recognized that the burnt offering was offered to make atonement. But, as Wenham says, "This is the clearest clue to the purpose of the burnt offering to be found in the Levitical law."[74] Even on the Day of Atonement, in which the sin offering figures so prominently, there is no atonement without the presentation of a burnt offering (Lev 16:24). Whatever else is happening in the burnt offering, then, it is an offering by which atonement was made for the sinner who appears before YHWH.

Atonement for what? But for what does the burnt offering make atonement? Here we are confronted with a necessary question that is not answered by the text. Leviticus 1:4 clearly speaks of atonement, but it makes no mention of a particular sinful act that has made this atonement necessary. This creates a contrast with the sin and guilt offerings, which are always offered

---

[73] As sin both endangers and pollutes, so atonement comes by way of a "purifying ransom and ransoming purgation" (Sklar, *Sin, Impurity, Sacrifice*, 182).
[74] Wenham, *Leviticus*, 57.

in response to some identified transgression.⁷⁵ Similarly, the sin and guilt offerings typically include a promise of forgiveness in their pronouncements of atonement (e.g., "and the priest shall make atonement for him, and he shall be forgiven"; Lev 4:31; see Lev 4:20, 26, 35; 5:10, 13, 16; 6:7), but no mention of forgiveness is found in the description of the burnt offering. It would seem, then, that no particular transgression is in view. But if that is so, why is atonement necessary?

This question is not explicitly answered by the text. In my judgment, however, the text invites a reading that does provide an answer.⁷⁶ In the narrative context of Leviticus, the Israelite offeror who stands before YHWH has already been depicted as unclean. In Exodus 19, the people were warned not to touch the holy mountain, set aflame by the divine presence with a lethal holiness. The priests are allowed to approach, but only after consecration, "lest the Lord break out against them" (Ex 19:22). When the Lord's presence moves from Mount Sinai to the tabernacle, a similar prohibition is in order. The divine presence is dangerous for the Israelite offeror. And it is dangerous because he is unclean. To be able to approach, he must first be made clean, then consecrated.

This state of being unclean, to be sure, is a ritual state. It has to do with the offeror's access to and status in the grounds around the tent of meeting. But it is not merely a ritual state, as if it had no other meaning. The ritual state of being unclean points to the reality of an ontological and moral lack in the offeror. The offeror is not characterized by the life that God eternally possesses and shares with his people by his Word and Spirit. Instead, he is characterized by death, the wages of sin. What is being highlighted in the offeror's need for an atoning substitute is therefore a sinfulness in the offeror that goes beyond individual acts but that characterizes his very being. Accordingly, commentators often suggest that what is being atoned for in the burnt offering is the offeror's state or condition

---

⁷⁵I am assuming that the repeated phrase that the offeror "realizes his guilt" in Lev 4–6 means that the offeror(s) of the sin or guilt offering has come to a realization that he has committed some particular sinful act and does not simply suspect guilt based on his unfortunate circumstances.

⁷⁶Richard S. Briggs, *Theological Hermeneutics and the Book of Numbers as Christian Scripture* (Notre Dame, IN: University of Notre Dame Press, 2018), 18. Briggs helpfully explains how "texts invite readings." That is, they lend themselves to a range of valid interpretations, but a range that is limited by "the way the words go."

of sin. Knierim says it is "sin in a wider sense" that is being addressed.[77] Wenham labels it "sin in a more general sense."[78] Perhaps John Hartley is most perceptive: it is the offeror's "general sinful disposition" that makes atonement necessary.[79] I believe this suggestion points us in the right direction. We might go further, however. What these commentators call sinfulness in a wider or more general sense, I suggest, should be called original sin.

Original sin is the mysterious but all too obvious sin of the human race in Adam. Original sin names the truth that we are somehow made guilty by Adam's guilt and corrupted by his corruption.[80] This original corruption results in the habitual,[81] dispositional desire for sin that makes human nature "fertile and fruitful of every evil."[82] Original sin can therefore be described as a "state of deformity" caused by a fundamental "estrangement from God."[83] Bonaventure explains that human beings were "meant to accomplish [their] works with God as their source, in accordance with God's norms, and with God as their end." This describes the original justice with which humanity was created: humanity existing from God (as their source), through God (following his norms), and to God (as their end). But the corruption of original sin has turned all this on its head. There is a twofold "movement" of original sin, Bonaventure says: a habitual

---

[77] Knierim, *Text and Concept*, 82.
[78] Wenham, *Leviticus*, 57.
[79] Hartley, *Leviticus*, 19.
[80] Article 9 of the Thirty-Nine Articles of Religion (1571) is helpful: "Original sin standeth not in the following of *Adam*, (as the *Pelagians* do vainly talk;) but it is the fault and corruption of the Nature of every man, that is naturally ingendered of the offspring of *Adam*; whereby man is very far gone from original righteousness, and is of his own nature inclined to evil, so that the flesh lusteth always contrary to the Spirit; and therefore in every person born into this world, it deserveth God's wrath and damnation." This article goes on to explain that original sin consists of an "infection of nature . . . [a] concupiscence and lust [that] hath of itself the nature of sin."
[81] Scheeben speaks of original sin as a fault (in Adam) that has resulted in the deformity of "habitual sin." This sin is habitual in that it has become an "abiding tendency" of the soul. Sharing in Adam's faulty and the damage it did to the human constitution, humanity now lives in "a state of habitual aversion from God." Matthias Joseph Scheeben, *The Mysteries of Christianity*, trans. Cyril Vollert, SJ (New York: Herder & Herder, 1946), 274, 285.
[82] Herman Bavinck, *Reformed Dogmatics*, vol. 3, *Sin and Salvation in Christ*, ed. John Bolt, trans. John Vriend (Grand Rapids, MI: Baker Academic, 2006), 98. Aquinas speaks of original sin in terms of habitual, dispositional desire. Original sin is a habit, as in a disposition or inclination, that consists materially of concupiscence, which he describes as the turning of the will away from God and "inordinately to mutable good" (Aquinas, *Summa Theologica* 2.82.1, 3).
[83] Scheeben, *Mysteries of Christianity*, 285, 293.

turning away from God, matched by a habitual turning toward created goods.[84] By the corruption of original sin, the source of our works is no longer God but the nothingness and absurdity of sin; the norm for our works is no longer the law of God but the "law of the flesh"; and the end or goal of our works is no longer the beatifying vision of God but the created order viewed through lustful gaze of the flesh, which ultimately turns up empty.

In his *Compendium of Theology*, Thomas Aquinas speaks of corruption as a separation of a being from its form.[85] The corruption of original sin would therefore be a separation in some way of the human being from its formal or exemplar cause, which is the image of God. In this way, original sin is both moral and legal, since, as sin, it is also defined as a violation of divine law. But to a certain extent it is also ontological. Though it does not change *what* we are, original sin corrupts *how* we are what we are. It denotes a sinful mode of human existence alienated from its true form and directed to a false end. It is a humanity that is therefore corrupted and perverse and that needs to be healed.[86] Humanity in original sin needs to be both pardoned and restored, which would entail being returned to its true form and redirected to its proper end.

The burnt offering and atonement outside Leviticus. That the burnt offering was meant to address the offeror's original sin is at least a possibility opened to us by the text. And that possibility seems to be strengthened by the way the burnt offering makes atonement in texts outside Leviticus.[87] In Job 1, we read of righteous Job's weekly burnt offerings on behalf of his children, whom he feared may have sinned at their feasts (Job 1:5). Job does not know that his children have sinned. Though he fears his children may have "cursed God in their hearts," he is not presenting his offering for any specific transgression. Instead, Job is presenting burnt offerings out of a knowledge of his children's sinful condition or corruption, from which whatever actual transgressions they might commit would issue.

---

[84]Bonaventure, *Breviloquium* 3.1.2; 3.6.3.
[85]Aquinas, *Compendium of Theology* 74.
[86]See how Cornelius Plantinga Jr., *Not the Way It's Supposed to Be: A Breviary of Sin* (Grand Rapids, MI: Eerdmans, 1995), relates the perversity of an action with a divorce from its proper end (40).
[87]Wenham points to Gen 8:21; Num 15:24; 2 Sam 24:25; Job 1:5; 42:8; 2 Chron 29:7-8 as texts outside Leviticus that link the burnt offering with atonement (*Leviticus*, 57-58).

There may also be a connection between the burnt offering and original sin in the Genesis account of the flood. In Genesis 6, a locus classicus for the doctrine of original sin, we read of God's sorrow over the corrupted state of humanity. The violence and corruption of humanity are met by the flood, God's great act of judgment. Then, after the waters recede, Noah offers a burnt offering that to some degree "reverses" God's attitude toward humanity.[88] When God "smelled the pleasing aroma," we are told, he "said in his heart, 'I will never again curse the ground because of man, because the intention of man's heart I evil from his youth'" (Gen 8:20-22). This text does not explicitly mention atonement, and some argue it is improper to read this as an atoning sacrifice. But the concept of atonement seems present in the text. Humanity, we read here, is deeply corrupted by sin, even the humanity represented by righteous Noah after the flood—we learn soon enough that the intention of their heart is still evil. Previously, this kind of corruption had led God to curse the ground; as God says to Adam in Genesis 3:17, "Cursed is the ground because of you." The idea of the ground being cursed because of humanity's guilt and corruption is reminiscent of what happened at the tabernacle—the altar was defiled by Israel's sin and required regular cleansing through rites of atonement. On the basis of that atonement, God would continue to dwell in the tabernacle, and Israel could continue to approach him there. Similarly, in Genesis 8, the LORD seems to accept the earth and its creatures as clean through Noah's offering. The effect of Noah's burnt offering is the same as that mentioned in Leviticus: the LORD receives it as a pleasing aroma (Gen 8:21; Lev 1:9). Consequently, he will not again curse the ground, nor will he again put to death every living creature. By Noah's burnt offering, the corrupted state or way of humanity, and the guilt that accompanies it, is somehow overcome (or at least offset).[89] God will allow human beings to continue on the land, despite their corruption, because of his pleasure in this burnt offering.

Atonement through the substitution of the Son of God. I believe we are warranted in reading the burnt offering as a means of addressing the original

---

[88] Wenham, *Leviticus*, 57.
[89] To be clear, I believe the guilt and corruption of original sin are simultaneous and inseparable. There is in original sin both imputation and impartation. As "in Adam," every individual is guilty due to the imputation of Adam's guilt, and every individual is corrupted due to the impartation of the corruption that took hold of Adam after his sin.

sin of the offeror. In fact, I believe the basic mechanism for addressing original sin through this offering has already been identified: substitution. The original sin of the offeror constitutes an absolute disqualification for the presence and service of YHWH. For the offeror stands before God as a falsified son of God, one who no longer lives from God, through God, and to God, as he was meant to, but whose mode of existence has been perverted by his election (in Adam) of a false end. He can stand before God, therefore, only through a substitute. The substitute must be what the offeror is meant to be. In the words of Leviticus 1:3, he must be תָּמִים—in conformity with the Word of God. And the offeror must somehow come to share in the cleanness of the substitute. This is the first component of the mechanism of atonement in the burnt offering. Atonement begins with substitution.

To identify substitution as a mechanism of atonement is to identify it as a partial explanation for why the ritual acts of the burnt offering have an atoning effect for the offeror.[90] At the moment of this substitution, that ritual is far from over. But by calling attention to this mechanism of relationship, the text alerts us to what will be happening in the remainder of the ritual. The offering will stand in for the offeror, doing (and suffering) what the offeror should do (and suffer) but cannot. Not all readers will see things the same. Some will say that the idea of substitution is absent from the text, that all that is happening here is the presentation of a gift that pleases the LORD. But that interpretation downplays the substitutionary implications of Leviticus 1:4, which states that the offering is accepted for the offeror who seeks acceptance; it gives too little weight to the way in which the burnt offering represents the movement of the entire Levitical cult, which is a movement of the offeror himself (and not just his gift) into the presence of God; and it fails to recognize that the character of the offering reflects the ideal character of the offeror.

The burnt offering, we will see shortly, is what the offeror should be—conformed to the Word of God and fully devoted to God. As something given to Israel by God and completely returned to God, the blameless offering

---

[90] As I argue in the introduction, I believe there can be more than one mechanism of atonement. Sacrificial atonement seems to require what we could call mechanisms of relationship (such as substitution) and of achievement (an example would be satisfaction). In other words, the offering accomplished something to make atonement, and that accomplishment must somehow be shared with the offeror. Substitution is a necessary but not sufficient condition for atonement.

represents true creaturehood: an entity whose origin and end lie in God. In that way, the offering itself reflects the character of the incarnate Son of God, whom we have identified as the hero of the Levitical cult, as he enacts his eternal relationship to the Father—his being *from* and *to* the Father—in human flesh. In the burnt offering, we see, even if only dimly, a picture of the substitution of the Son of God. This may be why the victim is identified in Leviticus 1:5 as בֶּן הַבָּקָר—literally, "a son of the herd."[91]

Perhaps that exegesis appears strained at this point. But I believe it receives further justification from the witness of the rest of this ritual.

THE ACT OF OBEDIENCE UNTO DEATH

In the exegesis above, I said both that the burnt offering was a gift, devoted fully to God, and that it represented a test. The offeror stands with gift in hand before the throne of YHWH, and as he does so he is subject to the divine scrutiny. Will this offeror prove true? The quick answer, we have seen, is no; there must be a substitute. But what, then, of this substitute? What must it be and do? As we keep reading, we see how the substitute, which is clean by conformity to the Word of God, passes the test in the offeror's place and pleases God on his behalf.

How and why does this offering please God? The following verses seem to tell us, as they lay out a sequence that culminates in the promise of God's delight in the offeror and his gift. A key moment, no doubt, is when the priests throw the blood against the altar (Lev 1:5). God declares in Leviticus 17:11, "The life of the flesh is in the blood, and I have given it for you on the altar to make atonement for your souls, for it is the blood that makes atonement by the life." Surely, then, the application of blood to the altar is central to the atoning efficacy of the burnt offering.

But what does the blood actually do, and how? These are essential questions, and I will try to answer them by paying close attention to the entire movement of the burnt offering.

The meaning of the slaughter. וְשָׁחַט אֶת־בֶּן הַבָּקָר לִפְנֵי יְהוָה—"Then he shall slaughter the bull before the LORD." The next stage in the burnt offering,

---

[91]Leithart calls attention to this terminology and suggests the burnt offering is thereby described as a uniquely filial offering. Peter J. Leithart, *Delivered from the Elements of the World: Atonement, Justification, Mission* (Downers Grove, IL: IVP Academic, 2016), 108n39.

what Kleinig calls the blood rite, begins with the slaughter of the offering, performed by the offeror.[92] Perhaps the most striking thing about the prescriptions for the offering's slaughter is the brevity with which it is treated. The instructions are plainly stated, and the text quickly moves on. As Eberhardt notes, "No interpretive comment appears in connection with the act of slaughter," either in Leviticus 1 or later in the book.[93]

Yet the slaughter of the offering has often been the center of attention in Christian readings of Leviticus. No doubt this is due to the Christian practice of reading these offerings typologically. If the death of Jesus, the fulfillment of all sacrifice, is as important as the Gospels suggest it is, then surely the death of the Levitical offerings must be important too. The slaughter of the offering has therefore been dwelled on at length in Christian thinking about atonement. And, as noted earlier, there has been a great deal of debate about what that death means. Leon Morris argues that the death of the victim, as a penal substitution, is in fact the mechanism of atonement: "It is the termination of life, the infliction of death that atones."[94] Wenham is open to understanding the death differently—it may be a symbol of the offeror's own death, not a substituted penalty—but still attaches great importance to it.[95] Frank Gorman does not explain the rite's meaning but assures us that slaughter is "at the heart of the ritual interaction of Yahweh and Israel."[96] Others, however, attach little importance to the slaughter, other than being a means to the blood and fat that were to be placed on the altar.[97]

---

[92] Kleinig, *Leviticus*, 63. That the slaughter is performed by the offeror is my reading of the instructions of Lev 1. But this is admittedly uncertain. According to Ezek 44:11, the Levites slaughtered the burnt offering "for the people." The LXX takes the same view, as it makes the verb plural, implying the priests would perform the slaughter (Hartley, *Leviticus*, 13). The reason for this apparent uncertainty begins with the Hebrew text. Sklar suggests the Hebrew of Lev 1:5 might be translated passively: "the bull shall be slaughtered," instead of "he [the offeror] shall slaughter." Milgrom too translates the verb as a passive but also argues that anyone was able to perform the slaughter, relying partly on rabbinic evidence (*Leviticus 1–16*, 154). In my judgment, it seems most natural to take the verb as active with the offeror as its subject, since "the sons of Aaron" are introduced as a new subject following this statement. The translation, however, does not bear significant theological weight.
[93] Eberhardt, *Sacrifice of Jesus*, 65.
[94] Leon Morris, *The Apostolic Preaching of the Cross*, 3rd ed. (repr., Grand Rapids, MI: Eerdmans, 1976), 119.
[95] Wenham, *Leviticus*, 62.
[96] Gorman, *Divine Presence and Community*, 25.
[97] De Vaux gives this impression; see *Studies in Old Testament Sacrifice*, 42, for example.

What, then, can we say about the meaning of the slaughter in the burnt offering ritual? We can start by noting how the burnt offering's slaughter differs from that of the sin and guilt offerings. The carcass of the burnt offering is flayed, arranged, further cleaned, and placed entirely on the altar of the LORD (Lev 1:6-9; 6:8-13).[98] It is not so with the sin and guilt offerings. In cases of sin among the priesthood or the entire congregation of Israel, while some of the fat of the offering is burned on the altar, the rest of the carcass of the sin offering is discarded. It is removed from the camp—a kind of exile—and completely burned at "the ash heap . . . on a fire of wood" (Lev 4:11-12; cf. Lev 4:20-21). On other occasions, the flesh of the sin offering is eaten by the priests and the priests alone. Whatever the reasons for these differences, the differences in how the body of the slaughtered victim is used seem to point to a difference in the intention of the slaughter and therefore in the meaning of the slaughter.

The slaughter does not tell the whole story of sacrifice and atonement.[99] For the burnt offering, in addition to the slaughter, there must be an approach to the altar, from which the offering is sent up in smoke, as we will see. However, it would be wrong for that reason to overlook just how essential the slaughter of the victim is to the action of the burnt offering. The slaughter occurs at a critical moment in the movement of the rite: after the substitution of offering for offeror, before the application of blood and the burning. The slaughter thus provides a transition between these moments. It is, on the one hand, the most serious of claims as to the offering's fitness to be offered to YHWH; only because it is blameless may it be presented to the LORD through slaughter. And only because it has been slaughtered may it actually be "transferred" to YHWH as his property and placed on his altar; only through death may the gift of the burnt offering be given.[100] In fact, we can say that the death of the victim allows for an exchange of gifts between YHWH and Israel: by death, YHWH gives Israel the blood of atonement on the altar (Lev 17:11); by death, Israel presents YHWH with a food offering in

---

[98] De Vaux, citing Lev 7:8, notes that the skin of the burnt offering was given to the officiating priest (*Studies in Old Testament Sacrifice*, 29).

[99] Earlier I labeled the death of the victim the crisis of Levitical sacrifice—the point at which the fate of the offeror is sealed. But there is nevertheless much that has to happen *after* the slaughter before the offering is complete.

[100] Knierim, *Text and Concept*, 40.

which he delights. The gifts that proclaim and enact the covenant bond between God and his people are given through death—surely that is a point for reflection.

Perhaps this adds something to our understanding of the necessity of the offering's death. Given the way sin locks humanity out of the presence of God, the communion that God desires to have with humanity, manifested in the exchange of gift and gratitude, can take place only through death. And perhaps the text highlights this dynamic by stating that the slaughter of the offering occurs "before the LORD." That phrase separates this ritual act from profane slaughter (as does the Hebrew verb that is used, שָׁחַט); the killing of this animal is a solemn act, for the victim is slaughtered on the tabernacle grounds and devoted to the LORD.

De Vaux's description of the burnt offering is therefore apt: in the burnt offering, there is a "total and unreserved making over of a gift" that is enacted in the slaughter.[101] The slaughter therefore represents the offering's devotion to the LORD and honors the deity of the LORD; to this God belong worship and honor and offerings. Here we are reminded of sacrifice's essentially religious character: though it may be more than an act of worship, it is never less.

Slaughter and consecration. And here too we are reminded that a basic meaning of sacrifice is devoting something to God so that it is made holy. The offering, as we have seen, is already clean—of a class of animals that may be offered to YHWH. Further, it is without blemish, a blameless representative of that class. But by its slaughter, the offering becomes not only clean but consecrated. In the slaughter, the offeror has renounced his rights to the possession and use of this offering; the slaughter is "the actualization, the execution, of the offeror's surrender of this animal to death."[102] The slaughter, along with the flaying, allows the offering to be placed on the altar, making the slaughter a bridge between the presentation of Leviticus 1:3-4 and the burning in Leviticus 1:6-9. Perhaps, then, we can see the slaughter as the beginning of the offering's consecration.[103] As said above, the death opens

---

[101]De Vaux, *Studies in Old Testament Sacrifice*, 37.
[102]Knierim, *Text and Concept*, 47.
[103]As evidence that it is not yet holy, we have Milgrom's observation that the offeror, not the priest, performs the slaughter (*Leviticus 1–16*, 154).

the way for the offering to be received by YHWH. By its death, the offering can be returned to God—and the offeror can follow.

The death of the offeror? So what did this slaughter mean for the offeror? It may be more than an act of piety. It seems likely that the offeror would be aware that he is offering a substitute for himself. When he slaughters this substitute, does it not therefore symbolize his own slaughter? Wenham thinks it does: "The death of the animal portrays the death of [the offeror]. In the animal's immolation on the altar his own surrender to God is portrayed." He adds later that this surrender means "dying for his sin and giving himself entirely to God."[104] Morales too speaks of self-sacrifice as "implicit in the symbolism of the cult." He adds specifically of the burnt offering that the burning of the entire animal conveys a "sense of self-denial and utter consecration . . . absolute surrender and total dedication."[105] Sklar is similar but notes in the slaughter a penal element. Noting the high cost of this offering, he states, "By giving the whole animal to the Lord, offerors acknowledged that their sinfulness before a holy God was so great that only a full and costly ransom payment would suffice."[106] Klawans makes an observation that raises the possibility of a penal element even higher. There is conceptual and terminological overlap in the biblical instructions for sacrifice and capital punishment: both are forms of ritualized killing, both address moral defilement and involve the laying on of hands.[107] It seems likely, then, that in the death of the offering there would be a note of surrender, a confession that the offeror should die for his sins, even a ritual representation of that death.

I suggest that the offeror would be symbolically surrendering his own life—submitting to the verdict of death he justly deserves—when he slaughters his offering. There is in this submission both penitence and penalty. The offering's death is both a death *to* sin—a death that means the consecration of a life to God and in which the offeror shares by repentance. But it is also a death *for* sin—a death by which the integrity of the divine law is maintained. This conclusion fits well with what I have called the plot of

---

[104]Wenham, "Theology of Old Testament Sacrifice," 77-78.
[105]Morales, "Atonement in Ancient Israel," 29, 34.
[106]Sklar, *Leviticus*, 94.
[107]Klawans, *Purity, Sacrifice, and the Temple*, 72n119.

Levitical sacrifice, a return to God through death. It also fits well with what we will see in the rest of the burnt-offering ritual, which seems to bring the offeror into the presence of God as the offering, transformed by divine fire, rises to heaven and satisfies God. It fits, too, with the idea that the offeror's original sin is what is being addressed by this offering. What can be done for one under the guilt and corruption of original sin? The consistent biblical witness is that the only solution is death and resurrection. Given the guilt of original sin and the divine promise that "the wages of sin is death" (Rom 6:23; cf. Gen 2:17), a death for sin is necessary. In the words of Athanasius, there is a "law of death" hanging over humanity in its corrupted state that must be fulfilled by a death.[108]

But, as Athanasius would also say, if God's intentions for humanity are to be fulfilled, there must be not only death but new life. The death must be not only for sin but also to sin, since the one corrupted by sin must die to sin in order to be made new. The slaughter of the offering, on this reading, would represent in New Testament terms the death of the "old self," the "body of sin" that is enslaved to sin (Rom 6:6), a death that is at the same time a condemnation of sin in the flesh (Rom 8:3). Whoever would see the kingdom of God must be born again (Jn 3:3). The burnt offering seems to be testifying to this reality in the slaughter of the substitute.

Blood on the altar. וְהִקְרִיבוּ בְּנֵי אַהֲרֹן הַכֹּהֲנִים אֶת־הַדָּם וְזָרְקוּ אֶת־הַדָּם עַל־הַמִּזְבֵּחַ סָבִיב אֲשֶׁר־פֶּתַח אֹהֶל מוֹעֵד—"The priests shall bring [offer] the blood and throw the blood against the sides of the altar." As critical as the death is to the rite, no less critical is what comes next: the priests approach the altar and apply blood on the worshiper's behalf. Here there is a noticeable shift in agency; the priests collect, bring near, and throw the blood against the altar, not the offeror. This may reinforce the offeror's need of atonement. Because he is not clean, he may not have contact with the altar, where YHWH dwells in the fire.[109]

---

[108]Athanasius, *On the Incarnation* 8. This translation, "law of death," is Archibald Robertson's in *A Select Library of Nicene and Post-Nicene Fathers of the Christian Church*, Second Series, ed. Philip Schaff and Henry Wace, vol. 4, *St. Athanasius: Select Works and Letters*, ed. Archibald Robertson (Buffalo, NY: Christian Literature, 1892). Behr's translation is "law concerning corruption" Popular Patristics Series 4a (Yonkers, NY: St. Vladimir's Seminary Press, 2011).

[109]Geerhardus Vos, *Biblical Theology: Old and New Testaments* (Grand Rapids, MI: Eerdmans, 1948), 181. Ross refers to the fire on the altar as "the fire of the LORD." Allen P. Ross, *Holiness to the Lord: A Guide to the Exposition of the Book of Leviticus* (Grand Rapids, MI: Baker

It would be a mistake, however, to see the priests as the only or primary agent here. As we read of blood on the altar, we are reminded of the divine agency by which blood becomes a means of atonement: "For the life of the flesh is in the blood, and I have given it for you on the altar to make atonement for your souls" (Lev 17:11). The blood of atonement appears on the altar by an act of divine mercy. It is applied there by priests who are ordained and empowered by God to minister at the altar, and it is made effective by the divine Word that "instituted and empowered the rituals in the Leviticus so that they accomplished something."[110] The further we go in this ritual, the more conspicuous is the LORD's agency.

The application of blood in the ritual for the burnt offering is different from that of the ritual for the sin offering. When the blood of the sin offering is applied to this altar, some of it is applied by the priest to the horns of the altar, while the rest of it is poured out (Heb. שָׁפַךְ) at the base of the altar (e.g., Lev 4:25).[111] With the blood of the burnt offering, by contrast, the priest is instructed to bring near or "offer" the blood (Heb. קָרַב) and then throw or splash (Heb. זָרַק) it on the sides of the altar.[112] The difference in ritual suggests a difference in meaning. The application of blood in the ritual for the sin offering seems to intend a cleaning of the altar. But in the ritual for the burnt offering, the application of blood to the altar seems to be the means of the offering of the blood. To place the blood on the altar is to offer it to YHWH, an act that reinforces the notion that the *entire* offering is presented to YHWH.

If the blood is the life of the offering (Lev 17:11), then the application of blood in this ritual represents the total devotion of the offering to the LORD. We might even call it a devotion unto death. The blood on the altar

---

Academic, 2002), 92. Milgrom puts it differently, describing the altar as a "the earthly terminus of a divine funnel for man's communion with God" (*Leviticus 1–16*, 251). His idea is that the prayers and offerings of Israel ascend into heaven along the path created by the smoke that ascends from the altar to heaven. Thus, in a tradition of later Judaism, he says, "The air space above the altar is an extension of its sanctity."

[110]Kleinig, *Leviticus*, 23. I would remind the reader that though the accomplishment of the Levitical cult was limited, it was real, as I argue in the introduction.

[111]The blood of the sin offering is also applied to the veil of the sanctuary and to the altar of incense. Afterward, it is poured out at the base of the altar of burnt offering. See, e.g., Lev 4:5-7.

[112]Wenham notes that while it is not clear what was entailed in offering the blood, the verb does denote "a particular action in the sacrifice. Perhaps the priest lifted it up [after collecting it in a bowl] and said a prayer" (*Leviticus*, 54).

symbolizes that a life has been offered to the LORD *through* death. Though the offering was already in conformity with the Word of God, the law of the particular kind of creatureliness stipulated for its species, that conformity is now perfectly enacted when the creature's blood returns to God at the altar in an act of praise and obedience. The law of all creaturehood instructs us that "from him and through him and to him are all things" (Rom 11:36). In the burnt offering's devotion through death, that law is perfectly honored.[113]

Substitutionary obedience, doxology, and contrition. Again, the substitutionary relationship between offering and offeror is crucial here. In this ritual, the Israelite offeror was acknowledging what he must—yet cannot—be to return to God and therefore acknowledging his need for death and resurrection. At the same time, however, he was through his substitute offering a life in conformity to the Word of God and offered to God as a gift of praise. The offering of the burnt offering therefore appears to be an act of what Khaled Anatolios calls "doxological contrition," in which there are notes of both praise and repentance.[114] In other words, the burnt offering seems to represent a deep *agreement* with God about the righteousness of God, the goodness of his law, and the just deserts of those who fail to conform to that law. Surely this speaks to what the offeror should be as image of God—or, as argued previously, a son of God.

In the ritual for the burnt offering, the offeror was acknowledging what he ought to be. Yet this acknowledgment, good and right as it is, only serves to highlight the problem addressed by the burnt offering: that no one is what he ought to be. The offeror must bring a substitute, and he can approach God in praise and repentance only through that substitute.[115] Even after this point of the ritual, the offeror's need for a substitute does not cease. Though the blood on the altar reestablishes contact with God, the divine acceptance promised earlier in the ritual is not yet realized. Though

---

[113]Eberhardt reads things this way, suggesting that the application of blood on the altar was itself a way of returning the "life" of the creature to God, the giver of life (*Sacrifice of Jesus*, 65).

[114]Khaled Anatolios, *Deification Through the Cross: An Eastern Christian Theology of Salvation* (Grand Rapids, MI: Eerdmans, 2020), 32-39.

[115]And though the priests play an intercessory role in Leviticus, the substitute is notably not human. It is tempting here to see a testimony of the necessity of the incarnation—there is no true human capable of appearing before God. An (re-)incarnation of the image of God is required.

the offeror has gone with his substitute into death, he is yet to rise to the new life that his atonement requires.

The Act of Ascension

After the substitution, testing, and slaughter of the offering comes the ascension. This is truly the end of the ritual, both its terminus and its telos. As the offering is placed on the altar, the divine fire will transform it, and it will ascend toward heaven. As it does so, the offering will be received by God, and the offeror will find the acceptance he seeks. The ascension of the burnt offering is therefore not only a constituent element of the ritual but an element of unique importance. As the offeror reaches his goal, the meaning of the ritual and all its particular activities is disclosed (at least to some extent).[116] Roy Gane speaks of Levitical ritual as a "dynamic transformation process."[117] The end of the burnt offering shows that to be an apt description of this ritual.

Ascending to the altar. After the blood is applied to the altar, the remainder of the ritual action (Lev 1:6-9) may seem to be merely procedural. In Leviticus 1:6-8, the offeror skins and butchers his offering before washing its entrails and legs with water. When a bird is offered, the procedure necessarily differs; the bird is torn open instead of butchered, and instead of washing, the crop and its contents are removed and thrown to the east side of the altar.[118] These instructions may reveal merely pragmatic concerns. The animal is butchered (or torn open) simply to make an orderly arrangement on the altar, and it is washed so that nothing foul will have immediate contact with the altar.[119]

---

[116] Roy Gane, *Cult and Character: Purification Offerings, Day of Atonement, and Theodicy* (Winona Lake, IN: Eisenbrauns, 2005), 12. Gane interprets Levitical rituals (especially that of the Day of Atonement) as a "system." In a system, he stresses, the meaning of any action is not inherent in that action itself but is only discernible in light of the goal of the system of which that action is a part. The meaning of any action within the ritual of the burnt offering, say the hand-leaning or slaughter or burning, is only discernible in light of the goal of that offering. Gane's argument may just be an elaborate way of saying an action is defined by its intention, but is nevertheless helpful when reading Lev 1.

[117] Gane, *Cult and Character*, 12.

[118] The translation "crop" is uncertain. It might actually refer to the anus and tailfeather of the bird, along with its intestine. Either way, it is a kind of excrement, "something filthy," that is removed from the offering (Kleinig, *Leviticus*, 58).

It is tempting to see the east as symbolic of exile. As Adam and Eve were cast eastward out of the garden, as Judah was cast eastward into Babylonian exile, so the excrement was cast eastward at the altar.

[119] Sklar, *Leviticus*, 92.

But there may be more here as well.[120] The care taken at this point in the ritual—the careful removal of the skin, the more or less precise dismemberment, the washing—may signal that the high point of this ritual is imminent: the priest is preparing to ascend the altar.[121] There may also be here another reminder of divine judgment. Klawans sees Levitical sacrifice in general as a matter of imitating God, and in this case, there would be an imitation of God's all-discerning eye. As God examines the heart and kidneys (see Ps 7:9; Jer 11:20), so the offeror is instructed to dissect the animal with discernment.[122] Maybe it is proper here to remember Hebrews 4:12: "For the word of God is living and active, sharper than any two-edged sword, piercing to the division of soul and of spirit, of joints and marrow, and discerning the thoughts and intentions of the heart." Maybe we can say that through and even after its death, the offering was being tested.

Regardless of whether we should follow this line of thought, an emphasis of this ritual is that the entire offering, save the skin and what was washed away or discarded, was placed on the altar, from which it ascended to heaven. It should be noted, however, that the placement on the altar was in itself an ascent, in the sense that it initiated contact with God. For the altar is God's holy table, the place where the divine fire consumes the offerings. The ascent on the altar begins the greater ascent of the offering to the heavens as it is turned into smoke. The offering, after its death, is now rising in a return to God, a return that is empowered by God.

Turning into smoke. וְהִקְטִיר הַכֹּהֵן אֶת־הַכֹּל הַמִּזְבֵּחָה—"And the priest shall burn all of it on the altar." Though Christian theology has often seen the slaughter as *the* essential act of sacrifice, the burning was no less significant for the rituals described in Leviticus.[123] If the slaughter meant the death of

---

[120]Perhaps a lot more. Radner compares the butchering of the burnt offering to the dismembering of the Levite's concubine in Judg 19–20. See Ephraim Radner, *Leviticus*, Brazos Theological Commentary on the Bible (Grand Rapids, MI: Brazos, 2008), 44. The parallel would be in the violence done to flesh, "an act that alerts the world to the reality of sin and danger." In other words, the dismemberment may be a reminder of the curse of sin and the necessity of death.

[121]Milgrom notes that this care was unusual. Elsewhere in the ancient Near East, flaying, quartering, and washing were not part of rituals for burnt offerings; the victim was simply placed on the altar (*Leviticus 1–16*, 157).

[122]Klawans, *Purity, Sacrifice, and the Temple*, 64.

[123]Kleinig claims that the burning was the "main part of the whole ritual procedure" (*Leviticus*, 60). Eberhardt goes so far as to call burning on the altar "the constitutive element of sacrifice" in the Levitical system (*Sacrifice of Jesus*, 98).

the offeror, the burning means new life for the offeror, for in this culminating rite of the burnt offering we see the transformation and ascension of the offeror through his offering.

Kleinig notes that the *hiphil* verb used here (הִקְטִיר) is a technical term used specifically for cultic burning. The translation "burn," he argues, is in fact misleading, since the purpose of this burning is evidently not to destroy the offering but to turn it into smoke.[124] Similarly, Eberhardt speaks of the "metamorphosis" of the offering in the fire. The altar fire "changes the sacrificial material and transforms it into a new, ethereal essence," which belongs no longer to the earthly realm but to "the heavenly or transcendent sphere."[125] So also F. C. N. Hicks, whom Milgrom quotes approvingly: "The offering is not destroyed but transformed, sublimated, etherealized, so that it can ascend in smoke to the heaven above, the dwelling place of God."[126] In short, the עֹלָה was turned to smoke so that it might עָלָה ("ascend") to God.

But if this offering is ascending to God, that movement is empowered by contact with God. The altar was holy, itself a dwelling of God, as the theophanic flame of the exodus indwelled the altar. "The coming upon the altar," Vos states, "is a most significant thing: it means the direct consumption of the sacrifice by Jehovah, for Jehovah dwells in the altar."[127] Or, as Kleinig puts it, the altar was "the hearth of God's house ... the place of God's theophany ... the place of atonement ... and the reception of blessing from God."[128] The flame of the altar was a divine consecrating fire, a fire of transformation. And in that fire, the LORD was taking possession of the offering that he might make it fully his own. "The transformational burning was for the sake of transferring the animal, as a vicarious substitute, from the ordinary earthly plane to the divine heavenly realm, to the ownership of God."[129]

Following this line of thinking, Morales identifies a twofold significance for the offeror in the burning of the עֹלָה. First, as the entire offering was consumed by the divine flame and thereby raised to heaven, so this offering

---

[124] Kleinig, *Leviticus*, 56.
[125] Eberhardt, *Sacrifice of Jesus*, 67.
[126] F. C. N. Hicks, *The Fullness of Sacrifice*, 3rd ed. (London: SPCK, 1953), 13; quoted in Milgrom, *Leviticus 1–16*, 161. The same quotation is found in Morales, "Atonement in Ancient Israel," 35.
[127] Vos, *Biblical Theology*, 181.
[128] Kleinig, *Leviticus*, 55.
[129] Morales, "Atonement in Ancient Israel," 35.

represented the devotion of the entire person to God. The burning conveys "the sense of self-denial and utter consecration—a life yielded entirely unto YHWH, in full submission to his will and complete obedience to his law." Morales even goes so far as to see in this sacrifice the symbol of "a positive fulfillment of the Torah" and its greatest commandment, that is, to "love YHWH with all your heart, with all your soul, and with all your strength." On the interpretation of covenant pursued in this study, this fulfillment would mean the demonstration of faithful sonship. Morales would seem to agree. Reflecting on the daily burnt offerings that were offered every morning and evening, he sees a pattern that is fulfilled in Christ's incarnate sonship: "As obedient Son his daily life, morning and evening, was conformed to the ascension offering."[130] The burning and ascension of the entirety of this offering seem to speak the reality of a life perfectly oriented to God and perpetually devoted to God. That is the life of incarnate sonship, whose ways perfectly image and honor the will of the Father.

Second, Morales adds, the burning represented the offeror's vicarious ascension to heaven "via the sacrificial fire of the ascension offering." Through the fire, the offering is given over to God. But given the relationship between offering and offeror at work through this ritual, this must mean that the offeror is given with it. As the offering is now possessed by God, so too is the offeror. In other words, the offeror himself is consecrated through the burning of his offering, and in that consecration he is received by the LORD. "Through the הִקְטִיר rite," Morales states, "the Israelite ascends, as it were, ushered into YHWH's presence with the clouds. The altar 'of the ascension offering' thus existed for Israel's cultic ascent to God." Morales therefore speaks of "the ascension theology at the heart of Israel's understanding of atonement."[131] The burning of the offering represented the goal of the Levitical cult: the offeror's return to God. In broad terms, this is atonement. That it is atonement is confirmed in the last lines of instruction for the burnt offering, in which we see the "results" of the burnt offering as it is received by the LORD.

---

[130] Morales, "Atonement in Ancient Israel," 35, 37.
[131] Morales, "Atonement in Ancient Israel," 36. Morales's mention of "the clouds" is a reference to the "cloud" created by the burning of incense in the holy of holies, a movement he believes is paralleled by the burnt offering's smoke literally rising toward the clouds.

New creation. The burnt offering thus appears to signify the new creation of the offeror. Having come through death, the offering rises to new life and is then received by God, who is satisfied by the death and resurrection. Again, the offering is not destroyed but *transformed* by the fire. And as it is, it speaks the promise of the offeror's own transformation. The burnt offering is an offering of new creation.

We can look to Noah's burnt offering to highlight the theme of renewal in the burnt offering. Similar to the burnt offering of Leviticus 1, Noah presents his burnt offering after coming through divine judgment and death. And as he presents his offering, new creation is in the air. After returning to a primordial state of decreation in the flood, the earth has been renewed as the waters return to their place. The newness of the earth's situation after the flood seems to be affirmed by God as he blesses Noah with the same words with which he blessed Adam: "Be fruitful and multiply and fill the earth" (Gen 9:1). It is therefore fitting that Noah presents his offering at the beginning of a new year. "In the six hundred and first year [of Noah], in the first month, the first day of the month," the waters have dried, Noah leaves the ark, and he then presents his offering (Gen 8:13). Moreover, Noah presents his offering on ground renewed by the flood—the curse on the ground has been lifted, or at least alleviated, as Lamech prophesied (Gen 5:29). New creation is at the heart of Noah's offering and perhaps even explains why God is so pleased with Noah's offering. God's reception of the burnt offering seems to signal that his wrath has abated, and he is satisfied with the new creation.

Whether or not this reading of Noah's offering persuades, the transformation and elevation of creaturely life certainly seems to be at the heart of this offering. And that becomes even more evident in God's reception of the offering.

Reception and perfection. עֹלָה אִשֵּׁה רֵיחַ־נִיחוֹחַ לַיהוָה—"a burnt offering, a food offering, a pleasing aroma to YHWH." At this point, the prescriptions for the offering have ended. The work of offeror and priest is done, and YHWH states his intention to receive the gift along with an assurance of acceptance. What is testified to here is therefore the achievement or effect of this offering. This is the *end* of the עֹלָה.

There may be a sense, or even multiple senses, in which we can think of this consumed offering as being perfected. First, we could think of the offering as being perfected as it achieves its goal or serves its proper function. As the offering is transformed into smoke, the creature placed on the altar is received as a "food offering" (Heb. אִשֶּׁה) by YHWH. Having been first received by the offeror from the Lord, the animal is now returned to the Lord, transferred into his possession for his use.[132] The offering thus shows itself to be what it is intended to be: a creature existing both *from* and *to* the Lord, fully devoted to his good purposes. In this case, those purposes are covenantal. Through this food offering, the Lord and his offeror have fellowship through the covenantal movement of reception and return. In this movement, both offering and offeror reach their telos, for each is made by and for the Lord.

This may look to be a strange way of reaching one's telos, for the idea of being offered as a food offering may appear to entail being consumed. But Scripture states plainly that YHWH does not eat the flesh of bulls (Ps 50:13). What, then, is the meaning of presenting this God with a food offering? It is a supplication by the offeror to be united with God in worship. As argued in chapter two, the presentation of food to YHWH enacts a covenantal reciprocity on the part of the offeror that marks him as a faithful son of YHWH. YHWH does not eat the food presented to him but receives it (without destroying it), consecrates it, and then employs it as a medium of covenant communion with the offeror. In this offering, then, the Lord perfects the offering because he employs it for its given purpose: nurturing the life of his people, a life ultimately found in communion with himself through his Word and Spirit.[133]

Second, and perhaps we are on better footing here, we could think of the offering's perfection as a state of immortality. This, at least, is a suggestion opened to us if the epistle to the Hebrews is allowed to inform our reading. David Moffitt argues convincingly that the perfection Hebrews ascribes to Jesus—a perfection that is communicated to those who receive him in faith—is an outcome of his resurrection. In general, Moffitt admits, the

---

[132] David Moffitt, among others, argues that to sacrifice just is to transfer something to God for his use (*Rethinking the Atonement*, 163).

[133] This is not to say that the food God provides his people does not have the more mundane use of nurturing their bodies. But there is more than one way to "perfect" something. Here I am arguing that the perfecting of the offering comes through its use in the offeror's fellowship with God.

language of perfection in Hebrews is "closely bound up with the purification of the human being such that humanity and God's presence can dwell together. Perfection has to do with making the human being fit to enter the world to come." But on a cultic logic, such as Hebrews is following, purification is a prelude to the fullness of life that characterizes one who has been freed from death. It makes good sense, then, that Hebrews would link Jesus' perfection with his resurrection. The author of Hebrews, Moffitt shows, construes Jesus' perfection as a "postmortem state" and links it with his possession of an "indestructible life" (Heb 7:16). This is why Jesus can serve as high priest: by his bodily resurrection from the dead and consequent possession of "a heavenly, enduring life," he has "been made perfect forever" (Heb 7:28).[134]

In all this, Moffitt never links his argument to the burnt offering. But I believe he could. As it is turned to smoke on the altar and ascends to heaven, the burnt offering has certainly been made fit for the divine presence; the statement of Leviticus 1:9 that God will treat it as "a food offering, a pleasing aroma" testifies to that much. Furthermore, the burnt offering's fitness for the divine can, like Jesus' perfection, be seen as a postmortem state. The ascending offering exists in a kind of life after death; though it has died, it is still active, especially in the spiritual realm. I suggest, then, that the rising smoke of the burnt offering can be seen as a resurrection of sorts and therefore as the perfection of the offering.[135] Having traveled the cultic path through death, the offering rises to the realm of the immortal. It is now fit for the presence of God and therefore received into that presence with joy, an offering in which God delights.

If all this seems tenuous, then appeal can also be made to what Leviticus 9 shows to be the *end* of Levitical sacrifice, the vision of God. As Aaron has completed the full sequence of Levitical sacrifice for the first time and descends the altar to bless the people, the "glory of the LORD" appears to all the people, and a divine fire consumes the burnt offering. The consumption of the burnt offering, which produces the smoke, is here associated with the

---

[134]David M. Moffitt, *Atonement and the Logic of Resurrection in the Epistle to the Hebrews*, Supplements to Novum Testamentum 141 (Leiden: Brill, 2013), 200, 195, 207-8.

[135]To be sure, the rising smoke of the burnt offering would not be the bodily resurrection that Scripture ascribes to Jesus. But I believe the ascending smoke can be taken as a token or promise of that greater resurrection that is ours through the one who fulfills this offering.

Action   145

vision of divine glory. This too seems to speak of the perfection of the offering. Hans Boersma speaks of the vision of God's glory as the conclusion of the "beatifying process."[136] The process of our transformation begins with the incarnation of Christ and the gift of the Spirit and is completed with the sight of God. In my judgment, Boersma's logic follows that of 1 John 3:2: "When he appears we shall be like him [i.e., perfected], because we shall see him as he is." And this is a logic we can see at work in the burnt offering. The burnt offering's movement toward the heavens is a movement toward the divine glory, which implies the offering's perfection. It is that perfection that explains God's delight in the offering.[137]

A pleasing (and appeasing) aroma. As the offering is completed in the ascension of the smoke, the ritual of the burnt offering concludes with God's gracious reception of the offering as a "pleasing aroma to the LORD." The phrase is startling. The one who declares himself YHWH, "I AM WHO I AM," who makes all things from nothing, who assures his people that he does not need their offerings—this one communicates a nearly sensual delight in the properly offered עֹלָה.

The translation of the Hebrew phrase רֵיחַ־נִיחוֹחַ is sometimes the subject of heated debate. The difficulty is tied to concerns about the doctrine of God. May we say that God is "appeased," "soothed," or "placated" by this offering, as some take these words?[138] Or should we reject such translations and the theology of propitiation that would seem necessarily to accompany them?

Two answers can be given in defense of reading רֵיחַ־נִיחוֹחַ in terms of appeasement. First, there is the function of the burnt offering outside Leviticus. Morales notes that in 2 Samuel 24, appeasement appears to be the

---

[136]Hans Boersma, *Seeing God: The Beatific Vision in the Christian Tradition* (Grand Rapids, MI: Eerdmans, 2018), 418.
[137]It is tempting to see here an allusion to the transforming presence and energy of the Holy Spirit in the fire. As we read in C. F. Keil and F. Delitzsch, *Commentary on the Old Testament*, vol. 1, *The Pentateuch* (repr., Peabody, MA: Hendrickson, 2011): "Fire is employed as a symbol and vehicle of the Holy Spirit (Acts 2:3, 4) and the burning upon the altar was a symbolical representation of the working of the purifying Spirit of God; so that the burning of the flesh of the sacrifice upon the altar 'represented the purification of the man, who had been reconciled to God, through the fire of the Holy Spirit, who consumes what is flesh, to pervade what is spirit with light and life, and thus to transmute it into the blessedness of fellowship with God'" (509). The authors are quoting a source they label "Kahnis."
[138]E.g., Wenham, *Leviticus*, 56.

result of David's burnt offering. When David, against God's clear command, orders a census of Israel and Judah, the LORD sends a pestilence against Israel in judgment. But when, by the LORD's command through the prophet Gad, David offers up burnt offerings, the LORD "responded" and the plague is averted (2 Sam 24:25). The role of the burnt offering in this narrative, Morales states, "underscores vividly its uniquely effective function of appeasing" YHWH. For this reason, he states, the translation of רֵיחַ־נִיחוֹחַ as "propitiating savor" is "fully justified."[139] Appeasement also seems to be implied in Genesis 8. Though God's judgment had already been enacted by the flood, he responds to the burnt offering Noah offered upon leaving the ark as one who seems to be appeased: "And when the LORD smelled the pleasing aroma [Heb. אֶת־רֵיחַ הַנִּיחֹחַ], the LORD said in his heart, 'I will never again curse the ground because of man'" (Gen 8:21). Based on the use of the same Hebrew terminology in Genesis 8 and the propitiatory force of the expression there, it seems right to translate the phrase as "soothing" or "appeasing" aroma in Leviticus 1.

Second, there is the issue of how exactly we use the language of propitiation or appeasement. This language can easily go wrong. Conceivably, and sometimes in reality, it can be pressed to suggest the idea of a passible God, one who is directly affected by the world, sometimes in a manner that is less than becoming of one thought to be the source and standard of all virtue. If we take things just a step further, we might begin to think that God suffers from frustrated appetites that he is all too eager to satisfy—for example, an appetite for vengeance. This would be a tragic understanding of God's character and relationship to creation. But can we really avoid it while using the language of propitiation?

I think we are helped here by Kevin Vanhoozer's idea that God's emotions, of which the appeasement communicated in the burnt offering would be an example, are "covenantal concern-based theodramatic construals." By this, Vanhoozer means that biblical statements about divine emotion are "reality-depicting." That is, they are not mere anthropomorphisms that in reality can be explained away. Instead, they truly express something of the way God in his unchanging nature judges the object or event that is said to arouse his

---

[139]Morales, *Who Shall Ascend*, 133.

emotion. Biblical talk of divine jealousy, for instance, "represents God's true construal of the theodramatic situation and expresses God's legitimate (and constant) concern to preserve an exclusive relationship."[140]

This construal of divine emotion can help us when it comes to interpreting the רֵיחַ־נִיחֹחַ of the burnt offering. What is happening here is not the kind of appeasement sometimes associated with pagan gods and their lustful responses to sacrifice. Instead, this language expresses both God's evaluation or judgment of the offeror and how that judgment has changed as a result of the offering. In other words, while God has not changed, the offeror's situation has changed. His standing before God has changed. Or, to draw on Vanhoozer's language, God's construal of the "theodramatic situation" in which the offeror finds himself has changed. Whereas the offeror was in a state of condemnation, he is now judged acceptable. Instead of playing the part of God's enemy, he is now cast as a friend. God's covenantal concerns, it seems, have been met.

In my judgment, this understanding of the language of "pleasing aroma" is significant, for it testifies to the reality of satisfaction.[141] If divine emotion attests the realities of God's covenant concerns and judgments, then the language of the burnt offering's "pleasing aroma" just is the language of satisfaction. In this offering, something has been done to change the offeror's standing in the covenant and satisfy God's covenantal concerns. Any breach in the terms of the covenant has somehow been compensated for in this offering in such a way that God no longer stands against the offeror but embraces him. In short, satisfaction has been made.

There is therefore a twofold effect of the burnt offering. On the one hand, the offering is perfected and thus is the offeror vicariously. On the other, God is appeased (or propitiated) and satisfied.[142] This is the atonement we

---

[140]Kevin J. Vanhoozer, *Remythologizing Theology: Divine Action, Passion, and Authorship* (Cambridge: Cambridge University Press, 2010), 414.

[141]It seems necessary here to note again that I do not simply equate satisfaction with compensation or payment. There are also aesthetic and teleological aspects to satisfaction, and those aspects seem to be prominent in the burnt offering's reception by God.

[142]I do not take the terms *propitiation* and *satisfaction* to be synonymous. Propitiation, properly speaking, denotes a change in divine "emotion" from wrath to favor, while satisfaction speaks to the meeting of certain conditions. But these terms do complement each other, as each speaks to the realities of reconciliation and the fulfillment of God's purposes in creation and covenant.

have been waiting for, promised in Leviticus 1:4. Here at last the offering is fully delivered, fully accepted, and the offeror thereby makes his return to God as one requalified for the presence and service of God. God's happy reception of the offeror's gift signals that the compensation and cleaning of atonement have at last taken place.

Synthesis: Satisfaction and Recapitulation in the Burnt Offering

If the exposition offered in these pages has any value, then there was a great deal happening in the ritual for the burnt offering—more, indeed, than I have been able to adequately account for here. However, there is a central thrust to this offering, seen most clearly in its pattern of movement, that gives rise to a certain construal of the mechanism of atonement. If one were to label that mechanism, the phrase "satisfaction by recapitulation through the substitutionary obedience, death, and resurrection of the Son" would be a wordy but adequate expression. Perhaps "filial satisfaction" is a suitable abbreviation.[143] The following synthesis attempts to lay out the mechanism of atonement in the burnt offering more fully.

The offeror appears before God as a son of God, created by God and called into covenant with God. He is mercifully summoned to appear before God and enjoy the grace and glory of the divine presence. But he cannot. In his very being the offeror possesses a disqualification for the divine presence. In theological terms, this disqualification is called original sin. The guilt and corruption of original sin mark the offeror as a descendant of Adam and make him unfit for the presence and service of YHWH. Most fundamentally, this corruption is a misalignment with the Word of God that is meant to define and direct the offeror's existence. In Thomistic terms, we may say that

---

[143]It may be helpful to relate my term "filial satisfaction" to the idea of narrative necessity. One thing this phrase suggests is that the offering represents a fitting completion of Israel's story—in that sense it is a satisfaction. This fitting completion would, at the least, have to involve a legal aspect, so that God's law is fulfilled, and a teleological aspect, so that God's covenantal purposes are fulfilled in Israel's filial relationship to God. The necessity for both the legal and teleological aspects of this satisfaction is found, first, in the character of God, who cannot cease to be himself, and second, in his commitment to creation, since God cannot lie. As has often been said (e.g., Athanasius and Anselm), it would be unfitting for God to simply abandon his creation—or his covenant with Israel—and not lead it to its telos, since God's purposes for creation would in that case not be fulfilled. I would add to this that the covenant implicit in creation makes this reasoning all the more forceful.

the offeror is separated from his form, and he is therefore disoriented to his true end. The offeror has lost his way, even lost himself. Made to be a son of God, made upright and in line with the word of God, the offeror has transgressed the Word of God, and by that transgression he has so corrupted himself that he no longer is what he was made to be, no longer does what he was made to do. He is unclean—out of line with the Word of God—and therefore incompatible with the holiness of God.

What, then, can be done with this offeror? He must be made new. A death is necessary. In one regard, this death is *for* sin, as God's word to Adam and Eve demands: "The day you eat of it"—or break the divine law in any other fashion—"you shall surely die" (Gen 2:17). But there must also be a death *to* sin. If the offeror is to return to God, he cannot do so in his corruption. He must be healed. His sinful form of life must be put to an end, and he must somehow receive a new mode of existence. In other words, he must die and rise again. For one stained by original sin, this is the only hope.

But how can a man be born again? How can one endure a death for sin and to sin without being utterly destroyed? The solution is found in a substitute, one who can die for the offeror while simultaneously carrying him through death to new life. This substitution is therefore recapitulatory—that is, it sums up all that the offeror is meant to be, traversing the whole course of obedience to which he is called, and in doing so both corrects and perfects the offeror. The substitute is what the offeror should be: a son who is conformed to the Word of God, defined and directed by that Word, and therefore clean. The testing of the substitute proves that conformity. The substitute then does (and suffers) what the offeror ought to do (and to suffer). The offering manifests total devotion to the service of YHWH, and yet it is put to death, for a death is owed by the one for whom the offering stands. Importantly, this is not the end of the sacrifice, nor of the story of atonement this ritual tells. As the offering was devoted to God in death, its blood being put on the altar, it proves to be true to the law of its creaturehood, the law whereby it exists from God and to God. The LORD therefore raises the slaughtered body of the offering, first through the agency of the priests placing the body on the altar, then the divine fire that transforms the carcass into a pleasing aroma and transfers it into the heavenly realm in the ascending smoke. As the offering ascends to heaven, God is satisfied.

A crucial point for the mechanism of atonement in the burnt offering is that as the offering passes the test, dies, and rises, so too does the offeror. The offeror is included in the movement of his substitute.[144] As a gift from his own herd or flock, and as that with which he has been identified in the hand-leaning rite, the offering acts for the offeror in such a way that the offeror somehow participates in the test, death, and ascension of his substitute. In other words, the offeror is able to follow in the cultic way into the divine presence opened by his offering, since the offering has satisfied God on his behalf, and he is able to stand in that presence because he is now clean in God's sight as a creature reborn in the holiness of the divine fire. The uncleanness that barred the offeror from the presence of the Lord does so no longer, because through his offering—meaning both his identification with his offering and what that offering achieved—he has been cleansed and renewed. The offeror so fully shares in his substitute that both the cleanness of the substitute and the outcome of its obedience, death, and ascension are communicated (i.e., imputed) to him.[145] In short, the offeror has found his way back to God through death. Cleansed of the guilt and corruption of original sin, the offeror now stands before God as a true son, renewed by the Word and Spirit.[146]

The offering therefore works both *for* and *in* the offeror, and the result is atonement. Because of the compensation and cleansing effected by the offering as his substitute, the offeror is (re)qualified for the presence and service of God.[147] Through this paradigmatic act of worship, the offeror is

---

[144] Of course, it is important to note that Levitical sacrifice was not "automatically" efficacious, *ex opera operato*. The genuine faith and repentance of the offeror were necessary for the offering to be regarded by God. This, I take it, is what the prophetic critique of sacrifice established.

[145] The concept of imputation is controversial in the doctrine of atonement. It is sometimes dismissed as a legal fiction. But something very much like it seems necessary to account for the way in which the offering benefits the offeror. In my judgment, so long as the idea of imputation can be tied to some sort of union between the offeror and offering, a union not is not *merely* legal; the concept is helpful. What I have in mind is something similar to Martin Luther's concept of imputation in his "Two Kinds of Righteousness," in which he likens imputation to marriage: "Just as a bridegroom possesses all that is his bride's and she all that is his." Martin Luther, *Martin Luther's Basic Theological Writings*, 3rd ed., ed. Timothy F. Lull and William R. Russell (Minneapolis: Fortress, 2012), 119.

[146] To be sure, the efficacy of the Levitical burnt offering was limited and temporary. Or, to repeat the argument of Ben Ribbens, the efficacy of these offerings was dependent and sacramental, found not in the offerings themselves but the promise of God who gave Israel these offerings to typify the work of Christ.

[147] Note that this is the definition of atonement sketched out earlier in this study. Atonement is an act of consecration and cleaning that requalifies a sinner for the presence and service of God.

transformed by the fire of God's holiness and transferred into the realm of holiness. Here, then, we have the fulfillment of the demands of covenant, as the offeror draws near to his God and Father as a son. Here, too, is the fulfillment of the demands of creation, as the one made by God is once again rightly oriented to God. Here, finally, is the fulfillment of the demands of consecration, as the offeror, like his offering, is now conformed to the Word of God and filled by the Spirit of God.[148] The offering of the burnt offering was therefore an offering given for satisfaction of God's will, specifically of his will that his children be united to him in holiness. More specifically, it was an offering for satisfaction achieved by the new creation of the offeror through the Word and Spirit by virtue of the substitutionary obedience, death, and resurrection of a filial substitute. It was, in short, an offering of filial satisfaction.

It is important to note that on this interpretation, every act in the sequence that makes up the ritual for the burnt offering is atoning. From the offeror's selection (testing) of the animal to YHWH's transforming reception, the entire action of the burnt offering has atoning import. In other words, each step in the sequence is necessary to make satisfaction. Perhaps some steps are more important than others. Earlier, I argued that the slaughter of the offering should be considered critical, even though it is not the essence of sacrifice, as some have argued. Moffitt, alternatively, argues that in the logic of Levitical sacrifice, the presentation of the slaughtered offering on the altar (and the application of its blood to the sancta) is the most important moment, for this is when the offering is actually presented to God and received into his presence.[149] But if my reading of the Levitical cult is right—if the plot of the cult is return to God through death—then both the slaughter and the presentation, along with all the testing of the offering, the laying on of hands, the butchering, and so on, are essential to the mechanism of atonement in Levitical sacrifice. It is the movement through death

---

[148] If this all sounds too grand for the burnt offering, it should be remembered that the cult ultimately served a sacramental and prophetic function; even though it was by God's grace truly effective, its efficacy lay in the greater reality to which it pointed, the obedience, death, and ascension of Jesus Christ. So, the burnt offering did not by itself perfect the Israelite worshipers. Nevertheless, it truly testified to the offering that does perfect, the eternal burnt offering presented in the heavenly tabernacle by Jesus Christ, and being received as a sign of that greater offering, it was efficacious for the atonement of the Israelite worshiper.

[149] Moffitt, *Rethinking the Atonement*, 172.

back to God as a clean and consecrated creature that satisfies God.[150] And that movement involves the entire ritual, beginning with the selection of the offering, moving through the testing and slaughter and placement on the altar, and culminating in its transformation and reception in the heavenly places. Each step in the movement is necessary for atonement.

Similarly, it is important to remember that this action is divine. Although the offeror and priests have their part to play, God's agency is primary. Without the authority of the divine Word and the enlivening (and fatal) power of the divine Spirit, the rituals are empty and ineffective. It is God who tests, God who gives the blood, God who makes holy, God who transforms the offering, and God who causes it to ascend, so that God can receive the offering and thereby be satisfied. Ultimately, what is attested to in the burnt offering is the cauterizing yet healing embrace of the offeror by the Word and Spirit, restoring the offeror as a son of the Father. By the offeror's fellowship with the Word and Spirit of God, satisfaction is made for his sin, his corruption is purified, and his telos is reached. The burnt offering thus testifies to God providing atonement for sinners through the work of his own two hands.

The purpose of this chapter has been to examine in detail the action of the burnt offering as prescribed in Leviticus 1 in hopes of discerning the logic of atonement in this offering. Following the whole sequence of acts in this sacrifice, and attempting to think theologically with that sequence, I have argued that the logic or mechanism of atonement in this offering is one of filial satisfaction. As the offering is tested, put to death, and rises, so too does the offeror, who participates in the full movement of his filial substitute. The offeror is therefore carried through death by his offering. Compensation is offered, cleansing is effected, and the offeror is now

---

[150]Similarly, and in words that anticipate part of the argument of the following chapter, Douglas Farrow writes, "the ascension of Jesus Christ is also an act of perfecting grace, completing what was begun when the Spirit, who long ago brooded over the waters and brought forth life on earth, hovered over Mary, who brought forth a son. Not only does it fully erase the alienation between God and man introduced by the fall, it fully establishes the communion between God and man at which God was already aiming in the creation itself.... In bearing our humanity home to the Father, Jesus brings human nature as such to its true end and to its fullest potential in the Holy Spirit. He causes it to be entirely at one with God, and so to become the object (and, for other creatures, the mediator) of God's eternal blessing. The ascension, in both senses, is atonement: the 'one-ing' of God and man that is the goal of the incarnation." Douglas Farrow, *Ascension Theology* (London: Bloomsbury T&T Clark, 2011), 122.

qualified for the presence and service of YHWH. In short, atonement has been achieved.[151]

If this reading of the burnt offering has merit, then what is needed now is a reading of the life, death, and resurrection of Jesus that helps us see how Jesus fulfills the pattern and promise of the burnt offering and that gives rise to a theologically coherent account of atonement. I aim to meet that need in the following chapter.

---

[151] It must be remembered, however, that the burnt offering was not the only atoning offering. When a specific transgression had been committed, a sin or guilt offering was also necessary for atonement. This account is therefore not meant to be comprehensive.

FIVE

Meaning

Jesus Christ and the End of the Story

IS THERE A MEANING in the text of Leviticus 1? Throughout this study, I have tried to show that there is. The LORD gives the Levitical cult (including the burnt offering as a summary of the cult) to Israel because it serves his intentions for Israel.[1] These intentions are defined by the identity and character of the LORD; they involve a return to the LORD by sinners, a return that runs through death; and they are satisfied by the LORD's reception of Israel as son of God, as the filial community God had called Israel to be. It is these intentions that give the burnt offering meaning.

These same intentions give the story of Israel meaning. The story of the Levitical cult is the story of Israel as we find it in the ages of the Old Testament. That story is in the first place the story of the Pentateuch. Leviticus itself is part of the pentateuchal narrative, and, as I argued earlier, Levitical ritual was a way of enacting that narrative. Genesis and Exodus are especially important to this story as I have told it: they allow us to

---

[1] At least since J. L. Austin's *How to Do Things with Words*, the meaning of a text has often been associated with the author's intended action, or what the author means to accomplish by their words. This would apply to the biblical text, too; see Timothy Ward, *Words of Life: Scripture as the Living and Active Word of God* (Downers Grove, IL: IVP Academic, 2009). To be sure, the referent of the text is also essential to meaning, and the questions of the text's referent is important for my reading of Lev 1: does this text really refer to Christ? But, in fact, textual referent and authorial intention are tightly intertwined and cannot be understood apart from each other. I cannot understand what an author is doing if I do not understand what he is referring to, and vice versa. Following the NT, especially Hebrews, I read the burnt offering, and all the Levitical sacrifices, as types of Christ, meaning they are symbols that refer to Christ that God instituted for the sake of announcing Christ.

identify the setting, plot, and hero of the story told by the Levitical cult, all of which, in turn, help us follow the action of the burnt offering more closely.

But the exodus, of course, is not the end of Israel's story, and neither does it exhaust the meaning of the burnt offering. The offeror's return to God through death in this offering recalls the triumph of the exodus—Israel is delivered by the blood of the Passover Lamb and the trial at the Red Sea so that they may worship at the mountain of God. At the same time, however, the burnt offering seems to forecast the exile and return yet to come.[2] Isaiah speaks of the exile as a purifying fire, divinely appointed to purge Jerusalem of its sin and idolatry, giving rise to a new, consecrated life for the faithful remnant.[3] By the fiery trial of exile, the Lord would renew his people and bring them back to himself. If this is sound, then as much as the burnt offering of Leviticus 1 was recapitulating the narrative of Genesis–Exodus, it was also forecasting what was to come for Israel, who would one day face another pilgrimage of return.

Even in this postexilic return, however, we do not find the true end of the Levitical story. As the writings of postexilic prophets such as Malachi attest, Judah's return from Babylon was not truly a return to the Lord, at least not the full and final return the voice of earlier prophets might lead us to expect. And neither was it the end of the story as foretold by the burnt offering. To follow the lead of Hebrews, we can say that as the smoke of the burnt offering continued to rise from the postexilic altar, so it continued to testify to a greater return to God that was yet to come. The repetition of the burnt offering attested that the return and purification that the offering promised was not yet realized. Something greater than the burnt offering was

---

[2] I affirm Moses as the primary author of Leviticus. I am open to the idea that the exile had a decisive influence on the shape and content of the OT canon. But even if that is the case, we can still affirm a prophetic quality in Leviticus. It is possible that the exilic community gave great attention to Levitical ritual (and its limitations) because of the experience of exile. If they took time to refine Levitical prescriptions, it is likely because they had already found that Levitical ritual spoke meaningfully to their situation.

[3] This theme runs throughout the book and is already apparent in Is 1:21–2:5. N. T. Wright agrees that there was a link between the process of sacrifice and the Babylonian exile-return in Isaiah. See Wright, *The New Testament and the People of God* (Minneapolis: Fortress, 1992), 276. It is worth noting here that my reading of the burnt offering shows parallels with Wright's idea (found in the same work) that in the death and resurrection of Jesus, Israel was finally rescued from exile.

necessary—something that could fulfill the promise of that offering once and for all.

As it is in Jesus Christ that all the promises of God find their yes and amen, so it is in Jesus Christ that we find the end and prophetic meaning of the burnt offering. What the burnt offering ultimately foretells is the humiliation and exaltation of Jesus Christ, the Son of God incarnate, as he fulfills Israel's story. In him, God's demands for creation, covenant, and consecration have been fully and finally satisfied as the true Son returns to God through death, opening a way for all who would trust him to follow (see, e.g., Heb 10:19-23). Therefore, in the Son's incarnation, obedience, death, resurrection, and ascension—the whole sequence of his saving action—those joined to him by faith have the atonement promised by the burnt offering.

The aim of this chapter is to state how Jesus fulfills both the pattern and the promise of the burnt offering. I aim to demonstrate, that is, how the Son's saving mission follows the pattern of substitution, testing, death, and exaltation established in the Levitical instructions for the burnt offering. I aim also to demonstrate how the burnt offering's promise of atonement is fulfilled in these events, and is fulfilled in a way that follows the logic of atonement found in the burnt offering, a logic of satisfaction and recapitulation through filial substitution. To put it plainly, in this chapter I will proclaim Jesus' atoning work as the meaning of the story told by the burnt offering.[4]

---

[4]This chapter will at times read something like a sermon. My defense: one litmus test for a doctrine of atonement is, "Can you preach it?" There is a kerygmatic element in all Christian theology, just as there are elements of doxology, apologetics, and catechesis in all theology. In this chapter the kerygmatic element will at times be decidedly more pronounced than the others.

As stated above, meaning has to do with both the referent of an author's words and the author's purpose for speaking or writing. These have been labeled locution and illocution, respectively. A story, in this view, has a meaning just like any other piece of writing, since the author has a purpose for it. I believe, as I said in the beginning, that God has given Leviticus to his church for the sake of testifying the atoning work of Christ to us and so that we might trust and honor Christ accordingly. Or, in the words of Calvin: "The sacrifices of the law . . . plainly and openly taught believers to seek salvation nowhere else than in the atonement that Christ alone carries out." John Calvin, *Institutes of the Christian Religion*, ed. John T. McNeill, trans. Ford Lewis Battles (Louisville, KY: Westminster John Knox, 1960), II.vi.2. That said, I do not claim that this is the only reason God gave Lev 1 to his people, and so I do not claim that Christ's sacrifice exhausts all possible meaning of the burnt offering. Much less does my understanding of that sacrifice! Nevertheless, with all proper qualifications in place, I do believe we can speak confidently of Jesus Christ as the meaning of the Levitical instructions for the burnt offering, the point of the story inherent in those instructions.

This chapter will therefore proceed by following the saving course of events that constitute the life and ministry of Jesus Christ.[5] As it recounts these events, it will seek to demonstrate what significance the burnt offering ascribes to them. In other words, my aim is simply to demonstrate how the burnt offering proclaims Christ on the basis of my reading of Leviticus 1, and how its witness contributes to our doctrine of atonement.[6] That contribution, I believe, is manifold and not reducible to a single idea. Nevertheless, there is one idea I will be highlighting throughout this chapter: that the efficacy of Christ's atoning sacrifice lies in his identity as eternal Son of God incarnate. This will support my thesis that, according to the logic of the burnt offering, atonement is made by filial satisfaction.

Incarnation and Substitution

To begin, the incarnation. If the burnt offering truly proclaims Christ, then it begins by proclaiming his incarnation as an act of substitution. As with the burnt offering, this act of substitution is where Christ's atoning work begins, and it is what gives the acts that follow his incarnation their atoning value.

The necessity of a substitute. In my exposition of the burnt offering in the previous chapter, I argue that substitution is essential to the logic of the burnt offering, at least as it is presented in Leviticus 1. Context is determinative: the Israelite offeror is graciously summoned by YHWH, who is eager to accept him as son. But as he is, the offeror cannot be accepted. The offeror approaches the Lord as one who is both guilty and corrupted, unclean. He is not blameless, he has not done what is right, and he does not speak the truth in his heart. He therefore may not dwell on YHWH's holy hill (Ps 15:1-2), even though he is summoned to do so. So, for the sake of receiving this wayward son back into his house, the Lord provides legislation for a substitute.

---

[5] I should reiterate here a point made in the introduction of this study. I do not intend simply to point out how the NT draws on the language and logic of the burnt offering. That the NT does so is important, of course, and I am eager to follow its lead. However, the burnt offering must be allowed to testify to Christ without being reduced to the NT's use of the burnt offering.

[6] As I write that final sentence of this paragraph, I confess that I feel like a fool rushing in where angels fear to tread. And yet I believe that we are invited to tread this ground by the Word of God. Still, "Who is sufficient for these things?" (2 Cor 2:16). Surely my labors will fall short. May God have mercy on me and my words, and may those words honor the reality of the atonement even as they fail to comprehend it.

The Israelite's disqualification for the presence and service of YHWH speaks to the reality of original sin and thus to the condition of all people. This much is confirmed by Paul's epistle to the Romans: "For all have sinned and fall short of the glory of God" (Rom 3:23). In fact, it is helpful here to consider the particular way in which all fall short of that glory according to Romans. Created by God, and receiving good from God, humanity is meant to offer itself in return as a living sacrifice (Rom 12:1-2). The human being of Romans is *homo adorans*, a priestly being, whose natural reaction to the world and his existence in it ought to be gratitude (Rom 1:21), "to bless God in return, to thank him," and thereby to honor him as God.[7] But we have rejected this priestly way of being. Although we know our Creator (Rom 1:19), we have not acknowledged him. As a result, our hearts have been darkened (Rom 1:21). We no longer know what is right. Even when we do know what is right, with the good being declared to us in God's law, written either on our hearts or in the words of Scripture, we still transgress it. Deep in the heart of humanity, then, there is a refusal of our vocation and a rejection of the Word of God. Like the Israelite offeror, we are God's and are called to stand before him as sons and daughters in the knowledge that "from him and through him and to him are all things" (Rom 11:36). But we reject this knowledge and the life to which it gives rise, and we worship the creature rather than our Creator. In this way, we all "fall short of the glory of God," failing to acknowledge his glory, thus being barred from entering into it. In other words, we are disqualified for God's presence and service, so that we may not dwell on his holy hill.

But God is rich in mercy, and he has loved his people with a great love. And so he provides a substitute.

The most fitting substitute. According to the instructions for the burnt offering, the substitute, which will be "accepted for" the offeror who seeks

---

[7]Alexander Schmemann, *For the Life of the World: Sacraments and Orthodoxy*, rev. ed. (Crestwood, NY: St. Vladimir's Seminary Press, 1973), 15. Perhaps my calling this a natural reaction to the world will be objected to. Calvin speaks of the fact that the natural now testifies to God's wrath, as Rom 1:18 suggests. "Our eyes—wherever they turn—encounter God's curse. . . . We cannot by contemplating the universe infer that [God] is Father." But Calvin admits this in the beginning, it was not so. "The natural order was that the frame of the universe should be the school in which we were to learn piety, and from it pass over to eternal life and perfect felicity" (*Institutes* 2.6.1). Paul, who taught that the wrath of God is being revealed in this world, could also proclaim that he has left witness to himself in the good and pleasant things that he has given to us (Acts 14:17).

acceptance (Lev 1:3-4), must be blameless, or "without blemish" (Lev 1:3).[8] That is, it must be both clean (that is, from an approved class or species for consumption and sacrifice) and true to form, an "exemplar" of its species.[9] The offering will be tested and must prove itself blameless; it must show itself conformed to the Word that defines its particular proper way of being. And then it will be accepted for the offeror to make atonement for him (Lev 1:4).

In light of these instructions, and of the priestly anthropology of Scripture as sketched out above, the incarnation of the Son of God is seen to be the most perfect act of substitution. Perhaps some other substitute could have been put forward; perhaps God could have devised some other means of atonement. But "no other way would have been so fitting or so appropriate," and it is hard to imagine a way that could elicit so much praise as the incarnation of the eternal Son of God.[10]

In thinking through the fittingness of this action, as well as the way this action makes atonement for sins, it is helpful to highlight how the incarnation entails the communication of the Son's personal property, his filial act of being, to his human nature. Sacrifice is a communicative, dialogical act between God and humanity. Just above, I noted that a kind of dialogue is meant to characterize all of human life; we are made to receive good from God and return to him our praise, which is part and parcel with receiving his word and returning obedience. This, I believe, is part of what it means to image God. In the incarnate Son of God, and only in him, we finally see one living out this identity and vocation.[11] The "core" of Jesus' personality, writes Cardinal Joseph Ratzinger, "was his dialogue with the Father." According to the testimony of Scripture, Ratzinger says, Jesus' entire life is drawn up into his communication with the Father. His entire earthly existence is at once a "mission," a "sending," communicated to him by the Father, and also a prayer offered to the Father. "In all the words and deeds of Jesus,

---

[8] The term translated "without blemish" in Lev 1:3 (תָּמִים) means "blameless" when applied to human persons. See, e.g., Gen 17:1.

[9] Rolf P. Knierim, *Text and Concept in Leviticus 1:1-9: A Case in Exegetical Method* (repr., Eugene, OR: Wipf & Stock, 2010), 31.

[10] Bonaventure, *Breviloquium*, trans. Dominic V. Monti, OFM, Works of St. Bonaventure 9 (Saint Bonaventure, NY: Franciscan Institute, 2005), 4.1.1.

[11] "Image of God," like "son of God," is both an identity and a vocation in Scripture. In fact, identity and vocation are always intertwined. One always implies the other.

this filial relationship always shines through. . . . We perceive that his whole being is at home in this relationship."[12]

It is in just this way, Ratzinger continues, that Scripture reveals Jesus' identity as eternal Son of God, consubstantial with the Father.[13] For what has happened in the incarnation, on this account, is the union of the Son's eternal relation to the Father with the human nature he has assumed for himself. The Son's eternal mode of subsistence—his being "God from God," eternally generated by the Father—is what makes him a unique divine person, distinguished from the Father and Spirit. And when the Son assumes human nature, that nature is characterized by this mode of subsistence; in the words of Dominic Legge, "by the filial mode of existing proper to the divine Son who subsists in that human nature." In other words, "everything in Christ's humanity takes on the filial mode of the Son."[14]

It is this communication of the Son's filial mode of subsistence that makes him such a fit substitute, indeed, an atoning substitute, the true hero of this story (as I argued in chap. 3). Precisely by enacting his identity as divine Son in human flesh, Christ proves to be clean, an acceptable substitute, one able to fulfill the demands of appearing before God placed on the Levitical offeror and on every other human being. When the Son becomes incarnate, the result could be nothing other than a human being who is (and proves to be) the faithful Son of God, conformed in all his being and acting to the Word of God and always offering a "perfect and personal obedience" to that Word, as he lives from, through, and to God as a living sacrifice.[15]

Incarnation and the negation of original sin. In other words, we can say that the incarnation of the Son means the negation of original sin and, with that, the promise of humanity's restoration. As Christ's humanity "subsists in the very subsistence" of God the Son, it is brought into union with the divine nature, the attributes of which "inwardly impact [Christ's] human nature."[16] His humanity, remaining humanity, shares in the holiness of God

---

[12]Joseph Ratzinger, *Behold the Pierced One: An Approach to a Spiritual Christology*, trans. Graham Harrison (San Francisco: Ignatius, 1986), 18, 22, 21.

[13]Ratzinger, *Behold the Pierced One*, 36.

[14]Dominic Legge, *The Trinitarian Christology of St. Thomas Aquinas* (Oxford: Oxford University Press, 2017), 111-12.

[15]Westminster Confession of Faith 7.2.

[16]Herman Bavinck, *Reformed Dogmatics*, vol. 3, *Sin and Salvation in Christ*, ed. John Bolt, trans. John Vriend (Grand Rapids, MI: Baker Academic, 2006), 3:309. "Subsists in the very subsistence"

the Son in a way befitting its creaturely condition. For this reason, among others, his humanity does not share in the guilt and corruption of original sin. To be sure, Paul tells us that God sent his Son "in the likeness of sinful flesh" (Rom 8:3) and to bear the curse of sin (Gal 3:13). The Son assumed a weak human nature, one truly formed from Mary and not yet perfected. The Son's humanity was therefore passible, susceptible to temptation, and subject to suffering and death.[17] But these affirmations need not imply or even suggest that Christ shared in the guilt and corruption of original sin or that he assumed a fallen human nature.[18] In my judgment, the testimony of the burnt offering points us away from the affirmation of a fallen human nature in Christ, as it calls for a substitute that is without blemish and true to form. And what is a fallen human nature if not one *deformed* by original sin?

The incarnation of the Son holds the promise and certainty of humanity's restoration to form, because in this act "the restoring principle" takes our nature to himself.[19] As the incarnation of the one through whom all things were made, through whom all was originally "set in order," the Son's assumption of human nature could only mean the restoration, reordering, and healing of our nature.[20] Irenaeus proclaims that it is "the Maker of all, the Word of God, who molded man at first"—it is this one who has "healed it in every way" and "renewed the whole man, sound and entire" in the incarnation.[21] For Thomas and much of the Western tradition, the Son is the

---

comes from John of Damascus, *Exposition of the Orthodox Faith*, trans. S. D. F. Salmond, in *A Select Library of Nicene and Post-Nicene Fathers of the Christian Church*, Second Series, ed. Philip Schaff and Henry Wace (Grand Rapids, MI: Eerdmans, 1989), vol. 9, 3.7.

[17] Bavinck, *Reformed Dogmatics*, 3:310; cf. Bonaventure, *Breviloquium* 4.8.4.

[18] In my understanding, a fallen human nature would necessarily be one that has inherited original sin. Donald Macleod, *The Person of Christ*, Contours of Christian Theology (Downers Grove, IL: InterVarsity Press, 1998), argues cogently along these lines (224-30).

[19] Bonaventure, *Breviloquium* 4.8.3.

[20] Hilary, *On the Trinity* 4.21, ed. W. Sanday, trans. E. W. Watson and L. Pullen, in *A Select Library of Nicene and Post-Nicene Fathers of the Christian Church*, Second Series, ed. Philip Schaff and Henry Wace (Grand Rapids, MI: Eerdmans, 1989), vol. 9. While I am indebted to the work of T. F. Torrance, particularly the way he illuminates the importance of Christ's divine sonship for our understanding of atonement, it is necessary to clarify in this chapter that I disagree with his claim that the incarnation effects a union between Christ and human nature in general. The Son's assumption of humanity is healing, I believe, but it is healing only for those united to Christ by faith. The necessity of a union of faith between the offering and offeror may be implicit in Leviticus in the offeror's leaning on his offering. It is also implied in the prophetic critique of the cult, in which Israel is accused of not sharing in the virtues of their offering and therefore receiving no benefit from them.

[21] Irenaeus, *Against Heresies*, trans. John Keble (repr., Nashotah, WI: Nashotah House, 2012), 5.12.6.

exemplar or formal cause of creation.[22] When humanity is joined to the Son, what could it mean but our return to form—in Levitical terms, our being made clean and without blemish? For Maximus, the eternal *Logos* contains within himself the *logoi* of all creatures, the various divine orderings or scripts for different creatures, the divine Word that gives them their proper place and function in the world.[23] When that eternal Logos is united with humanity, what could it mean but our realignment with the divinely given ordering or script that is meant to govern us?

Moral and ontological aspects of atonement. Here we can see both moral and ontological aspects of atonement. The correction and perfection and human nature in Christ lies not simply in the fact that his humanity was morally flawless and so free from guilt but also in that it was (and is) properly filial. Christ's obedience exceeds that prescribed by positive divine law and reached into his very way of being human. To speak of Jesus' way of being human is to make an ontological claim, for ontology concerns not only *what* a being is but *how* a being is. For creatures, ontology includes matters of purpose and orientation, not just material components. As there is an ontological aspect to sin, namely, original sin, so there is an ontological aspect of the Son's incarnation (and subsequent atoning acts) that remedies original sin.

The incarnation as mechanism of atonement. Thus, in my judgment, the burnt offering tells us that the incarnation itself, this supreme act of substitution, is essential to the mechanism of atonement.[24] The substitute does what the offeror cannot do for himself—what we cannot do for ourselves. The substitute is accepted for us, who come seeking acceptance. And the substitute is acceptable because he is in truth the eternal Son incarnate, the Word become flesh. The eternal Son, Fred Sanders tells us, "lived out in his human life the exact same sonship that makes him who he is from all eternity as the second person of the Trinity;" Jesus Christ is "the Son behaving filially

---

[22]Gilles Emery, OP, "Trinity and Creation," in *The Theology of Thomas Aquinas*, ed. Rik van Nieuwenhove and Joseph Wawrykow (Notre Dame, IN: University of Notre Dame Press, 2005), 58-76.
[23]Paul M. Blowers, *Maximus the Confessor: Jesus Christ and the Transfiguration of the World* (Oxford: Oxford University Press, 2016), 112-13.
[24]Though we might rarely put it in these terms, thinking of the incarnation as a mechanism or means of atonement is nothing new. It is obviously fundamental to the logic of Anselm in *Cur Deus Homo*.

in human nature."²⁵ And it is as he lives out his filial identity that he is an acceptable and atoning substitute for us (that is, those united to Christ by faith), filling out our true form and offering the loving obedience that we should offer but cannot.

To be clear, it is not the incarnational union considered in itself, in isolation from the obedience, death, and resurrection of Jesus, that is atoning, as if atonement were made in an impersonal or merely physical union of the divine and human natures. The incarnation, of course, is anything but impersonal. It is a dynamic and lived union of a particular divine person, God the Son, and the human nature he personalizes.²⁶ Anything that suggests a static union of abstracted divine and human natures is simply ruled out from the start and should not be allowed to influence our thinking on atonement. (With apologies to Anselm, this is why the question "Why the God-man?" should perhaps be replaced with the question "Why the Son of God made man?") What it means for the incarnation to be essential to the mechanism of atonement, then, is that the union of the Son's filial mode of being with his human nature ensures the correction and perfection of our nature and the satisfaction of God's demands. The humanity of God the Son was initially clean but not yet perfected in holiness. Nevertheless, by virtue

---

²⁵Fred Sanders, *Fountain of Salvation: Trinity and Soteriology* (Grand Rapids, MI: Eerdmans, 2021), 22.

²⁶T. F. Torrance, *Incarnation: The Person and Life of Christ*, ed. Robert T. Walker (Downers Grove, IL: InterVarsity Press, 2008), 201, distinguishes between understanding the hypostatic union "dynamically" and "statically." Torrance believed that understanding the union dynamically went hand in glove with affirming a fallen human nature assumed and corrected by Christ. Though I am following Torrance to some extent here, as my vocabulary alone shows, I again do not think that it is necessary affirm with him that Christ's human nature was at some time, in some way, fallen. The substitute in the burnt offering takes the offeror's place, is tested like the offeror, dies to and for sin on behalf of the offeror. Yet, throughout, that substitute is itself *clean*. Similarly, Jesus Christ takes our place. He is tested on our behalf, lives under the conditions of life outside the garden, dies to and for sin, and even suffers some level of alienation from God; this is his state of humiliation (see Macleod, *Person of Christ*, 229). Yet for all that, he is clean. At all times, his human nature is conformed to the Word of God, to which it is united. Perhaps it is possible to argue that Christ's human nature was *anhypostatically* fallen but *enhypostatically* sanctified, so that "Christ's human nature is able to sin in abstraction from the incarnation . . . and it is made sinless (but still peccable) through assumption by the Word. Its hypostatic impeccability . . . has nothing to do with any natural property of the human nature assumed by the Word." Oliver Crisp, "On the Vicarious Humanity of Christ," *International Journal of Systematic Theology* 21, no. 3 (July 2019): 247. That account of Christ's humanity may in some way square with my thesis in this chapter. But, again, I do not believe it is necessary, nor am I ready to endorse such an account.

of its union with God the Son, it was incapable of not being perfected.[27] The testing, death, and resurrection of Christ were all means to that perfecting, as I will argue shortly. "The Son's fleshly presence in time does not atone but for its finale," and for that matter, all the events leading up to that finale.[28] But as God cannot deny himself, it was impossible that the Son would lose his distinctively filial manner of being—that he would cease to be the holy Son. With the assumption of our flesh, the outcome of his life—that he would prove to be the Son of God—was inevitable.

The work of Christ is what it is because of who Christ is. "The significance of his death"—and life and resurrection and every other atoning action—"depends entirely on the identity of its subject."[29] In other words, *who* Christ is, the eternal Son of God, is essential to the explanation of *how* he makes atonement for our sins.

Atonement and union with Christ. Thus the incarnation, in my judgment, is an explanation for why the acts of Christ achieve atonement; why they make satisfaction to God, why they effect the healing of our humanity. In the introduction to this work, I called this a mechanism of achievement. The incarnation is not, however, a full explanation of who ultimately receives the benefits of the incarnation; it is not to be taken as a mechanism of relationship.[30] John of Damascus explains that while in Christ our human nature has been delivered from death and received into heaven, not all human persons have.[31] Though Christ is truly in our flesh, not all are in Christ. There must be some additional mechanism of relationship at work for Christ's incarnational life, death, and resurrection to be atoning for individuals. In the previous chapter, I argued that the laying on of hands in the

---

[27]This is another way of affirming Christ's impeccability. I believe Jesus' temptations were genuine temptations because his humanity was not yet perfected. As I will argue below, he was still under trial. His humanity was therefore passible. Being created for growth, as Irenaeus said human nature to be (*Against Heresies* 4.11.1), it was still growing in its determination to the good throughout the whole time of Christ's life.

[28]Ivor J. Davidson, "Atonement and Incarnation," in *T&T Clark Companion to Atonement*, ed. Adam J. Johnson (London: Bloomsbury T&T Clark, 2017), 51.

[29]Davidson, "Atonement and Incarnation," 35.

[30]In my judgment, election also belongs to the mechanism of relationship between Christ and the Christian as a precondition for union with Christ. Only those who are regenerate can be united to Christ by faith, and only those who are elected by God will be regenerated. This would mean that I deny a hypothetically universal atonement. That said, I do not believe the account of atonement I sketch out in these pages depends on my affirmation of soteriological election.

[31]John of Damascus, *Exact Exposition of the Orthodox Faith* 3.6.

burnt offering ritual most likely signified an identification or union between offeror and offering. This union is necessary for the offeror to receive the benefit of the offering's mediation. So it is with Christ. The burnt offering proclaims that union with Christ is a necessary condition for atonement. Without such a union, Calvin famously teaches us, we have no share in Christ's achievement: "As long as Christ remains outside of us, and we are separated from him, all that he has suffered and done for the salvation of the human race remains useless and of no value to us. . . . All that he possesses is nothing to us until we grow into one body with him."[32] The incarnation is a means to the achievement of atonement, but it does not apply a universal application of that achievement.

Testing and Obedience

Moving on to the testing of the substitute: as the substitution of the burnt offering comes in a context of testing, so too does the substitutionary life of Jesus Christ. The offeror of Leviticus fails the test; he is not blameless and so not able to approach without mediation. He therefore puts forth a substitute that is tested in his place and found blameless. So it is that Christ, the true Son of God, is tested for us. He is found blameless—vindicated and exalted—and in his acceptance, we are accepted.

Testing is a key feature in the setting of the burnt offering. The Lord who indwells the tabernacle has shown himself to be a consuming fire at Sinai, manifesting his holiness there to test the children of Israel (Ex 20:20). When he summons them from the tent, he does so as their King and Judge, the one whose throne is established in righteousness, as he has proven in the exodus, and whose footstool, the ark of the covenant, houses his law. To appear before this God is to be subject to his judgment; to be accepted by this God is to pass the test of his judgment. What the burnt offering makes clear to us is that the Israelite offeror passed the test only by his substitute. The offering is examined by the divine eye and tried in the divine flame on the altar before it is received as a pleasing aroma to the Lord. And so it is with Jesus.

Jesus' lifelong trial. The Gospels tell us that while Jesus Christ lived as the Son of God incarnate, eternally beloved of the Father, he nevertheless lived

---

[32]Calvin, *Institutes* 3.1.1.

a life of testing. The Son's assumption of human flesh did not immediately issue in exaltation. It was necessary, rather, that he first submit to a trial and be found obedient. The trial was necessary because of God's intentions for humanity. Leviticus, I have argued, teaches us that God wills human beings to be perfected and receive the grace of the beatific vision. That the glory of the LORD appeared to Israel at the inauguration of the cult, and that the holy place was designed to be resplendent with light—both hold out the promise of beatific vision.[33] It would seem, however, that God wills this perfecting to be gradual, not all at once; humanity is meant to grow into a perfection that is brought to completion in the beatific vision. This anthropology fits what we see in the Garden of Eden. The story of Adam's test and failure makes most sense when we assume with Irenaeus that while God made Adam upright, he nevertheless "formed him for augmentation and growth." Humanity was made to receive good from God and thereby to grow up in goodness, to be "the receptacle of His Goodness" and "continually get on towards God" by being so. God formed us, Irenaeus insists, not because he needs us but that "He may do good to those who abide in His service," and that they might continue in the communion with God that is their glory.[34] But continuing is essential. To be "formed for growth and augmentation" brings with it the possibility of degeneracy, the possibility of a fall. All the time before Adam's perfection, before he attained to the fullness of life and immortality held out to him by God, was therefore to be a time of testing.

The burnt offering shows us that Adam, having failed the test, is still summoned forward by God and still seeking perfection in communion with God. And with that, it shows us Jesus, the new Adam, the substitute Adam, under the same trial as Adam. According to all the Gospels, Jesus' life culminates in a trial, a trial that calls into question his every word and action, his very identity. Is this man truly the Son of God, as he has said? Are the actions by which he claimed divine authority justified? Or has it all been blasphemy? The same challenge Satan presents at the beginning of Jesus'

---

[33]Michael L. Morales, *Who Shall Ascend the Mountain of the Lord? A Biblical Theology of the Book of Leviticus*, New Studies in Biblical Theology (Downers Grove, IL: InterVarsity Press, 2015), 21: "Entering the house of God to dwell with God, beholding, glorifying, and enjoying him eternally ... *is* the story of the Bible, the plot that makes sense of the various acts, persons, and places of its pages," including those of Lev 1.

[34]Irenaeus, *Against Heresies* 4.11.1-2; 4.14.1.

ministry is repeated at the cross—"if you are the Son of God," then prove it, either by throwing yourself down from the temple (Mt 4:6) or coming down from the cross (Mt 27:40). In each case, Jesus answers the same. By entrusting himself to the Father and obeying his voice, he proves by his filial obedience that he is indeed the true Son of God.

Other moments in Christ's life manifest the same obedience. When the boy Jesus is left behind in Jerusalem and sought by his parents, Mary speaks in exasperation: "Son, why have you treated us so? Behold, your father and I have been searching for you in great distress" (Lk 2:48). Jesus responds, "Why were you looking for me? Did you not know that I must [Gk. δεῖ] be in my Father's house?" (Lk 2:49). Jesus was with the Father, he respectfully insists, as he was listening to the Scriptures at the temple. Throughout his ministry, this filial identity and devotion are only further confirmed. At his baptism, the voice from heaven identifies Jesus as "my beloved Son; with you I am well pleased" (Lk 3:22). When Jesus heals a man on the Sabbath, he assures his critics that he is working with his Father, doing only what he sees the Father doing (Jn 5:17, 20). When he cleanses the temple, he does so as a faithful Son: "Do not make my Father's house a house of trade" (Jn 2:16). When Jesus prays, he invokes God as his Father (e.g., Mt 6:9); when he preaches, he proclaims God as Father (e.g., Mt 6:25-34). In all his speaking and acting—and even in his suffering—Jesus shows himself to be the faithful Son of the Father.

Atoning obedience. It is in this way that, as Calvin puts it, Jesus has countered our transgression with his obedience and satisfied God's judgment.[35] In other words, Jesus' filial obedience is atoning. First, it effects our cleaning from sin. By his obedience, Jesus passes the test placed on him and is therefore accepted. Like the true burnt offering, he is accepted on our behalf as he proves to be clean and without blemish. Jesus' life manifests a proper humanity, a humanity not plagued by original sin and that is therefore true to its created form as image of God. Aquinas spoke of corruption as "separation from form."[36] As one true to the form of human nature, Jesus proves free from humanity's corruption and its concomitant guilt. Similar to

---

[35]Calvin, *Institutes* 2.12.3.
[36]Thomas Aquinas, *Light of Faith: The Compendium of Theology*, trans. Cyril Vollert (Manchester, NH: Sophia Institute, 1993), sec. 74.

Aquinas, Alexander of Hales held that the stain of sin consisted of "deformity or dissimilarity to God."[37] In Jesus Christ, that stain is removed, as he proves to be the eternal image incarnate, the divine Son whose being is the exact repetition of the Father's by virtue of his eternal generation from the Father.

Second, Jesus' obedience provides compensation for sin, satisfying God on our behalf. The obedience offered by the incarnate Son could be nothing less than perfectly righteous and even consummately beautiful, as it was a creaturely reflection of the divine character of which none greater could be conceived. As such, it was, in the words of Anselm, "more loveable [to God] than sins are hateful." Jesus' "life outweighs all the sins of mankind," Anselm reasons; the Son's incarnate life is, in the eyes of the Father, "so loveable [that it] can suffice to pay the debt which is owed for the sins of the whole world," or even infinitely more.[38] Anselm's words about the value of Christ's life assume a principle of reparative justice here, arguing that Jesus makes amends not by bearing punishment but by offering something other than punishment that relieves the demand for punishment.[39] The idea of reparative justice is by no means foreign to Leviticus; it is clearly present in the guilt offering, sometimes labeled "reparation offering," which stipulates that in the case of a "breach of faith," such as theft, the guilty party must repay more than he took and then must bring an offering for "compensation to the LORD" (Lev 6:1, 6). Something similar seems to be happening in Jesus' fulfillment of the burnt offering. Though the Levitical offeror is unacceptable, the offering is accepted for him and received with divine delight. God's delight in the offering compensates for the offeror's guilt and corruption. Thus it is with the obedience of Jesus. God's delight in the obedience of his incarnate Son covers and compensates for the sins of those who are in Christ. The Lord's reception of the burnt offering as a pleasing aroma suggests that

---

[37] R. S. Franks, *The Work of Christ: A Historical Study of Christian Doctrine* (New York: Thomas Nelson and Sons, 1962), 189.

[38] Anselm, *Why God Became Man*, in *Anselm of Canterbury: The Major Works*, ed. Brian Davies and G. R. Evans (Oxford: Oxford University Press, 1998), 2.14.

[39] These words come in a section of the *Cur Deus Homo* in which Anselm reflects on the value of Jesus' life poured out in death. The question of Jesus' death is still in the air, but Anselm's words speak directly to the value of his life, since it is such a beautiful life that is poured out in death. It thus cuts against the objection sometimes raised that Anselm's account "has no place for the active obedience of Christ." Michael S. Horton, *Lord and Servant: A Covenant Christology* (Louisville, KY: Westminster John Knox, 2005), 181.

he receives the offering as satisfaction for sin, and it also suggests an aesthetic element in sacrificial satisfaction. Thus it highlights, ultimately, God's deep pleasure in the incarnate Son, in whom all the fullness and beauty of divine holiness dwell bodily (see Col 2:9), and the capacity of the incarnate Son to offer a supremely pleasing gift for atonement.

Multiple mechanisms, a consistent logic. Following the lead of the burnt offering, we can begin to see multiple mechanisms of atonement at work in the testing and obedience of Jesus, all of which are necessary to bring us through death and into new life with God. Jesus' obedience effects cleansing and offers compensation; Christ restores us to form and offers a propitiatory gift for our reconciliation through his filial obedience, an obedience in which we participate in our union with Christ. But this is not yet a full account of atonement; much remains to be said about Christ's death and resurrection and ascension. So we see already why there is not just one model or mechanism of atonement. Christ's work is multifaceted. It consists of the "totality of a journey" from conception to life to death to resurrection, and atonement is made all along the way.[40]

However, I believe that while the burnt offering attests to a diversity of mechanisms in Christ's atoning work, it also reveals a principle of unity in that work. A single logic undergirds the entirety of Christ's action and infuses it all with atoning value: the incarnation of the Son of God "for us and our salvation." The foundational logic of atonement is the logic of the Son of God uniting our flesh to his sonship to do for us what we could not do for ourselves, and then making the fruits of what he accomplishes in that flesh available to us as individuals by union with himself. In the burnt offering we see atonement by substitution—a substitution of the healthy and whole for one who suffers the deprivation of sin, of the one without blemish for the one made guilty and corrupted by sin. This speaks to the substitutionary incarnation of the Son of God in Jesus Christ for the sake of countering our trespasses and healing our diseased nature.

The ancient formula holds that "he became what we are so that we might become what he is." Various models or accounts of atonement might add to this formula and help us fill out what exactly his becoming what we are

---

[40]Davidson, "Atonement and Incarnation," 31.

entails. A number of motifs or metaphors might be needed to specify what he has done to make us "what he is." But our atonement theology can never move away from this incarnational and substitutionary foundation. Just as the burnt offering provides a paradigm or framework for the entire Levitical cult, all other sacrifices (including the sin and guilt offerings) being enfolded into its movement, so the incarnational and substitutionary logic of atonement in Leviticus 1 provides a framework for all of our thinking about atonement.[41]

Death to Sin, Death for Sin

In light of the foregoing, it may strike us as paradoxical that God's delight in the offering does not set aside the necessity or fittingness of its death. It may too strike us as nearly heretical to say that Jesus was enacting his eternal divine sonship in human flesh when he took up his cross and laid down his life. How could this be?[42] By what logic does the life of the incarnate Word end in death? Only by the twisted logic of sin. When the Word became flesh and came to his own, he came to a world that was made through him. But the world did not receive him. Irrationally, the world put him to death. This death, however, was according to the purpose of God, his rational answer to the irrationality of sin.

The important point to make here is this: while "Jesus' human history is exhausted in the fact that it is the form of the divine descent into the world, acting out in time . . . the eternal relation of Father and Son," it is nevertheless "a commissioned history, the discharge of an office."[43] The Son came into the world not simply to manifest his Sonship but to fulfill a mission, a mission that required him to suffer, die, and rise.[44] In the burnt offering, a

---

[41]In my judgment, some foundational logic is desired in atonement theology. While the push of the last several decades toward multiple, complementary models or accounts of atonement has been helpful, the doctrine loses its meaning if it is not held together by some core logic or principle that is able to accommodate the various models and hold them together.

[42]Perhaps it would be a sign of an impoverished doctrine of atonement if it did not feel this tension. The NT seems astonished at the crucifixion of the Son of God, and so does much Christian theology throughout the centuries.

[43]John Webster, "'It Was the Will of the Lord to Bruise Him': Soteriology and the Doctrine of God," in *God Without Measure*, vol. 1, *God and the Works of God* (London: T&T Clark, 2016), 157.

[44]Webster, "'It Was the Will,'" 157. Davidson gives an apt reminder: "It remains vitally important that atonement is not so directly identified with the person of the incarnate Christ that the specific course of his personal history suffers eclipse" ("Atonement and Incarnation," 39). And

gift was given to YHWH. This gift represented the gratitude and devotion of the offeror. But that gift was also given in a particular historical and theological context. That context was marked by calling, testing, sin, and judgment, and thus one of the purposes for the gift was atonement. That is why the gift was given in death. It was the God-appointed purpose of the burnt offering that explains why the offering had to travel the particular path that it did and why that path would wind through the valley of the shadow of death.

The same is true of the death of Jesus. Christ's death is an answer to the reality of sin. Still, that death maintains a distinctly filial character. In chapter two, I spoke of the slaughter of the burnt offering as the crisis of the cultic plot, the decisive event on which the plot turns. This is not to say that it is the moment of greatest importance—it is not *the* essential act of sacrifice. But it is the moment at which the offeror's fate is sealed, so to speak. And so it is with the death of Jesus. The death of Jesus completes his life of obedience and self-giving and is the apex of his obedience and self-giving. It is the incarnate Son's "most perfect and definitive act" of self-giving by which he honors and enacts the proper order of the world.[45] As Ratzinger notes, "Jesus died praying." Indeed, "his dying was itself an act of prayer, his death was a handing-over of himself to the Father." By dying in the way he died, Jesus "fashioned his death into . . . an act of worship."[46] This may be one of the clearest contributions of the Levitical burnt offering to our understanding of atonement: it uniquely highlights the doxological aspect of Christ's death.[47] Viewed under the paradigm of the burnt offering, we can see that there is something distinctly filial in the death of Christ. In his death, he manifests his most perfect agreement with the will of the Father and his most earnest desire to glorify the Father.[48]

---

the personal history of Christ, he insists, is determined by his appointment to the office of Messiah.

[45] Sonderegger, "Anselmian Atonement," in *T&T Clark Companion to Atonement*, ed. Adam J. Johnson (London: Bloomsbury T&T Clark, 2017), 191.

[46] Ratzinger, *Behold the Pierced One*, 22, 24.

[47] On the doxological aspect of the death of Christ, see Khaled Anatolios, *Deification Through the Cross: An Eastern Christian Theology of Salvation* (Grand Rapids, MI: Eerdmans, 2020), esp. chap. 7. Anatolios explicates Christ's sacrificial death as an act of "doxological contrition."

[48] Thomas Weinandy points in a helpful direction that will be followed below: "Jesus, the all-holy Son, took upon himself sin's condemnation: death. Yet on the cross Jesus transfigured or transposed that condemnatory death into a prayerful hallowing act of worship by offering himself

Jesus' death to sin. The tragic element of this reading of the cross is that Jesus' gift of filial devotion must be given in death.[49] The gift is offered by the Son *incarnate*, one who, though not personally stained by sin, lives in a world under the tyrannous reign of sin and death. For this reason, it is fitting that he delivers his gift to the Father by a death *to* sin; "for the death he died he died to sin, once for all, but the life he lives he lives to God" (Rom 6:10). In his crucifixion, Jesus dies to sin in the sense that he passes away, once and for all, from the domain of sin. Michael Horton comments that, on the cross, Jesus was "in that life-long trial recapitulating and restoring what was lost in Adam." He continues, "That which [Jesus] offered was not only a sacrifice of atonement," understood by Horton primarily in terms of the guilt offering, "but an obedient *life*." "Christ's sacrificial life precedes his sacrificial death," and his "active self-offering" culminates in his death.[50]

As the culmination of his trial, the crisis moment of his trial, Jesus' death is his definitive act of obedience, an irrevocable yes to God. As such, it is also a final and irrevocable no to sin. On the cross, Jesus endures his most agonizing test. Not only do the mockers repeat the words of Satan's temptation, "If you are the Son of God, come down from the cross . . . for he said, 'I am the Son of God'" (Mt 27:40, 43), but Jesus himself seems to feel the question of his sonship as he cries out, "My God, my God, why have you forsaken me?" (Mt 27:46). But then with a loud voice Jesus "yielded up his spirit" (Mt 27:50), a voice with which, according to Luke, he uttered a final word of filial obedience: "Father, into your hands I commit my spirit!" (Lk 23:46). The Roman centurion understands what he witnesses: "Truly this was the Son of God" (Mt 27:54; Mk 15:39). In his death, Jesus gives confirmation of his sonship—a confirmation answered by that of the Father and the Spirit in Jesus' resurrection (e.g., Rom 1:4). In this way Jesus dies to sin: he definitively asserts the truth of his sonship against the falsity of sin

---

on humankind's behalf as an all-holy and loving sacrifice to his Father. . . . When Jesus lovingly placed his spirit in the hands of his Father, when he breathed his last, he who bears the name 'Son' perfectly hallowed him who bears the name 'Father,' and in doing so made reparation or satisfaction for humanity's sinful unhallowing acts, which desecrated and violated his Father's name." Weinandy, *Jesus Becoming Jesus: A Theological Interpretation of the Synoptic Gospels* (Washington, DC: Catholic University of America Press, 2018), 404.

[49]E.g., Lk 24:26: "Was it not necessary that the Christ should suffer these things?"

[50]Horton, *Lord and Servant*, 226, 223. Horton is seeking to integrate the Reformed concepts of Christ's active and passive obedience in this formulation.

and temptation with an irrevocable word of obedience unto death that is received and confirmed by the Father. His trial is therefore complete. Having resisted sin to the point of shedding blood, even all the way to death (Heb 12:4), Jesus conquers sin. Having been disciplined by his Father—learning the full extent of obedience by his trial and suffering (Heb 5:8)—his humanity has come to share fully in God's holiness (Heb 12:10).

It should be remembered, however, that while Jesus, like the burnt offering, dies alone, he does not die for himself. The death he dies, he dies "for us," even in a way that includes "us." As I argued in the previous chapter, there is an inclusive element in Christ's substitutionary act.[51] In the slaughter of the offering, the death of the offeror was enacted symbolically. And the symbolic death of the offeror was a death to sin. By his offering, the offeror manifested his contrition, his will to die to sin and be made new.[52] The offeror comes confessing his sin—perhaps implicitly, in the case of the burnt offering—and thereby confessing that he deserves death.[53] Similarly, we, through the death of Jesus, are to count ourselves dead to sin and alive to God (Rom 6:11). The death of Christ is "for us" in that it marks not only his but also our freedom from the tyranny of sin and death. Through our identification with his death, we die, being crucified with Christ so that we might be raised to new life.

Though this inclusive sense of the "for us" is not always given much attention in our theologies of atonement, the New Testament is replete with

---

[51] The notion of inclusive place-taking is usually attributed to Hartmut Gese, "The Atonement," in *Essays on Biblical Theology*, trans. Keith Crim (repr., Eugene, OR: Wipf & Stock, 2018), 93-116. While I agree with Simon Gathercole that Scripture teaches that Christ's crucifixion for us was an act of exclusive place-taking, I argue here that there is nevertheless an inclusive element in his substitution. As Rom 6 says, we are crucified with Christ. When he dies for us, we somehow die with him. This is not the only way in which his death is for us. It is important to maintain that he undergoes something (divine judgment) that we do not and does it so that we do not have to. This is just to say that there are both inclusive and exclusive elements of Christ's substitutionary atoning work.

[52] The offeror will contradict this contrition by his ongoing sin. Still, his act of contrition would not have been entirely meaningless. It would have been the act of a broken and contrite heart, which marks all acceptable sacrifice in God's sight; see Ps 51:17.

[53] The sin and guilt offerings are more obviously offerings accompanied by confession, for in these the offeror realizes his guilt. That is, he has become aware that he has committed some transgression of divine positive law and brings an offering for compensation and cleansing. Nevertheless, if all I have said about the context of the burnt offering in these pages is basically right, then the offeror would necessarily be coming with an awareness of his need to be forgiven and renewed, and thus with a confession of sin in his heart if not on his lips.

statements that tie our freedom from sin's power to the death of Jesus Christ. "He himself bore our sins in his body on the tree, that we might die to sin and live to righteousness. By his wounds you have been healed" (1 Pet 2:24). "He died for all, that those who live might no longer live for themselves, but for him who for their sakes died and was raised" (2 Cor 5:15). In his death, we are made new (2 Cor 5:16-17). God condemned sin in the flesh of Christ so that we might walk "not according to the flesh but according to the Spirit" (Rom 8:4). We have "died to the law through the body of Christ," released from the sin and death that held us captive by the law, "so that we may serve in the new way of the Spirit" (Rom 7:4, 6). The burnt offering represented the promise of the offeror's renewal or restoration, and this renewal included the offeror's vicarious death in the offering. Thus Jesus Christ, our true burnt offering, died so that we could die and be made new with him.

Jesus' death for sin. That said, would the burnt offering also teach an exclusive sense of the "for us"? Does Jesus, by the burnt offering's logic, die as a sin-bearing substitute, suffering a cursed death in our place, so that we do not have to? While penal substitution may not be the most obvious or prominent feature of the burnt offering, I believe it has its place in this offering, and, with that, its place in the atoning work of Christ. Again, the context is decisive. The offeror, I argued in the previous chapter, stands before YHWH under the guilt and corruption of original sin, and yet he seeks what is ultimately a reentry into the garden-temple of the LORD. To gain that reentry, he must come to terms with the "law lying against [him]."[54] This law is put forth in God's word to Adam: "In the day that you eat of it you shall surely die" (Gen 2:17). It is "unthinkable" that this law would simply be repealed. A death has been threatened by God; the conditions for that death have tragically been met; the sentence of death must therefore be fulfilled, lest God be made a liar, inconsistent in character.[55]

This context, of course, applies not simply to the ritual of the burnt offering but universally. Everyone is summoned to appear before God, our Creator who made us for himself. And yet everyone lives under the sentence of death.

---

[54] Athanasius, *On the Incarnation: Greek Original and English Translation*, trans. John Behr, Popular Patristics Series 44a (Yonkers, NY: St. Vladimir's Seminary Press, 2011), sec. 10.
[55] Athanasius, *On the Incarnation* 8, 7.

If, then, in Jesus we find that the way has been opened, that we have been brought back to God through the death of the righteous for the unrighteous (1 Pet 3:18)—as the offeror was brought back through the death of his offering—it could only mean that in Jesus the law that demands our death, and demands it as the penalty for our transgression, has been fulfilled. Jesus Christ "fulfilled in death that which was required" for our restoration. While our restoration requires more than satisfying the "law lying against us," which hangs over us because of our sin, it does not require less. Christ, "by the sacrifice of His own body," put an end to "the law of death that barred our way."[56] Even though we still die, "we no longer do so as those condemned but as those who will arise." Because of Adam's sin, in which all share, "there was need of death, and death on behalf of all had to take place, so that what was required by all might occur." And this is the reason the Son took our place: that he might offer the sacrifice on behalf of us all, "delivering his own temple to death in place of all, in order to make all not liable to and free from the ancient transgression."[57]

This Athanasian logic, I believe, explains how it is that Christ's death frees us from the guilt of original sin and does so in a way that agrees with the witness of the burnt offering.[58] Athanasius knew well that the death of Christ was not *only* a satisfaction of our debt of punishment—it also cleansed us of sin's corruption (i.e., death), as he makes plain. Nevertheless, he has more than a little to say about Christ's fulfillment of our sentence of death in his own death. What is this if not penal substitution?

Following Athanasius's logic—which in my judgment is simply a biblical logic, one that arises from a good reading of the biblical narrative—we can read the burnt offering as a testimony to Christ's penal-substitutionary death. But that does not mean that penal substitution is the sum total of atonement.[59] Again, it is not all that Athanasius had to say about atonement,

---

[56] Athanasius, *On the Incarnation* 9-10; this is Archibald Robertson's translation in *A Select Library of Nicene and Post-Nicene Fathers of the Christian Church*, Second Series, ed. Philip Schaff and Henry Wace, vol. 4, *St. Athanasius: Select Works and Letters*, ed. Archibald Robertson (Buffalo, NY: Christian Literature, 1892).

[57] Athanasius, *On the Incarnation* 10, 20.

[58] In the preceding, I have not sought to reduce Athanasius's account to penal substitution. But I have tried to highlight how a penal element is present in his reading of the biblical narrative and to note how much explanatory power this penal element has in regard to Christ's death freeing us from a condemnatory death.

[59] We could say that Christ's penal substitution is a necessary but not sufficient condition for atonement.

and it is not all that the burnt offering has to say about atonement either. In fact, I do not believe it to be the *heart* or center of what the burnt offering has to say about atonement (though that does not necessarily mean it is not the heart of what the entire biblical witness says about Christ's atoning work).[60] What seems to satisfy God in Leviticus 1 is ultimately the devotion to God of a transformed creature, a creature not under the guilt and corruption of original sin and which he receives with delight. Atonement, at least according to the burnt offering, is incomplete without ascension.

Resurrection and Ascension

The burnt offering shows Levitical sacrifice to be a "multi-step process" or "sequence of events."[61] David Moffit has recently emphasized this point and has argued that the process is only complete when the offering is received by God; Levitical sacrifice is "a process whose center rests on bringing the material of sacrifice into God's presence."[62] Applied to the work of Christ, this means that Jesus' sacrifice is not complete until he ascends to heaven and enters the true, heavenly holy of holies, where he presents his resurrected humanity to God.[63] "The entry of Jesus into heaven with his resurrection life and the offering of himself before God there mark the time,

---

[60] Joshua McNall, *The Mosaic of Atonement: An Integrated Approach to Christ's Work* (Grand Rapids, MI: Zondervan, 2019), part 2. This type of claim is common among proponents of penal substitution. In my opinion, it would be better to identify the heart as the point I am stressing in this chapter, the eternal Son of God taking on flesh for us and our salvation.

[61] David M. Moffitt, *Rethinking the Atonement: New Perspectives on Jesus' Death, Resurrection, and Ascension* (Grand Rapids, MI: Baker Academic, 2022), 31.

[62] Moffitt, *Rethinking the Atonement*, 203.

[63] It interesting to note a commonality between Moffitt's "rethinking" of the atonement and the work of Colin Gunton. Gunton repeatedly pushes back against Augustine's moralization of sacrifice, which he perceives to be a distortion. He instead argues for what he considers a properly material view of sacrifice. In his account, God delights in sacrifice because it is the return of perfected creation to God in praise and gratitude. See Gunton, *The Actuality of Atonement: A Study of Metaphor, Rationality, and the Christian Tradition* (London: T&T Clark, 1988), 161, where he says that, in Jesus, "humanity pure and undefiled is brought to the Father as a concentrated offering of worship and praise." Also see his "The Sacrifice and the Sacrifices: From Metaphor to Transcendental?," in *Trinity, Incarnation, and Atonement: Philosophical and Theological Essays*, ed. Ronald J. Feenstra and Cornelius Plantinga Jr. (South Bend, IN: University of Notre Dame Press, 1989), 226: "The humanity of Christ is the concentrated—and so representative—offering through the Spirit of true humanity to the Father." Gunton's account thus squares well with Moffitt's reading of the Levitical cult (though it predates it by decades). And I suspect that Gunton's influence on this study is evident.

place, and agent of atonement," at least on Moffitt's reading of the epistle to the Hebrews.[64] Even though Moffitt is not commenting directly on the burnt offering in these statements, I believe what he says is relevant to our reading of the burnt offering and points us in the right direction.[65] In Leviticus 1, it is not until the smoke rises from the altar toward heaven that God expresses his delight in the offering. God's satisfaction, if we may refer to his reception of the offering by that term, is connected with the offering's ascension through the transforming fire. It thus seems that the work of atonement is completed only in this ascension and not before. So if, as I am arguing, the logic of the burnt offering applies to the work of Christ, then Christ's ascension is necessary to his atoning work.[66] Atonement is not complete until Christ rises from the dead and enters the heavenly places, where he is happily received by the Father. Only then has humanity returned to God through death. Only then is the atoning work of cleansing and compensation complete.

Transformation, ascension, and reception. In Khaled Anatolios's reading of Exodus, he argues that "the manifestation of divine glory is by no means a merely esthetic or 'mystical' sideshow to God's work of salvation; it is concretely constitutive of the work. In the Exodus account, the beholding of divine glory is not only the goal of salvation; it is also the way to salvation."[67] Something similar could be said of the burnt offering. The end of the burnt offering, as the end of the entire Levitical cult, is an encounter with divine glory in the beatific vision. But before that encounter can take place, there must be a transforming encounter with the theophanic fire on the altar. Morales speaks of the "ascension theology at the heart of Israel's understanding of atonement," according to which the Israelite offeror ascends heavenward with his burnt offering through the burning rite, which was a kind of

---

[64]Moffitt, *Rethinking the Atonement*, 97.
[65]In the statements I have cited, Moffitt is addressing the entire movement of the Levitical cult considered as a whole. As I see the burnt offering as paradigmatic for the entire cult, and as gathering up the other offerings in its own movement, I have no problem with applying what he says about the cult as a whole to the burnt offering.
[66]In Lk 24:26, Jesus rebukes the disciples on the road to Emmaus for not understanding that it is "necessary that the Christ should suffer and on the third day rise from the dead." While Christian theology has tended to focus on the necessity of the suffering, and perhaps for good reason, Scripture confirms that the resurrection and ascension were no less necessary to the work of Christ.
[67]Anatolios, *Deification Through the Cross*, 104.

vicarious consecration.⁶⁸ The envelopment of his offering in the consecrating flame of the altar held out to the offeror the promise of his own consecration that would issue in his ascension, his entrance into the heavenly places.

Similarly, the Christian is made alive with Christ, raised with Christ, and seated with Christ in the heavenly places (Eph 2:5-6). In Christ's glorification, we have the certainty of our own: we shall "bear the image of the man of heaven" and be made to possess life immortal and imperishable by virtue of his resurrection and ascension (1 Cor 15:49). This is the victory over sin and death we have in Christ. Being transformed in and through the transformation of Christ, we live now in anticipation of final glorification and beatific vision. This is the end of atonement.

We can say with Moffitt, then, that Christ's sacrificial and atoning work is complete only when, similar to the burnt offering, Christ is received into heaven.⁶⁹ Again, it is in the ascension of the offering that divine satisfaction is expressed; it is in its ascension that the offering is finally and fully accepted for the offeror to make atonement for the offeror (Lev 1:4). So it is in Christ's ascension that he is accepted as our atoning offering, and satisfaction for sins is made. But if that is so, a crucial question must be answered: *Why* does ascension make satisfaction?

Christ's heavenly offering. The question may come down to what precisely is being received by God in Christ's ascension. What does Jesus present to God in the heavenly places? To return to Moffitt, he answers that it is a resurrected human life that is offered and received for atonement. "The offering of blood in the Mosaic cult did not symbolize the entry and presentation of death before the presence of God. This was instead an offering of life. In the same way, Hebrews' emphasis on Jesus' living presence

---

⁶⁸Michael L. Morales, "Atonement in Ancient Israel: The Whole Burnt Offering as Central to Israel's Cult," in *So Great a Salvation: A Dialogue on the Atonement in Hebrews*, ed. Jon C. Laansma, George H. Guthrie, and Cynthia Long Westfall, Library of New Testament Studies 516 (London: T&T Clark, 2019), 36.

⁶⁹It is worth noting with Douglas Farrow that the heaven to which Jesus ascends in Hebrews is a created realm. It is "not God's own place, which is simply God himself. . . . The heaven to which Hebrews refers, though not part of this world, is the place from which God's rule over this world is effected through the angels." It is, in other words, a created realm in which constitutes something like God's throne from which he guides and governs his creatures, to which he will glorify his redeemed. Douglas Farrow, *Ascension Theology* (London: Bloomsbury T&T Clark), 124.

in heaven ... implies that it is not the death/slaughter of Jesus that atones but the presentation of his life before God in the holy of holies."[70] Moffitt's reasoning is, of course, following the logic of the sin offering, especially the one that was slaughtered on the Day of Atonement, and his understanding of how Hebrews applies that logic to Christ. But a very similar logic might be seen to be at work in the burnt offering. The fire of the altar, I argued in the previous chapter, was not destructive but transformative. By it the offering was consumed, to be sure, but consumed in a manner that brought the offering into the heavenly sphere. The burning was not the end of the offering, then, but its exaltation.

Similarly, Moffitt would argue, we might understand that it is the exalted life of this offering that is received by God, testifying to Jesus Christ making atoning by virtue of his glorified, exalted, spiritual, and imperishable humanity. What satisfies God is his reception of Jesus' perfected humanity.[71] Here is a human being in heaven, cleansed forever by its reception into eternal life, able to compensate for the sin of the world because it has fulfilled God's purposes for creation and covenant.[72] In this man, God's will for humanity is realized, and this offering, once received, becomes the mediator of blessing to all who are in him, the means by which they will be perfected.[73]

While there is plenty of truth in this reading of Jesus' heavenly offering, I believe it is missing something essential. R. B. Jamieson has (appreciatively) critiqued Moffitt's thesis. Yes, Christ presents his offering in heaven after his ascension, according to Hebrews. But what he presents is not simply his life but his life-given-in-death. As much as Hebrews might make of Christ's ascension, and his priesthood by virtue of indestructible life, it is equally concerned with his death. Jamieson argues that Jesus' blood is a metonym for his death in Hebrews, or more technically for the life-for-life exchange that took place in sacrificial slaughter. He also emphasizes the clear statement of Hebrews 9:22, "without the shedding of blood there is no forgiveness,"

---

[70] Moffitt, *Rethinking the Atonement*, 97-98.
[71] Cf. Gunton, *Actuality of Atonement*, 161; Gunton, "Sacrifice and the Sacrifices," 226.
[72] Recall that association with death, or cycles of mortality, is the principle of uncleanness in the priestly worldview.
[73] Cf. Eugene Masure, *The Christian Sacrifice: The Sacrifice of Christ Our Head* (London: Burns, Oates & Washbourne, 1944), 47.

and what is the shedding of blood but death? What these words mean, he continues, is that "the giving of life in death is necessary for forgiveness . . . that death is integral to what makes blood a medium of atonement." The life that Jesus offers in the heavenly places is a life that has gone through death, and, according to Hebrews, it would not be able to make atonement if it had not done so. "As the material Jesus offers in heaven, his blood presents to God what his death achieved. Jesus' death-for-others is what makes his blood atoning; his blood atones by bearing his life-given-for-others to God."[74]

Jamieson, life Moffitt, is mainly following the logic of the sin offering that was slaughtered and presented on the Day of Atonement. But, again, I believe his thinking can and should be applied to the burnt offering and its witness to the atoning work of Christ. If, by the logic of the burnt offering, the humanity that Jesus presents is perfected, it is perfected only because it has died *to sin*. And if that exalted humanity is able to make atonement for others, to secure their place with him in the heavenly places, it can do so only because it has died *for sins*—only because, on their behalf, it has satisfied the divine promise that the wages of sin is death. In Hebrews 7:28, we read that Jesus is "a Son who has been made perfect forever." This perfection, on the basis of which he serves as high priest, is clearly connected with his being "exalted above the heavens." Nevertheless, that exaltation and perfection does not happen apart from his suffering and death. Jesus was in some sense made perfect through suffering (Heb 2:10), and it was "through death that he . . . destroy[ed] the one who has the power of death" and therefore made resurrection possible (Heb 2:14). Later, we read that Jesus was "made perfect" only as "he learned obedience through what he suffered" (Heb 5:9).

While Hebrews teaches that atonement depends on Christ's exaltation, it also reveals "an effective soteriological connection between Christ's death and subsequent exaltation."[75] If atonement depends on Jesus' exaltation, Jesus' exaltation depends on his death. God the Son, who for a little while was made lower than the angels by the assumption of our flesh, has triumphantly returned to God in that flesh by virtue of his obedience unto

---

[74]R. B. Jamieson, *Jesus' Death and Heavenly Offering in Hebrews* (Cambridge: Cambridge University Press, 2019), 166-68.
[75]Jamieson, *Jesus' Death and Heavenly Offering*, 169.

death, passing *through* death by maintaining faithful sonship in the face of death, and thereby bringing many sons to glory (Heb 2:10), sons "who have been sanctified through the offering of the body of Jesus once and for all" (Heb 10:10).

Exaltation, sonship, and atonement. As I stated earlier, Jesus' death is the completion of his trial. His is a death to sin that is not merely followed by exaltation but issues forth into exaltation, even *merits* exaltation, because it completes and seals his filial obedience.[76] Jesus' death *to* sin, once for all, is the basis of his own perfection and exaltation—he was made perfect through suffering (Heb 2:10). His death *for* sin—not his own but for the "many"—is the basis of the perfection and exaltation of those sanctified by his self-offering, allowing them to participate in his own sanctification by compensating for the guilt of original sin. The Christ who presents himself for our atonement in the heavenly places has been perfected by his suffering and resurrection alike, Hebrews seems to be telling us. Proving to be the faithful Son in his suffering, God has made him superior to the angels and coronated him as Son, whose throne is forever (Heb 1:5-9).[77]

In a 1944 book titled *The Christian Sacrifice*, Catholic theologian Eugene Masure calls attention to the way in which Christ's offering of humiliation and exaltation is rooted in his identity. As incarnate Son, Christ presents the atoning sacrifice "by following the law of his own being, that of returning to the Father." The Son's glorification, he argues, "is essential to His sacrifice." "The Son keeps in His humanity His eternal attitude, His single unvarying direction πρὸς τὸν θεόν." He does this while offering our sacrifice, as our head, and so "He had like us to approach the Father by the winding path which sin had made." His return to the Father will therefore come by way of a death for sins. Nevertheless, the incarnate Son's return to the Father is certain from the moment he takes up our flesh. His incarnate return "was a sort of replica of that immeasurable activity in which

---

[76]In the Reformed tradition, Christ's exaltation is typically seen as "a reward that he accomplished as the Servant of the Lord in the days of his humiliation." Christ "definitely merited something for himself" by his obedience, and "he also really obtained it in his exaltation" (Bavinck, *Reformed Dogmatics*, 3:433).

[77]Jamieson speaks of "the paradox of sonship" in Hebrews. This paradox is that the one who is eternally Son *becomes* Son through his obedience, death, and exaltation. See R. B. Jamieson, *The Paradox of Sonship: Christology in the Epistle to the Hebrews* (Downers Grove, IL: IVP Academic, 2021).

in the bosom of the Trinity the divine life flows back from the Son to the Father." As Jesus presents his offering, "the Father welcomes in a triumphal embrace His Christ, who is His glory, His love and His good pleasure [as] He is His Son eternally."[78] The exaltation of Christ is the perfection or completion (as in telos, not terminus) of the Son's incarnation. It is simultaneously the completion of his atoning work. Here again, we see a correlation between atoning sacrifice and incarnate divine sonship. It is by living out his filial divine identity in our flesh, even while bearing our sins, that Christ makes atonement.

In other words, Jesus Christ has made atonement by an offering of filial satisfaction. God is satisfied by the presentation of the Son's humanity as it has made its return to God through death. As incarnate Son, Jesus has passed the test, honoring all the demands of covenant, fulfilling the goal of creation, and devoting himself to God in absolute consecration. He has done all of this consummately in his death. Therefore, God has exalted him, raising him up in the flesh, and receiving that glorified flesh as the principle of cleansing and compensation for our sins. The Son's humanity, received by God to make atonement for us, is perfected by its suffering and exaltation alike. By faith in Christ, we share in that perfection. By faith, Christ's death *to* sin becomes *our* death to sin, *our* decisive renunciation of sin and the power by which sin is (progressively but assuredly) put to death in us.[79] And by Christ's death *for* sins, we are released from the penalty of sin, that we might be accepted by God.[80] Therefore, we share also in Christ's

---

[78]Masure, *Christian Sacrifice*, 166, 50, 144, 154, 147, 150.

[79]Here I am thinking of Augustine's statement that Christ's death is both an exemplar and a sacrament of our death: an exemplar of the death of our "outer man," a sacrament of the death of our "inner man" (*On the Trinity* 4.6). Aquinas, too, speaks of Christ's death as a sacrament and example, arguing that Christ willed to die "that his death might be for us not only a remedy of satisfaction but also a sacrament of salvation, so that we, transferred to a spiritual life, might die to our carnal life, in the likeness of His death." And Christ also "wished to die that His death might be an example of perfect virtue for us" (Aquinas, *Compendium of Theology* 227).

[80]Scholars debate whether Aquinas held to something like penal-substitutionary atonement, and applying that Peterson label to him may be anachronistic. Nevertheless, he clearly held that Christ suffered a penalty and we are thereby released from that penalty. "Christ willed to submit to death for our sins so that, in taking on Himself without any fault of His own the punishment charged against us, He might free us from the death to which we had been sentenced, in the way that anyone would be freed from a debt of penalty if another person undertook to pay the penalty for him" (*Compendium of Theology* 227). For a good treatment of whether Aquinas was a forerunner of penal-substitutionary atonement, see Brandon Peterson, "Paving the Way?

exaltation and glorification. By virtue of our union with Christ, God receives our cleansed humanity, for whose sins Christ has made compensation, when he receives Jesus Christ. In this way, Christ brings many sons to glory (Heb 2:10). In this way, Christ's flesh is our new and living way to God (Heb 10:20).

As Christ's sacrificial work is a process, a sequence of events, so there is atoning virtue throughout the sequence of incarnation, testing, death, and exaltation. At each point, that virtue is supplied by Christ's divine sonship, more specifically the union of the Son's eternal filiation with his human nature. Because the Son lives out his eternal relation to the Father in our flesh, he renews our humanity, passes our test, dies for our sins, and raises us up with himself to glory. With this, the Father is pleased. Satisfaction for sin and the perfection of our nature—in other words, the healing of original sin—are complete when the Father receives the incarnate Son as a pleasing aroma, the Son of his eternal delight. In other words, by fulfilling the telos of our nature through "the whole course of his obedience," Jesus Christ satisfies the terms of our creation, the calling to sonship that God has placed on us from our beginning.[81] "Christ's work is indeed an act of satisfaction," says Adam Johnson, "but one that brings to fullness and completion the plan of God for his creatures: his intention to share with us the divine life."[82] This is what is meant by "filial satisfaction."

And this, I argue, is what the burnt offering means for the Christian doctrine of atonement. The burnt offering preaches the good news of atonement through the entire sequence of events that constitute the life, death, and resurrection of Jesus Christ. In the incarnate Son, there is satisfaction for sins, as God receives something (the perfected humanity of Christ) that negates the debt of sin. In him, there is cleansing, as Christ passes the test and utterly consecrates himself to God in our flesh. In him, there is propitiation, as the Father rejoices in the Son's self-offering and consequently

---

Penalty and Atonement in Thomas Aquinas' Soteriology," *International Journal of Systematic Theology* 15, no. 3 (July 2013): 265-83.

[81]Calvin, *Institutes* 2.16.5.

[82]Adam J. Johnson, *Atonement: A Guide for the Perplexed* (London: Bloomsbury T&T Clark, 2015), 132. Johnson later adds helpfully: "the work of Christ was aimed above all at bringing to completion God's creative purposes as reaffirmed in the history of the covenants and promises God made to his people Israel."

relents of his judgment against us. In him, there is victory, as humanity has conquered sin and death. In him, there is restoration to new life, as those in Christ are freed from the burden of original sin. And in him there is redemption, as human beings in Christ are received and repossessed by God, and as they are now willing and able to acknowledge him as their origin and end. To sum it up: in the incarnate Son, there is atonement.

Conclusion

THE AIM OF THIS STUDY has been to make a contribution to the doctrine of atonement by way of a theological exegesis of the instructions for the burnt offering in Leviticus 1. This conclusion will state what that contribution is.

First, there is a methodological contribution. The exegesis found in these pages offers a close reading of the prescriptions for the burnt offering that draws heavily on the narrative context of Leviticus. Levitical sacrifice, I have argued, constituted the enactment of a narrative: a sequence of ritual actions that recalled the mighty acts of YHWH in the exodus and enacted the theology revealed by those acts. This study has accordingly considered Levitical sacrifice to be telling a story and has found it useful to make ad hoc use of some of the categories of narrative analysis in its exposition of Leviticus 1. Perhaps there is some small contribution in that; these categories may illumine the theology of the Levitical cult in a fresh way.

The more significant methodological contribution, however, lies in the decision to take the burnt offering seriously as an *atoning* offering. This study has made an effort to discern a coherent logic of atonement in the action of the burnt offering. In other words, it has proceeded under the assumption that the burnt offering tells its own story of atonement and that that story should be heard as a witness to the atoning work of Christ. Even if scholars disagree with the particular reading of the burnt offering I have put forward, I believe I have demonstrated that this approach to the Levitical cult is legitimate. Levitical sacrifice was not illogical, nor is its logic completely hidden from those without firsthand experience of its rituals; it is possible to discern at least something of the logic of the burnt offering through the text of Leviticus.[1] More specifically, it is possible to discern a mechanism of atonement in the burnt offering and then to see how that mechanism shows up in the life, death, and resurrection of Jesus Christ.[2]

I happily admit that the burnt offering does not tell the *whole* story of atonement. It is not even the whole story of atonement in the Levitical cult, since the sin and guilt offerings obviously have a lot to tell us about atonement as well. However, here I will suggest that as the sin and guilt offerings were accompanied by the burnt offering, and even to some degree swept up into the larger movement of the burnt offering, so the sin and guilt offerings should be read both *with* and *in light of* the burnt offering.[3] The three atoning offerings of Leviticus are complementary, each making atonement in different ways and on different occasions, while together serving the same end: requalifying Israel for the presence and service of YHWH. But if there is a certain primacy of the burnt offering in the Levitical cult, as I argued in chapter four, then perhaps the burnt offering should also be given a certain primacy in our understanding of atonement in the Levitical cult. The logic of atonement in the sin and guilt offerings might be understood within the framework of the logic of atonement found in the burnt offering. This is only a suggestion; more work on all three of these offerings would be necessary before this argument can be taken more seriously. This suggestion may point the way, however, to a fuller understanding of atonement in the Levitical cult (and, by extension, in the work of Christ).

In addition to these methodological contributions, I believe there is a *material* contribution in this study: the particular reading of the burnt offering it has offered. I have argued that the instructions for the burnt offering contain an account of atonement through a movement of testing,

---

[1] I again call attention to the valuable argument of Stephen R. Holmes, "Death in the Afternoon: Hebrews, Sacrifice, and Soteriology," in *The Epistle to the Hebrews and Christian Theology*, ed. Richard Bauckham et al. (Grand Rapids, MI: Eerdmans, 2009), that the meaning of Levitical sacrifice is capable of being mediating through the biblical text.

[2] My assumption is that this is the case in the sin and guilt offerings as well. It may be possible to discern a discrete mechanism of atonement in these offerings, too, so that we are able to hear more of what the cult has to say about the work of Christ.

[3] Recall that Morales sees the sin and guilt offerings as being "pre-fixed" to the burnt offering. Michael L. Morales, "Atonement in Ancient Israel: The Whole Burnt Offering as Central to Israel's Cult," in *So Great a Salvation: A Dialogue on the Atonement in Hebrews*, ed. Jon C. Laansma, George H. Guthrie, and Cynthia Long Westfall, Library of New Testament Studies 516 (London: T&T Clark, 2019), 27-39.

substitution, death, transformation, and reception. The offering, whose very being is conformed to the Word of God (and thus clean), takes the place of the offeror. It is tested, dies to and for sin, is transformed by the divine fire on the altar, and is then received into the heavenly places. Indeed, the LORD receives this offering as a pleasing aroma—a phrase I have argued denotes divine satisfaction. This satisfaction is marked by legal, aesthetic, and teleological elements: legal, in that it means the fulfillment of God's law; aesthetic, in that it elicits God's delight, as the offering reflects the filial movement and mode of being of God's beloved Son; and teleological, as the perfected offering and its reception into God's holy presence represents the fulfillment of God's purposes for creation. Thus, as the offeror participates in his offering's return to God through death, atonement (which consists of both cleansing and compensation) is made. Cleansing is effected as the offeror shares in his offering's conformity to the Word of God and sanctifying transformation by the Spirit. And compensation is made as the offering is received on the offeror's behalf as the fulfillment of God's intentions for creation—in other words, as a representation of the perfection (as in, reaching one's telos) that the offeror truly owes to God. Notably, on this reading, atonement is not fully complete until the reception of the offering in the heavens. Correspondingly, we are led to an account of atonement that highlights the importance of the entire incarnate mission of the Son, from his assumption of human nature, to his testing and death, all the way to his exaltation in heaven. This is part of the contribution the burnt offering makes to our doctrine of atonement: a strong statement that it is the entire movement of the incarnate Son back to God through death that makes atonement for us.

I have used the phrase "filial satisfaction" to summarize this atoning movement present in the burnt offering—and, by way of fulfillment, in the self-offering of Christ. The key idea is that Christ, through his filial obedience, fulfills the human vocation and makes satisfaction by offering a perfected humanity to God in the heavenly temple. The satisfaction, in its legal, aesthetic, and teleological aspects, is bound up with the recapitulation of humanity in the incarnate Son. Indeed, true sonship is precisely what Jesus Christ has offered in his life and death. Christ fulfills the movement and logic of the burnt offering by proving, throughout "the whole course of his obedience," to be the true Son of God.[4] And he does so in a way that reflects the truth of his eternal sonship, his distinctive mode of being as the Second Person of the Trinity, eternally begotten of the Father. The Son's eternal generation from the Father is the archetype of the Levitical offeror, an act that is mirrored in a creaturely way by the essential act of sacrifice (if it may be called that), the act of reception and return. This, I have argued, is what makes it fitting that the Son, in particular, became incarnate for us and our salvation.

Relatedly, I have argued that, according to the logic of the burnt offering, it is the incarnation that should be considered essential to the mechanism of atonement.[5] By communicating his filial mode of existence, by which he exists from and to the Father, to his humanity—and by living out this mode of existence in his humanity, constantly recognizing God as his origin and end—the Son does all that is necessary to make atonement. He fulfills every demand of creation, covenant, and consecration as he enacts the truth of his eternal sonship in human flesh. The filial obedience of Christ includes his death *to* sin and *for* sin, a reminder that his obedience was offered to God under the conditions of the economy—that is, in our place and on our behalf as sinners. But even that death is a distinctly filial act of obedience, as the Son entrusts himself to his Father while he breathes his last (Lk 23:46). It is the Son's communication to his human nature of his distinctive mode of subsistence, defined by his eternal generation, that gives his self-offering its atoning virtue.

This, I believe, is a contribution to our understanding of the mechanism of atonement. In these pages, I have highlighted the role of Christ's sonship in the satisfaction he makes to God on our behalf. Doing so has in turn allowed me to highlight the aesthetic and teleological aspects of that satisfaction (without, I hope, denigrating the judicial). Christ makes satisfaction

---

[4]John Calvin, *Institutes of the Christian Religion*, ed. John T. McNeill, trans. Ford Lewis Battles (Louisville, KY: Westminster John Knox, 1960), 2.16.5.

[5]As I have said above, I do not mean that the incarnation in itself, the initial act of the Son's assumption of humanity, is sufficient for atonement. With Brandon Crowe, I could say that "it is not the mere *fact* of the incarnation that accomplishes salvation but the *actions* of the Son of God in his incarnate state." Crowe, *The Last Adam: A Theology of the Obedient Life of Jesus in the Gospels* (Grand Rapids, MI: Baker Academic, 2017), 202. My intention is to highlight that the atoning efficacy of Jesus' actions (his obedience-unto-death and resurrection) is supplied by the incarnation of the Son.

for sin by repaying all that sin had taken away—God's "possession" of humanity as sons and daughters who reflect his goodness and character, and God's intentions to lavish on us an eternal inheritance of glory as we behold his face.[6] This account, I believe, fills out the notion of satisfaction in a helpful manner, as it relates satisfaction more to the "sum total of God's perfections."[7]

Perhaps more important, though, is the way in which this account locates the efficacy of Christ's work in his person. The heart of Christ's atoning work lies in his eternal sonship, his eternal act of being begotten of the Father. In my judgment, identifying the union of this sonship with Christ's humanity gives a coherent answer to the question of *how* exactly Christ saves us from our sins, which is surely part of the function of the doctrine of atonement. It also gives a pleasing sense of integrity to Christian theology, as it grounds the story of our salvation squarely in our theology, the confession of God as Father, Son, and Spirit—and surely we would want this too. But, importantly, it does all of this without "solving" the mystery of atonement, that is, without explaining away the incomprehensible and divine nature of the atonement. Rather, it elucidates the mystery of atonement while inviting us deeper into the central mystery of our faith: the mystery of the blessed triune life of God.[8]

To trace all our thinking and acting back to this mystery is the vocation of theology. If nothing else, then, I hope that this study has encouraged that kind of theological reflection. For in the end, what else could be hoped for? To contemplate atonement is to be led deeper into the mystery of the triune glory of God. And beholding the riches of that glory is not only the theologian's vocation but the Christian's hope. This hope is ours because of Jesus Christ, the Son of God, and our true burnt offering. Thanks be to God.

---

[6]Trevor Hart, *In Him Was Life: The Person and Work of Christ* (Waco, TX: Baylor University Press, 2019), 140.

[7]Kevin J. Vanhoozer, "Redemption Accomplished: Atonement," in *The Oxford Handbook of Reformed Theology*, ed. Michael Allen and Scott R. Swain (Oxford: Oxford University Press, 2020), 488.

[8]Thomas Weinandy, *Does God Suffer?* (Notre Dame, IN: University of Notre Dame Press, 2000), 36.

Appendix

Leviticus, Sacrifice, and Atonement

A (Very) Selective History

Thinking about atonement means thinking about sacrifice. The history of the doctrine of atonement proves the point. This short history highlights some of the developments and disputes in the church's reading of Levitical sacrifice (especially those concerning the doctrine of penal-substitutionary atonement, which came to be the most contentious issue in the church's understanding of Levitical sacrifice) and the consequences for the doctrine of atonement.

Patristic Precedent

It could only be expected that Levitical sacrifice, the primary background for the New Testament authors' understanding of sacrifice, would play a prominent role in the defense and development of the church's doctrine of atonement.[1] And, from the beginning, it has. The early church forcefully

---

[1] In an important essay on the topic, B. B. Warfield, writing at a time when theorizing on religious sacrifice was very much en vogue, noted that "the idea of sacrifice in general, conceived as a world-wide mode of worship" often plays too large a role in our efforts to understand what the NT says about sacrifice. Like Warfield, I consider this to be a mistake. The NT authors "work out the correspondence between [Jesus'] death and the different forms of Old Testament sacrifice. They show that a different acts of the Old Testament sacrificial ritual were repeated in Christ's experience." They do not, on the other hand, seem concerned to relate the death of Jesus to any particular pagan view of sacrifice. It is the OT, then, that grounds the NT use of sacrificial imagery and language. See B. B. Warfield, "Christ Our Sacrifice," in *The Person and Work of Christ*, ed. Samuel G. Craig (Phillipsburg, NJ: Presbyterian & Reformed, 1950), 392-94. This is not to say that the Levitical system was the *only* influence on the NT authors' view of sacrifice. Jarvis Williams, for example, argues that the account of "sacrificial" martyrdom in 4 Maccabees

asserted the typological relationship between Levitical sacrifice and the death of Christ, particularly in its apology to the Jews. In his *Dialogue with Trypho*, Justin Martyr argues that while all the cultic ceremonies of Israel were commanded on account of their hardness of heart (*Dialogue with Trypho* 43), they nevertheless prefigured Christ and his church. Not only, he claims, did the two goats offered on the Day of Atonement declare Christ as "an offering for all sinners willing to repent" (40), but the offering of fine flour too proclaimed Christ by prefiguring the bread of the Eucharist by which the church remembers his suffering (41). After the death and resurrection of Christ, Justin argues further, it is the Eucharist and prayers of Christians that God accepts as pleasing sacrifices, not the offerings of the Jews, which have been fulfilled and replaced (their doctrine of sacrifice being "corrected") in Christ and his body (117).[2]

Irenaeus, following a similar line of argument, calls Christ the "final cause" of the Mosaic law—that is, the goal or purpose of the law, which fulfills it, a statement Irenaeus saw as necessary for maintaining the unity of the two Christian testaments (*Against Heresies* 4.12.4). "It would be endless," Irenaeus states, "to recount the occasions upon which the Son of God is shown forth by Moses" (4.10.1). God, the self-same God as revealed in Jesus Christ, appointed the Levitical legislation, but not for his own sake, as Israel should have recognized. He did not need their oblations, nor was he propitiated by them (4.17.1). Rather, he meant to direct them by those rites to the true sacrifice, the obedience offered to God by Jesus Christ, by which God *is* appeased (4.17.2) and by imitation of which Christians present their own pleasing sacrifices to God (4.18).

In making these arguments, the early church was not only claiming the Old Testament as its own, a claim of no small importance for Christian doctrine, but was also establishing Levitical sacrifice as a major paradigm through which to understand the saving work of Christ, working out an

---

influenced Paul's conception of Jesus' atoning sacrifice. See Williams, *Maccabean Martyr Traditions in Paul's Theology of Atonement: Did Martyr Theology Shape Paul's Conception of Jesus' Death?* (Eugene, OR: Wipf & Stock, 2010). But the Maccabean depiction of martyrdom as an atoning sacrifice was itself deeply influenced by the Levitical system. And my claim here is that the Levitical system, and developments of understanding thereof evident in the OT canon, remains the *primary* background for NT presentation of sacrifice, even if not the only relevant background.

[2]Jaroslav Pelikan, *The Christian Tradition: A History of the Development of Doctrine*, vol. 1, *The Emergence of the Catholic Tradition (100-600)* (Chicago: University of Chicago Press, 1971), 15.

understanding of typology that subsequent generations of theologians would assume.³

SACRIFICE AND SATISFACTION IN MEDIEVAL THEOLOGY

By the fourth century, sacrifice was the "dominant" soteriological image in the East and West alike.⁴ And especially in the West, it began to be aligned more consistently with a certain way of thinking about atonement. Hilary, probably the first theologian to apply the term *satisfaction* to the death of Christ, linked sacrifice with satisfaction.⁵ Christ's death, he states, was "voluntarily undertaken to satisfy a penal obligation." And this he did by "offering Himself voluntarily as a victim to God the Father."⁶ While Hilary's association with sacrifice and satisfaction may seem perfectly natural to many readers, the significance of this move is difficult to overstate. "Here first in the history of theology," states R. S. Franks, "the concept of satisfaction, and not merely the concept but the term itself, definitely appears as a rational interpretation of the idea of sacrifice."⁷ While the notion of sacrifice remained flexible, capable of being understood to effect propitiation of God, cleansing from sin, the expulsion of evil forces, and so on, it was beginning to become more definitely associated with the idea of satisfaction.⁸

By the Middle Ages, the association of sacrifice with satisfaction had only grown stronger, as the major works of the period show. Anselm, for

---

³To be sure, Justin, Irenaeus, and many other early Christian theologians held that God instituted Levitical sacrifice as an accommodation. It was the golden calf incident, which proved Israel's stubborn proclivity to idolatry, that led to God's institution of the sacrificial system as a way for Israel to redirect her idolatrous impulses toward himself. This is a view that has been popular for centuries; Maimonides, for example, takes it in his *Guide for the Perplexed* 3.32.

On the early church claiming the Old Testament as its own, see Pelikan, *Christian Tradition*, 1:19. Pelikan references Justin Martyr's statement in his *Dialogue with Trypho*, "The Scriptures [of the OT] are much more ours than yours. For we let ourselves be persuaded by them, while you read them, without grasping their true import."

⁴J. N. D. Kelly, *Early Christian Doctrines*, rev. ed. (San Francisco: Harper & Row, 1978), 384-86.

⁵Pelikan, *Christian Tradition*, 1:147. See also Kelly, *Early Christian Doctrines*, 388: "Hilary must be regarded as one of the pioneers of the theology of satisfaction."

⁶As cited in R. S. Franks, *The Work of Christ: A Historical Study of Christian Doctrine* (New York: Thomas Nelson and Sons, 1962), 82.

⁷Franks, *Work of Christ*, 85. Franks explains that Hilary's idea of satisfaction was not necessarily shared by all other theologians. Notably, it was not shared by Tertullian. He adds, however, that the notion of satisfaction in the Western tradition may not be as uniform or as tidy as we are prone to think. At least two streams of thoughts appear side by side and are often conflated, that of satisfaction as "a merit which pays a debt" and as "a substituted punishment" (86).

⁸Frances Young, *Sacrifice and the Death of Christ* (repr., Eugene, OR: Wipf & Stock, 2009), 91.

instance, may not have employed the vocabulary of sacrifice all that often, but the argument of his *Cur Deus Homo* depends on a sacrificial substructure, in which something is offered to God to meet a divine demand and effect reconciliation.[9] Jaroslav Pelikan, in fact, sees one of Anselm's chief contributions to be his translation "of the biblical and liturgical image of sacrifice—that the redemption of mankind by Christ was an act addressed to God, not the devil—into a form that was compatible with the immutability of God." For Anselm, Pelikan states, satisfaction was "another term for sacrifice."[10]

The conceptual overlap between sacrifice and satisfaction may not be as complete in later medieval theologians, but it is nonetheless significant. According to Franciscan theologian Bonaventure, through his "fully satisfactory obedience," Christ "offered for God's appeasement a fully satisfactory sacrifice."[11] It is the same with the great Dominican doctor, Thomas Aquinas. "A sacrifice properly so called," Thomas states, "is something done for that honor which is properly due to God, in order to appease Him. . . . Therefore it is manifest that Christ's passion was a true sacrifice."[12] This appeasement, he explains, ultimately comes by way of charity: as a voluntary offering undertaken on behalf of humankind, Christ's Passion manifested the perfect love that fulfills the Mosaic law in both its moral and ceremonial aspects.[13] While Thomas's commentary on Hebrews 10 shows how rich and varied his understanding of sacrifice could be, satisfaction was undoubtedly central to that understanding.[14]

---

[9] Asle Eikrem, *God as Sacrificial Love: A Systematic Exploration of a Controversial Notion* (London: Bloomsbury T&T Clark, 2018), 19-23.

[10] Jaroslav Pelikan, *The Christian Tradition*, vol. 3, *The Growth of Medieval Theology (600–1300)* (Chicago: University of Chicago Press, 1978), 139, 143. Cf. Eikrem, *God as Sacrificial Love*, 23. For Anselm, Eikrem states, "sacrifice achieves satisfaction."

[11] Bonaventure, *Breviloquium*, trans. Dominic V. Monti, OFM, Works of St. Bonaventure 9 (Saint Bonaventure, NY: Franciscan Institute, 2005), 4.9.3.

[12] Thomas Aquinas, *The Summa Theologiae of St. Thomas Aquinas*, trans. Fathers of the English Dominican Province, 2nd rev. ed. (London: Burns, Oates & Washbourne, 1920–1922), 3.48.3, rev. and ed. for New Advent by Kevin Knight, www.newadvent.org/summa/.

[13] Matthew Levering, *Christ's Fulfillment of Torah and Temple: Salvation According to Thomas Aquinas* (Notre Dame, IN: University of Notre Dame Press, 2002), 53-61.

[14] Thomas Aquinas, *Commentary on the Letter of Saint Paul to the Hebrews*, ed. J. Mortensen and E. Alarcón, trans. F. R. Larcher, OP, in *Biblical Commentaries*, vol. 41, *Latin/English Edition of the Works of St. Thomas Aquinas* (Lander, WY: Aquinas Institute for the Study of Sacred Doctrine, 2012), 209-22.

From the statements considered here, we can see that all three of these medieval theologians are conceiving of Christ's sacrifice as an essentially positive offering, not merely a negation.[15] Sacrifice satisfies, according to this way of thinking, because of what is given to God, not simply by what is taken away from the offeror or suffered by the victim. As Aquinas states, "He properly atones [Latin: *satisfacit*] for an offense who offers something which the offended loves equally, or even more than he detested the offense."[16] However, the conceptual work that allows sacrifice and satisfaction to be viewed in more negative terms, as essentially a penal infliction, was already underway during this period. In Franciscan theologian Alexander of Hales, a penitential understanding of satisfaction is evident, in which satisfaction is conceived of as a "voluntary endurance of punishment," wherein the penitent "punishes himself and offers to God the gift of his self-humiliation and austerity." This proves an important and lasting complement to, and eventually modification of, the Anselmic doctrine. "No sin is reduced to order," Alexander states, "except in punishment." Therefore, "satisfaction for sin ought to be penal and afflictive.... The redemption of man ought to be by a walk in the way not of prosperity, but of penal adversity." Satisfaction, on this understanding, is therefore "at once a positive gift and a passive endurance, not merely a positive gift only as in Anselm."[17] What is new here is not the notion of penal suffering in the passion and death of Christ (which, as we saw, was present in Hilary) but the clarity with which penalty is related to satisfaction. It is now easier to conceive the debt of sin being erased not by a gift meeting or exceeding that debt but by a substituted infliction of penalty. And it is conceivable, given the nature of the relationship forged between satisfaction and sacrifice, to understand sacrifice as a penal substitution.

PENAL-SUBSTITUTIONARY SACRIFICE IN THE REFORMATION

While sacrifice and the satisfaction it makes for sin continued to be put in terms of homage and worship in later Roman Catholic theology, the

---

[15]Levering, *Christ's Fulfillment*, 56.
[16]Aquinas, *Summa Theologiae* 3.48.2; cf. Levering's translation in *Christ's Fulfillment*, 57n22.
[17]Franks, *Work of Christ*, 184-87.

Protestant Reformers spoke of satisfaction in terms of penalty.[18] Henri Blocher, deeply sympathetic to the Reformers, writes that "Luther broke the lock that kept Anselm from going further, the adage 'either satisfaction or punishment.' His profounder sense of sin made him realize that there is no other satisfaction than punishment." Luther therefore "takes literally the words of Scripture: 'he was made a curse for us.'"[19] Christ, Luther says in his commentary on Galatians 3:13, is "the Lamb of God cursed for us." "Our most merciful Father," he explains in a famous passage,

> seeing us to be oppressed and overwhelmed with the curse of the law and held by it . . . sent his only Son into the world and laid upon him all the sins of everyone, telling him to be Peter the denier, to be Paul the persecutor and blasphemer and oppressor, to be David the adulterer, to be the sinner who ate the fruit in paradise, the thief who hung on the cross—in short, to be the person who has committed the sins of everyone. . . . Christ is made guilty of all the sins that we have committed.[20]

Luther's rhetoric here marks a development. Medieval theologians may have spoken of Christ bearing the penalty of sin, but never of his being made guilty.[21] It also carries significance for the interpretation of sacrifice, as he speaks of "the Lamb of God, cursed for us." During and after the Reformation, sacrifice, at least in its expiatory mode, increasingly became associated with curse bearing.[22] While John Calvin could state that even in Christ's death, "his willing obedience is the most important thing," he also states that the sacrifice of Christ, like the Mosaic sacrifices that prefigured

---

[18]L. W. Grensted, *A Short History of the Doctrine of the Atonement* (repr., Charleston, SC: BiblioLife, 2010), 205.
[19]Henri Blocher, *La Doctrine du Péché et de la Redemption, Deuxième Fascicule* (Vaux-Sur-Seine: Faculté Libre de Théologie Evangélique, 1983), 172.
[20]Martin Luther, *Galatians*, Crossway Classical Commentaries (Wheaton, IL: Crossway, 1998). 153.
[21]See, e.g., Thomas Aquinas, *Light of Faith: The Compendium of Theology*, trans. Cyril Vollert (Manchester, NH: Sophia Institute, 1993), 227, 231. Cf. Luther's remarks on why the cross should terrify us in "A Meditation on Christ's Passion (1519)," in Martin Luther, *Martin Luther's Basic Theological Writings*, 3rd ed., ed. Timothy F. Lull and William R. Russell (Minneapolis: Fortress, 2012), 126-31.
[22]During the time of the Reformation, due to polemics surrounding the Protestant critique of the Roman Mass, the distinction between expiatory and eucharistic sacrifice became more commonly cited and began to play a larger role in the doctrine of the atonement. John Calvin, for example, states that while Christ offered a sacrifice that "blotted out our death and made satisfaction for our sins," we, being his "companions in this great office" of priesthood, offer "the sacrifices of prayers and praise" (*Institutes* 2.15.6).

it, consisted in vicariously bearing "the curse due for sins." What was prefigured in the Mosaic sacrifices—the imputation of punishment—is "manifested in Christ, the archetype of the figures."[23] To be sure, neither Luther nor Calvin reduces the meaning of sacrifice to punishment. Calvin, for instance, states that Christ's sacrificial blood saves "not only as a satisfaction, but also a laver."[24] Nevertheless, it is the penal aspect of sacrifice that proved to be the legacy of the Reformers' doctrine and came to dominate later conversations. And it was precisely in those conversations, conversations about atonement, sacrifice, and penalty, that the interpretation of Leviticus became of ever greater importance for the doctrine of atonement and even began to serve as an arbiter of doctrinal disagreement.

The Socinian Challenge

It was with the rise of the Socinian challenge to the Protestant doctrine of atonement and sacrifice that the debate over the meaning of sacrifice became more urgent. When Faustus Socinus and his followers attacked the cogency of the penal-substitutionary atonement theory developed by the Reformers, they appealed to Levitical sacrifice.[25] Their argument centered on a single claim: that the slaughter of the sacrificial victim was not directly related to the efficacy of the sacrifice. According to the Racovian Catechism, in the Levitical prescriptions for the Day of Atonement, expiation was made only after the high priest entered the most holy place. Therefore the slaughter of the sacrifice, to which Reformed theologians gave so much attention, did not directly contribute to the expiation of sin in that rite, a point the Socinians believed to be affirmed by the epistle to the Hebrews.[26] As with the

---

[23] Calvin, *Institutes* 2.16.5-6.

[24] Calvin, *Institutes* 2.16.6.

[25] Faustus Socinus (1539–1604) published his views on the person and work of Christ in a work titled *De Jesu Christo Servatore*. R. S. Franks refers to his theology as "a union between the humanism of Erasmus and the logical criticism of the school of Duns Scotus" (*Work of Christ*, 362).

To be sure, there were forerunners to the doctrine of penal-substitutionary atonement. Notably, the Reformers crystallized the doctrine by using Bernard of Clairvaux's language of imputation. See Anthony N. S. Lane, *Bernard of Clairvaux: Theologian of the Cross*, Cistercian Studies Series 248 (Collegeville, MN: Liturgical Press, 2013).

[26] Interestingly, a current debate over the reading of Hebrews mirrors that of the Socinians and their opponents. See David M. Moffitt, *Atonement and the Logic of Resurrection in the Epistle to the Hebrews*, Supplements to Novum Testamentum 141 (Leiden: Brill, 2013); cf. R. B. Jamieson, *Jesus' Death and Heavenly Offering in Hebrews* (Cambridge: Cambridge University Press, 2019).

type, so with the antitype: "It would not follow from the type of the sacrifices," they asserted, "that God was, by the death of Christ, satisfied for our sins in the sense contended for, since the Scripture never inculcates that those sacrifices had the effect of satisfying God for sin."[27]

Reformed theologians were not left without response, and they directly challenged the Socinian reading of Leviticus. Genevan theologian Francis Turretin, noting that the Levitical offerings "must have been instituted primarily to represent the sacrifice and satisfaction of Christ," argued that while the satisfaction made by those offerings was only "typical and ceremonial," it was nonetheless ordained by God for the purpose of testifying to the satisfaction of Christ, understood by Turretin to consist of paying the precise debt of punishment demanded of the sinner by the law of God. Moreover, he argued, this typological satisfaction took on the form of penal substitution: the sacrificial victim was "substituted in the place of sinners to bear the punishment of death due to them, as evinced by the rite of imposing the hands upon the head of the offering and making a confession of sin over it," an allusion, it seems, to Leviticus 16:21. The effect of these offerings in respect to God was the propitiation of his wrath.[28] Turretin's argument was not based solely on Levitical sacrifice, of course; he had much to say about the theological necessity of satisfaction that did not depend directly on the sacrificial system. Yet he does seem to judge the exegesis of key passages in Leviticus to be necessary, and he shows a concern that his argument always be consonant with what is found in Leviticus even when he is not directly engaging it.

When John Owen responded to the English Socinians in *Vindiciae Evangelicae*, he too engaged them on the grounds of Levitical priesthood and sacrifice.[29] Owen acknowledged that, as the Socinians were saying, on the Day of Atonement the high priest atoned for Israel's sins by offering blood in the most holy place, and he knew well that Hebrews describes the ascension of Christ as the fulfillment of this Levitical type. When Christ

---

[27] *The Racovian Catechism, with Notes and Illustrations*, trans. and ed. Thomas Rees (London, 1818), sec. 5, chap 8, 320, https://archive.org/details/racoviancatechi00unkngoog/page/n4/mode/2up.

[28] Francis Turretin, *Institutes of Elenctic Theology*, vol. 2, *Eleventh Through Seventeenth Topics*, ed. James T. Dennison, trans. George Musgrave Giger (Phillipsburg, NJ: P&R, 1994), 431-32, 427-28.

[29] Owen's defense of Reformed theology in this work is a response to a catechism written by the English Socinian John Biddle. See John Owen, *Vindiciae Evangelicae, or, The Mystery of the Gospel Vindicated, and Socianisme Examined* (Oxford: Leon Lichfield, Printer to the University, 1655), https://archive.org/details/vindi00owen/page/n7/mode/2up.

ascended into heaven, the true High Priest entered the archetypal most holy place and presented his offering. Owen insisted, however, that there is a crucial distinction to be made, both in Leviticus and in the priestly work of Christ, between the enactment and the presentation of that offering: "We do not deny that Christ offers himself in heaven,—that is, that he presents himself as one that *was so offered* to his Father; but *the offering* of himself, *that* was on earth: and therefore there was he a priest."[30] The result is that, contrary to what the Socinians claimed, Christ's sacrifice does in fact consist in bloodshed, through which he satisfied the justice of God. By thus pressing into the details of this Levitical ritual, Owen sought to defend his case for penal-substitutionary atonement.

It should be noted, however, that while theologians of all stripes rose up to oppose Socinus's views, the reaction was not uniform, a point of continuing significance for contemporary debates over atonement. Arminian theologians, such as Philip Van Limborch and Hugo Grotius, argued (against the Reformed) that while Christ offered a bloody sacrifice in our stead, that sacrifice, like those of the old covenant, satisfied "not the rigour of Divine justice, but the will of God."[31] Satisfaction, in both human and divine courts, can sometimes be "opposed to payment in the strict sense."[32] Christ's sacrifice, in this view, did not accomplish what Turretin would call a "real" or "true" satisfaction but was offered in lieu of strict satisfaction of the divine law.[33] At work here is the Scotist doctrine of acceptation, in which the sacrifice of Christ is accepted as satisfaction not on account of its "inherent dignity" (as Turretin would complain) but simply because it pleased God to do so, a viewpoint Socinus himself adopted.[34] While still opposing Socinus, then, the Arminians pay some heed to his critique of the Reformed doctrine of satisfaction.

---

[30] Owen, *Vindiciae Evangelicae*, chap. 20.

[31] Limborch, *Theologia Christiana*, as cited in Franks, *Work of Christ*, 387.

[32] Grotius, "Defense of the Catholic Faith Concerning the Satisfaction of Christ Against Faustus Socinus of Siena" (1617), as cited in Franks, *Work of Christ*, 400.

[33] Turretin, *Institutes of Elenctic Theology*, 2:439.

[34] Franks, *Work of Christ*, 393n5. See Turretin, *Institutes of Elenctic Theology*, 2:439. To be more precise, the doctrine of acceptation stipulates that Christ's satisfaction does not actually meet the full demand of the divine law, nor does its moral worth merit atonement in itself, yet it is reckoned by God to do so. For a helpful essay on this doctrine, see Oliver Crisp, "Salvation and Atonement: On the Value and Necessity of the Work of Jesus Christ," in *God of Salvation: Soteriology in Theological Perspective*, ed. Igor J. Davidson and Murray A. Rae (Burlington, VT: Ashgate, 2011), 105-20.

The Socinian controversy reveals two important developments in Christian thinking about sacrifice that still affect the conversation today. First, for most Protestant theologians, sacrifice has now come to be equated with penal substitution. Whether the strict satisfaction view of the Reformed, in which sacrifice entails a transfer of the actual penalty for sin; figuratively in the types and literally in Christ; or the Arminian view, in which sacrifice is the infliction of a lesser yet actual penalty, sacrifice is conceived of as a penal transaction of some sort. Second, the interpretation of Leviticus and the details of its ritual prescriptions have become more important for the doctrine of atonement than ever before. While Levitical sacrifice had always been significant for the church's doctrine of the work of Christ, it is now being appealed to in order to settle a doctrinal disagreement. For all parties involved, the nature and efficacy of Christ's work of atonement was closely tied to the nature and efficacy of Levitical sacrifice. Each camp saw interpreting Leviticus as part of the task of developing and defending the doctrine of atonement, increasingly so as disagreements intensified. These two developments in the interpretation of sacrifice and the place of Leviticus in the doctrine of atonement carry profound implications for the way atonement is understood and talked about today.

The Ongoing Dispute

The discussion around the doctrine of atonement has continued to develop in the last few centuries, of course, but the basic lines of argument that grew out of the Socinian critique remain live. The nature of the atonement is still very much disputed, and the interpretation of Levitical sacrifice remains an important point of controversy. The most volatile point of contention continues to be the idea of penal substitution.

Proponents of penal-substitutionary atonement have continued to contend (like Turretin and Owen) that Levitical sacrifice is a penal transaction and that the slaughter of the sacrifice is therefore the essential atoning act. A prominent defender of this view in the early twentieth century, whose influence remains to this day, was B. B. Warfield. By Warfield's day, the discussion over the meaning of sacrifice had become not only an exercise of theologians but an obsession of sociologists, which introduced a new level of difficulty and sophistication to the conversation. Warfield identified two rival conceptions of sacrifice present in anthropological and theological circles alike, which, when used toward that end, imply very different accounts of the work of Christ: a gift theory and piacular (or expiatory) theory. The former conceives of human beings as "mere" creatures who offer their homage to God in sacrifice, the latter as *sinful* creatures who offer a penal substitute.[35] Against the trend of his day, Warfield is clear that it is the biblical (i.e., Levitical) view of sacrifice that should inform the church's understanding of the work of Christ, not the theories put forth by anthropologists. And, in his judgment, while some of the Levitical sacrifices may be understood as gifts, the system as a whole was an "elaborate embodiment of the piacular idea." The Levitical system, he argued, was appointed as a means of propitiating God, and it did so through the death of the victim, the "essential act of sacrifice."[36] It is therefore in Christ's death that the "essence of his sacrificial character is found," a death that Leviticus (along with many NT passages) leads us to interpret as an act of penal substitution.

Leon Morris, in an important work of biblical scholarship, affirms and extends Warfield's argument. In the course of examining the meaning of the word *blood* in Scripture, particularly as it refers to the work of Christ, Morris argues that "sacrifice is inherently the destruction of the victims."[37] This is the view, he claims, of the New Testament and Old Testament alike. Arguing against the view that sacrifice makes atonement by way of the offeror's participation in the *life* of the victim, an argument made on the basis of Leviticus 17:11, Morris claims that it is "the *termination* of life, the infliction of death that atones."[38] In this, he asserts, the Levitical prescriptions and the New Testament witness are in full agreement.[39]

---

[35] Warfield, "Christ Our Sacrifice," 400. John Stott helpfully notes that these views should be considered complementary, "for both kinds of sacrifice were essentially recognitions of God's grace and expressions of dependence upon it." John R. W. Stott, *The Cross of Christ*, 20th anniv. ed. (Downers Grove, IL: InterVarsity Press, 2006), 135.

[36] Warfield, "Christ Our Sacrifice," 408, 413, 404.

[37] Leon Morris, *The Apostolic Preaching of the Cross*, 3rd ed. (repr., Grand Rapids: Eerdmans, 1976), 121.

[38] Morris, *Apostolic Preaching*, 119, emphasis added. Leviticus 17:11 reads, "For the life of the flesh is in the blood; and I have given it for you upon the altar to make atonement for your souls; for it is the blood that makes atonement, by reason of the life" (RSV). Morris's critique is most immediately directed at Vincent Taylor, *Jesus and His Sacrifice* (1939).

[39] Morris notes that in some cases, Leviticus speaks of atonement being made apart from death (e.g., Lev 14:18; 16:10). In his judgment, however, these examples are not relevant to the question at hand (*Apostolic Preaching*, 121).

The view of sacrifice put forth by Turretin, Owen, Warfield, and Morris appears in many textbooks of evangelical theology today. Michael Horton, for instance, echoes the arguments of Warfield and Morris, as does Millard Erickson.[40] For these theologians, the penal view of sacrifice (and, with it, of atonement) is *the* biblical view.

The critics, however, are far from persuaded, and they have put forth a plethora of alternatives for understanding the atoning sacrifice of Christ. Often, the most problematic element of the penal view of sacrifice is identified as the idea of propitiation, which stipulates that there is something in God that requires a sacrifice before forgiveness can be extended—of which, as I understand it, the doctrine of satisfaction is a species.[41] Critics of this idea often follow (or amend) and build on the argument of C. H. Dodd, who in a famous essay on the translation of the Greek term ἱλάσκομαι argues that propitiation is a pagan, not biblical idea.[42] Levitical sacrifice, and with it the sacrifice of Christ, did not propitiate or placate God. Rather, it expiated ("covered" or "wiped away") sin, a distinction of the greatest importance to disputes over the mechanism of atonement. The thrust of Dodd's argument is that sacrifice affects not God, who always stands ready to reconcile, but some creaturely entity (either sin or the sinner). In this way, Dodd, intentionally or not, echoes a theme of the Socinian critique.

Among other critics of penal substitution, proponents of nonviolent theories of atonement are prominent. A notable example is Denny Weaver. According to Weaver, Levitical sacrifice was not "ritualized blood payment to satisfy guilt" but "ritual self-dedication and self-giving." Satisfaction of a legal penalty had no place in the Levitical offerings. The blood of the sacrifice

---

[40]Millard Erickson, *Christian Theology*, 3rd ed. (Grand Rapids, MI: Baker Academic, 2013), 735-36; Michael Horton, *The Christian Faith: A Systematic Theology for Pilgrims on the Way* (Grand Rapids, MI: Zondervan, 2011), 493-500. To his credit, Horton goes beyond the argument of Warfield by arguing that Christ fulfills the "thank offering (owed by humanity apart from sin)" as well through his active obedience, which consists of a life of gratitude. Horton's effort to speak of the work of Christ in a more active voice is commendable.

[41]As noted above, Jaroslav Pelikan convincingly argues that the doctrine of satisfaction came into its own when Anselm more fully integrated the ideas of propitiatory sacrifice and the impassibility of God in *Cur Deus Homo* (Pelikan, *Christian Tradition*, 3:139).

[42]C. H. Dodd, "Atonement," in *The Bible and the Greeks* (London: Hodder & Stoughton, 1954), 82-95. Cf. Young, *Sacrifice and the Death*, 72-74. Young argues that the pagan concept of propitiation replaced the more biblical idea of expiation as the church's connection to its Jewish roots weakened and the influence of Greek thinking grew stronger.

did not denote a penal death substituted for that of the offeror but a consecrated life representing the worshiper to God. The sacrificial work of Jesus is thus to model the "Christian life as a self-offering," not to propitiate God through submission to divine judgment.[43] Contra the claim of Warfield and others that a vicarious, penal death is the essence of sacrifice, Weaver and company see the death of the victim as more or less accidental to sacrifice.

Another example is Darrin Snyder Belousek, whose account largely agrees with Weaver's while demonstrating more familiarity with recent trends in the interpretation of Leviticus. Appealing to Jacob Milgrom's interpretation of the sin offering, Belousek argues that God prescribed sacrifice not as a mechanism for penal substitution but as a means of purification.[44] Sacrifice was "directed" at the uncleanness of sin, not at God. In other words, God was never the object of atonement in the Levitical rites. Sacrifice, Belousek admits, may have served the purpose of averting God's wrath, but "*averting* God's wrath by removing uncleanness and *appeasing* God are two different things." Levitical sacrifice, and thus its fulfillment in Jesus Christ, was about purification and separation, not satisfaction of retributive divine justice.[45]

We should not forget, of course, that some theologians reject the typological approach altogether. Impossible to ignore for writers on sacrifice and atonement today is the work of René Girard. Girard and the theologians influenced by his theory, such as Mark Heim and Brad Jersak, have insisted that Christ "fulfills" all sacrifice not by completing or perfecting it but by "exposing and annulling" the fallacy of sacrificial atonement.[46] Sacrifice was not

---

[43]Denny Weaver, *The Nonviolent Atonement*, 2nd ed. (Grand Rapids, MI: Eerdmans, 2011), 70, 79. Weaver is quoting Michael Hardin, "Sacrificial Language in Hebrews," in *Violence Renounced: René Girard, Biblical Studies, and Peacemaking*, ed. William M. Swartley (Scottdale, PA: Herald, 2000), 121.

[44]Milgrom argues that the sin offering effects purification, not reparation. Jacob Milgrom, *Leviticus 1–16: A New Translation with Introduction and Commentary*, Anchor Yale Bible 3 (New Haven, CT: Yale University Press, 2009), 253-54. Furthermore, "sin offering" is not the right translation in the view of Milgrom, who argues fairly persuasively for the translation "purification offering." But since that translation is seldom the one adopted in English translations of the Bible, and since it is contested by some, "sin offering" will be used for the time being.

[45]Darrin W. Snyder Belousek, *Atonement, Justice, and Peace: The Message of the Cross and the Mission of the Church* (Grand Rapids: Eerdmans, 2012), 180-81, 190.

[46]Brad Jersak, "Nonviolent Identification and the Victory of Christ," in *Stricken by God? Nonviolent Identification and the Victory of Christ*, ed. Brad Jersak and Michael Hardin (Grand Rapids, MI: Eerdmans, 2007), 39. See S. Mark Heim, *Saved from Sacrifice: A Theology of the Cross* (Grand

divinely appointed and has no true religious value. Jesus came to expose the violence of sacrifice, which, according to this theory, is sufficient for its abolition. Salvation consists of life in communities set free from sacrificial violence. The sacrifice of Jesus, like all sacrifice, was about community formation, not a transaction with God. What makes Jesus' sacrifice unique is that it founds its community on love and truth instead of violence and deception. As can be seen, assenting to this proposal comes at a significant cost for Christians, whose Scripture and liturgies are filled with sacrificial terminology.[47]

It is still true that thinking about atonement means thinking about Levitical sacrifice. The church's theology of atonement has always evolved along with its theology of sacrifice. And, in my prognosis, it always will. For the sake of proclaiming and celebrating the gospel, in word and deed, we must continue to give our most careful thought to Levitical sacrifice.

Rapids, MI: Eerdmans, 2006). Similar to the method of Girard, Heim's work addresses various stories of sacrifice more than the ritual system of Leviticus. His arguments are easily extended to that system, however.

[47]Thus, while Girard's influence is far-reaching, his thesis is most often adopted with significant amendments and almost exclusively by those rejecting accounts of sacrifice in which a vicarious death is essential.

Bibliography

Allen, Michael. *Sanctification*. New Studies in Dogmatics. Grand Rapids, MI: Zondervan, 2017.

Anatolios, Khaled. *Deification Through the Cross: An Eastern Christian Theology of Salvation*. Grand Rapids, MI: Eerdmans, 2020.

Anderson, Gary A. *Sacrifice and Offerings in Ancient Israel: Studies in Their Social and Political Importance*. Harvard Semitic Monographs 41. Atlanta: Scholars Press, 1987.

———. *That I May Dwell Among Them: Incarnation and Atonement in the Tabernacle Narrative*. Grand Rapids, MI: Eerdmans, 2023.

Anselm. *Why God Became Man*. In *Anselm of Canterbury: The Major Works*, edited by Brian Davies and G. R. Evans, 260-356. Oxford: Oxford University Press, 1998.

Arcadi, James M. *Holiness: Divine and Human*. Minneapolis: Fortress Academic, 2023.

———. "Homo Adorans: Exitus et Reditus in Theological Anthropology." *Scottish Journal of Theology* 73, no. 1 (February 2020): 1-12.

Athanasius. *Against the Arians*. Translated by John Henry Newman. In *A Select Library of Nicene and Post-Nicene Fathers of the Christian Church*, Second Series, edited by Philip Schaff and Henry Wace, vol. 4, *St. Athanasius: Select Works and Letters*, edited by Archibald Robertson. Buffalo, NY: Christian Literature, 1892. Revised and edited for New Advent by Kevin Knight, www.newadvent.org/fathers/28162.htm.

———. *On the Incarnation: Greek Original and English Translation*. Translated by John Behr. Popular Patristics Series 44a. Yonkers, NY: St. Vladimir's Seminary Press, 2011.

Augustine. *Concerning the City of God Against the Pagans*. Translated by Henry Bettenson. London: Penguin Books, 1972.

———. *On the Trinity*. Edited by John E. Rotelle. Translated by Edmund Hill. Hyde Park, NY: New City, 1991.

Aulén, Gustaf. *Christus Victor: An Historical Study of the Three Main Types of the Idea of Atonement*. Translated by A. G. Hebert. 1931. Reprint, Eugene, OR: Wipf & Stock, 2003.

Averbeck, Richard E. "Offerings and Sacrifices." In *New International Dictionary of Old Testament Theology and Exegesis*, edited by Willem A. VanGemeren, 4:996-1022. Grand Rapids, MI: Zondervan, 1997.

———. "Sacrifices and Offerings." In *Dictionary of the Old Testament: Pentateuch*, edited by T. Desmond Alexander and David W. Baker, 706-33. Downers Grove, IL: InterVarsity Press, 2003.

———. "אָשָׁם." In *New International Dictionary of Old Testament Theology and Exegesis*, edited by Willem A. VanGemeren, 1:540-49. Grand Rapids, MI: Zondervan, 1997.

Ayres, Lewis. *Nicaea and Its Legacy: An Approach to Fourth-Century Trinitarian Theology*. Oxford: Oxford University Press, 2004.

Balthasar, Hans Urs von. *Theo-Drama: Theological Dramatic Theory*. Vol. 4, *The Action*. Translated by Graham Harrison. San Francisco: Ignatius, 1994.

Barclay, John M. G. *Paul and the Gift*. Grand Rapids, MI: Eerdmans, 2015.

Barth, Karl. *Church Dogmatics*. Vol. 4.1, *The Doctrine of Reconciliation*. Edited by G. W. Bromiley and T. F. Torrance. Translated by G. W. Bromiley. London: T&T Clark, 1956.

Bauckham, Richard. *Who Is God? Key Moments of Biblical Revelation*. Grand Rapids, MI: Baker Academic, 2020.

Bavinck, Herman. *Reformed Dogmatics*. Edited by John Bolt. Translated by John Vriend. 4 vols. Grand Rapids, MI: Baker Academic, 2003–2008.

Beale, G. K. *The Temple and the Church's Mission: A Biblical Theology of the Dwelling Place of God*. New Studies in Biblical Theology 17. Downers Grove, IL: InterVarsity Press, 2004.

Behr, John. *Irenaeus of Lyons: Identifying Christianity*. Christian Theology in Context. Oxford: Oxford University Press, 2013.

———. *The Mystery of Christ: Life in Death*. Crestwood, NY: St. Vladimir's Seminary Press, 2006.

Belousek, Darrin W. Snyder. *Atonement, Justice, and Peace: The Message of the Cross and the Mission of the Church*. Grand Rapids, MI: Eerdmans, 2012.

Biblia Hebraica Stuttgartensia: With Werkgroep Informatica, Vrije Universiteit Morphology. Bellingham, WA: Faithlife, 2006.

Blocher, Henri. *La Doctrine du Péché et de la Redemption, Deuxième Fascicule.* Vaux-Sur-Seine: Faculté Libre de Théologie Evangélique, 1983.

———. "The Sacrifice of Jesus: The Current Theological Situation." *European Journal of Theology* 8, no. 1 (1999): 23-36.

Blowers, Paul M. *Maximus the Confessor: Jesus Christ and the Transfiguration of the World.* Oxford: Oxford University Press, 2016.

Boersma, Hans. *Seeing God: The Beatific Vision in the Christian Tradition.* Grand Rapids, MI: Eerdmans, 2018.

Bonaventure. *Breviloquium.* Translated by Dominic V. Monti, OFM. Works of St. Bonaventure 9. Saint Bonaventure, NY: Franciscan Institute, 2005.

The Book of Common Prayer. Anglican Church in North America. Huntington Beach, CA: Anglican Liturgy Press, 2019.

Briggs, Richard S. *Theological Hermeneutics and the Book of Numbers as Christian Scripture.* Notre Dame, IN: University of Notre Dame Press, 2018.

Brümmer, Vincent. "Atonement and Reconciliation." *Religious Studies* 28, no. 4 (December 1992): 435-52.

Burns, J. Patout. "The Concept of Satisfaction in Medieval Redemption Theory." *Theological Studies* 36, no. 2 (May 1975): 285-304.

Calvin, John. *Institutes of the Christian Religion.* Edited by John T. McNeill. Translated by Ford Lewis Battles. Louisville, KY: Westminster John Knox, 1960.

Cassuto, Umberto. *A Commentary on the Book of Exodus.* Translated by Israel Abrahams. Jerusalem: Magnes, 1967.

The Catechism of the Catholic Church, with Modifications from the Editio Typica. New York: Doubleday, 1997.

Childs, Brevard S. *Biblical Theology of the Old and New Testaments: Theological Reflection on the Christian Bible.* Minneapolis: Fortress, 1992.

Clarke, W. Norris. *Person and Being.* Milwaukee: Marquette University Press, 1993.

Cockerill, Gareth Lee. *The Epistle to the Hebrews.* New International Commentary on the New Testament. Grand Rapids, MI: Eerdmans, 2012.

Cole, R. Allen. *Exodus.* Tyndale Old Testament Commentaries. Downers Grove, IL: InterVarsity Press, 1973.

Collet, Don C. *Figural Reading and the Old Testament: Theology and Practice.* Grand Rapids, MI: Baker Academic, 2020.

Collins, C. John. *Genesis 1-4: A Linguistic, Literary, and Theological Commentary.* Phillipsburg, NJ: P&R, 2006.

Coppedge, Allan. *Portraits of God: A Biblical Theology of Holiness*. Downers Grove, IL: InterVarsity Press, 2001.

Crisp, Oliver. *Approaching the Atonement: The Reconciling Work of Christ*. Downers Grove, IL: IVP Academic, 2020.

———. "On the Vicarious Humanity of Christ." *International Journal of Systematic Theology* 21, no. 3 (July 2019): 235-50.

———. *Participation and Atonement: An Analytic and Constructive Account*. Grand Rapids, MI: Baker Academic, 2022.

———. "Salvation and Atonement: On the Value and Necessity of the Work of Jesus Christ." In *God of Salvation: Soteriology in Theological Perspective*, edited by Igor J. Davidson and Murray A. Rae, 105-20. Burlington, VT: Ashgate, 2011.

Cross, Frank Moore. "Kinship and Covenant in Ancient Israel." In *From Epic to Canon: History and Literature in Ancient Israel*, 3-21. Baltimore: Johns Hopkins University Press, 1998.

Crowe, Brandon. *The Last Adam: A Theology of the Obedient Life of Jesus in the Gospels*. Grand Rapids, MI: Baker Academic, 2017.

Dalferth, Ingolf U. "Christ Died for Us: Reflections on the Sacrificial Language of Salvation." In *Sacrifice and Redemption: Durham Essays in Theology*, edited by Stephen W. Sykes, 299-325. Cambridge: Cambridge University Press, 1991.

Davidson, Ivor J. "Atonement and Incarnation." In *T&T Clark Companion to Atonement*, edited by Adam J. Johnson, 35-56. London: Bloomsbury T&T Clark, 2017.

Davison, Andrew. *Participation in God: A Study in Christian Doctrine and Metaphysics*. Cambridge: Cambridge University Press, 2019.

De Vaux, Roland. *Studies in Old Testament Sacrifice*. Cardiff, UK: University of Wales Press, 1964.

Derrida, Jacques. *Given Time: I. Counterfeit Money*. Translated by Peggy Kamuf. Chicago: University of Chicago Press, 1992.

Dillistone, F. W. *The Christian Understanding of Atonement*. London: SCM Press, 1968.

Dodd, C. H. "Atonement." In *The Bible and the Greeks*, 82-95. London: Hodder & Stoughton, 1954.

Douglas, Mary. *Purity and Danger: An Analysis of Concepts of Pollution and Taboo*. New York: Routledge, 2002.

Dumbrell, William J. *Covenant and Creation: A Theology of the Old Testament Covenants*. Reprint, Carlisle, UK: Paternoster, 2000.

———. *The Faith of Israel: A Theological Survey of the Old Testament.* 2nd ed. Grand Rapids, MI: Baker, 2002.
Eagleton, Terry. *Radical Sacrifice.* New York: Yale University Press, 2018.
Eberhardt, Christian A. *The Sacrifice of Jesus: Understanding Atonement Biblically.* Reprint, Eugene, OR: Wipf & Stock, 2018.
Eichrodt, Walther. *Theology of the Old Testament.* Vol. 1. Translated by J. A. Baker. London: SCM Press, 1961.
Eikrem, Asle. *God as Sacrificial Love: A Systematic Exploration of a Controversial Notion.* London: Bloomsbury T&T Clark, 2018.
Elliot, Mark W. *Engaging Leviticus: Reading Leviticus Theologically with Its Past Interpreters.* Eugene, OR: Cascade Books, 2012.
Emery, Gilles, OP. *The Trinitarian Theology of St. Thomas Aquinas.* Translated by Francesca Aran Murphy. Oxford: Oxford University Press, 2007.
———. *Trinity, Church, and the Human Person: Thomistic Essays.* Naples, FL: Sapientia, 2007.
———. *The Trinity: An Introduction to Catholic Doctrine on the Triune God.* Translated by Matthew Levering. Washington, DC: Catholic University of America Press, 2011.
———. "Trinity and Creation." In *The Theology of Thomas Aquinas,* edited by Rik van Nieuwenhove and Joseph Wawrykow, 58-76. Notre Dame, IN: University of Notre Dame Press, 2005.
Erickson, Millard. *Christian Theology.* 3rd ed. Grand Rapids, MI: Baker Academic, 2013.
Fairbairn, Donald. *Life in the Trinity: An Introduction to Theology with the Help of the Church Fathers.* Downers Grove, IL: IVP Academic, 2009.
Farrow, Douglas. *Ascension Theology.* London: Bloomsbury T&T Clark, 2011.
Fletcher-Louis, Crispin H. T. "Jesus as the High Priestly Messiah, Part 1." *Journal for the Study of the Historical Jesus* 4, no. 2 (2006): 155-75.
Frame, John M. *The Doctrine of God.* Vol. 2 of *A Theology of Lordship.* Phillipsburg, NJ: P&R, 2002.
———. *The Doctrine of the Word of God.* Vol. 4 of *A Theology of Lordship.* Phillipsburg, NJ: P&R, 2010.
Franks, R. S. *The Work of Christ: A Historical Study of Christian Doctrine.* New York: Thomas Nelson and Sons, 1962.
Gane, Roy. *Cult and Character: Purification Offerings, Day of Atonement, and Theodicy.* Winona Lake, IN: Eisenbrauns, 2005.
Gathercole, Simon. *Defending Substitution: An Essay on Atonement in Paul.* Grand Rapids, MI: Baker, 2015.

Gentry, Peter J., and Stephen W. Wellum. *Kingdom Through Covenant: A Biblical-Theological Understanding of the Covenants*. 2nd ed. Wheaton, IL: Crossway, 2018.

Gerson, Lloyd P. *From Plato to Platonism*. Ithaca, NY: Cornell University Press, 2013.

Gese, Hartmut. "The Atonement." In *Essays on Biblical Theology*. Translated by Keith Crim. Reprint, Eugene, OR: Wipf & Stock, 2018.

Goldingay, John. "Old Testament Sacrifice and the Death of Christ." In *Atonement Today: A Symposium at St. John's College, Nottingham*, edited by John Goldingay, 3-20. London: SPCK, 1995.

Gorman, Frank H. *Divine Presence and Community: A Commentary on the Book of Leviticus*. International Theological Commentary. Grand Rapids, MI: Eerdmans, 1997.

———. *Ideology of Ritual: Space, Time and Status in the Priestly Theology*. Journal for the Study of the Old Testament Supplement Series 91. Sheffield, UK: Sheffield Academic Press, 1990.

Gregory of Nyssa. *The Life of Moses*. Edited and translated by Abraham J. Malherbe and Everett Ferguson. Classics of Western Christianity. Mahwah, NJ: Paulist, 1978.

Grensted, L. W. *A Short History of the Doctrine of the Atonement*. Reprint, Charleston, SC: BiblioLife, 2010.

Gunton, Colin E. *The Actuality of Atonement: A Study of Metaphor, Rationality, and the Christian Tradition*. London: T&T Clark, 1988.

———. "The Sacrifice and the Sacrifices: From Metaphor to Transcendental?" In *Trinity, Incarnation, and Atonement: Philosophical and Theological Essays*, edited by Ronald J. Feenstra and Cornelius Plantinga Jr., 210-29. South Bend, IN: University of Notre Dame Press, 1989.

———. *The Triune Creator: A Historical and Systematic Survey*. Edinburgh Studies in Constructive Theology. Grand Rapids, MI: Eerdmans, 1998.

Habermas, Jürgen. *The Theory of Communicative Action*. Vol. 1, *Reason and the Rationalization of Society*. Translated by Thomas McCarthy. Boston: Beacon, 1984.

Hahn, Scott W. *Kinship by Covenant: A Canonical Approach to the Fulfillment of God's Saving Promises*. New Haven, CT: Yale University Press, 2009.

Halbertal, Moshe. *On Sacrifice*. Princeton, NJ: Princeton University Press, 2012.

Hardin, Michael. "Sacrificial Language in Hebrews." In *Violence Renounced: René Girard, Biblical Studies, and Peacemaking*, edited by William M. Swartley, 103-19. Scottdale, PA: Herald, 2000.

Harper, G. Geoffrey. *"I Will Walk Among You": The Rhetorical Function of Allusion to Genesis 1–3 in the Book of Leviticus*. Bulletin for Biblical Research Supplement 21. University Park, PA: Eisenbrauns, 2018.

Hart, David Bentley. "A Gift Exceeding Every Debt: An Eastern Orthodox Appreciation of Anselm's *Cur Deus Homo*." *Pro Ecclesia* 7, no. 3 (Summer 1998): 333-49.

Hart, Trevor. *In Him Was Life: The Person and Work of Christ*. Waco, TX: Baylor University Press, 2019.

Hartley, John E. *Leviticus*. Word Biblical Commentary 4. Grand Rapids, MI: Zondervan, 2015.

Hays, Richard B. *Reading Backwards: Figural Christology and the Fourfold Gospel Witness*. Waco, TX: Baylor University Press, 2014.

Heim, S. Mark. *Saved from Sacrifice: A Theology of the Cross*. Grand Rapids, MI: Eerdmans, 2006.

Hénaff, Marcel. *The Price of Truth: Gift, Money, and Philosophy*. Stanford, CA: Stanford University Press, 2010.

Hicks, F. C. N. *The Fullness of Sacrifice*. 3rd ed. London: SPCK, 1953.

Hilary of Poitiers. *On the Trinity*. Translated by E. W. Watson and L. Pullen. Edited by W. Sanday. In *A Select Library of Nicene and Post-Nicene Fathers of the Christian Church*, Second Series, edited by Philip Schaff and Henry Wace, 9:40-233. Grand Rapids, MI: Eerdmans, 1989.

Hodge, Charles. *Systematic Theology*. Vol. 1, *Theology*. Peabody, MA: Hendrickson, 2013.

Holman, Hugh, and William Harmon. *A Handbook to Literature*. 6th ed. New York: Macmillan, 1992.

Holmes, Stephen R. "Death in the Afternoon: Hebrews, Sacrifice, and Soteriology." In *The Epistle to the Hebrews and Christian Theology*, edited by Richard Bauckham, Daniel R. Driver, Trevor A. Hart, and Nathan MacDonald, 229-52. Grand Rapids, MI: Eerdmans, 2009.

Horton, Michael S. *The Christian Faith: A Systematic Theology for Pilgrims on the Way*. Grand Rapids, MI: Zondervan, 2011.

———. *Lord and Servant: A Covenant Christology*. Louisville, KY: Westminster John Knox, 2005.

Hundley, Michael B. *Keeping Heaven on Earth: Safeguarding the Divine Presence in the Priestly Tabernacle*. Tübingen: Mohr Siebeck, 2011.

Irenaeus. *Against Heresies*. Translated by John Keble. Reprint, Nashotah, WI: Nashotah House, 2012.

———. *On the Apostolic Preaching*. Translated by John Behr. Crestwood, NY: St. Vladimir's Seminary Press, 1997.

Jamieson, R. B. *Jesus' Death and Heavenly Offering in Hebrews*. Cambridge: Cambridge University Press, 2019.

———. *The Paradox of Sonship: Christology in the Epistle to the Hebrews*. Downers Grove, IL: IVP Academic, 2021.

Jenson, Philip Peter. *Graded Holiness: A Key to the Priestly Conception of the World*. Journal for the Study of the Old Testament Supplement Series 106. Reprint, London: T&T Clark, 2021.

Jersak, Brad. "Nonviolent Identification and the Victory of Christ." In *Stricken by God? Nonviolent Identification and the Victory of Christ*, edited by Brad Jersak and Michael Hardin, 18-53. Grand Rapids, MI: Eerdmans, 2007.

John of Damascus. *Exposition of the Orthodox Faith*. Translated by S. D. F. Salmond. In *A Select Library of Nicene and Post-Nicene Fathers of the Christian Church*, Second Series, edited by Philip Schaff and Henry Wace, vol. 9. Grand Rapids, MI: Eerdmans, 1989.

Johnson, Adam J. *Atonement: A Guide for the Perplexed*. London: Bloomsbury T&T Clark, 2015.

———. "Atonement: The Shape and State of the Doctrine." In *T&T Clark Companion to Atonement*, edited by Adam J. Johnson, 1-18. London: Bloomsbury T&T Clark, 2017.

Johnson, James. "Habermas on Strategic and Communicative Action." *Political Theory* 19, no. 2 (May 1991): 181-201.

Justin Martyr. *Dialogue with Trypho*. In *The Ante-Nicene Fathers: The Writings of the Fathers Down to A.D. 325*, edited by Alexander Roberts and James Donaldson, 1:194-270. London: Catholic Way, 2014. Kindle.

Keil, C. F., and F. Delitzsch. *Commentary on the Old Testament*. Vol. 1, *The Pentateuch*. Reprint, Peabody, MA: Hendrickson, 2011.

Kelly, J. N. D. *Early Christian Doctrines*. Rev. ed. San Francisco: Harper & Row, 1978.

Kiuchi, Nobuyoshi. *Leviticus*. Apollos Old Testament Commentary 3. Nottingham, UK: Apollos, 2007.

Klawans, Jonathan. *Purity, Sacrifice, and the Temple: Symbolism and Supersessionism in the Study of Ancient Judaism*. Oxford: Oxford University Press, 2006.

Kleinig, John. *Leviticus*. St. Louis: Concordia, 2003.

Kline, Meredith G. *Treaty of the Great King: The Covenant Structure of Deuteronomy: Studies and Commentary*. Grand Rapids, MI: Eerdmans, 1963.

Knierim, Rolf P. *Text and Concept in Leviticus 1:1-9: A Case in Exegetical Method*. Reprint, Eugene, OR: Wipf & Stock, 2010.

Lane, Anthony N. S. *Bernard of Clairvaux: Theologian of the Cross*. Cistercian Studies Series 248. Collegeville, MN: Liturgical Press, 2013.

Legge, Dominic. *The Trinitarian Christology of St. Thomas Aquinas*. Oxford: Oxford University Press, 2017.

Leithart, Peter J. *Delivered from the Elements of the World: Atonement, Justification, Mission*. Downers Grove, IL: IVP Academic, 2016.

———. *The Ten Commandments: A Guide to the Perfect Law of Liberty*. Bellingham, WA: Lexham, 2020.

Levenson, Jon D. *Creation and the Persistence of Evil: The Jewish Drama of Divine Omnipotence*. Princeton, NJ: Princeton University Press, 1988.

Levering, Matthew. *Christ's Fulfillment of Torah and Temple: Salvation According to Thomas Aquinas*. Notre Dame, IN: University of Notre Dame Press, 2002.

———. *Engaging the Doctrine of the Holy Spirit: Love and Gift in the Trinity and the Church*. Grand Rapids, MI: Baker Academic, 2016.

Lienhard, Joseph T., ed. *Exodus, Leviticus, Numbers, Deuteronomy*. Ancient Christian Commentary on Scripture Old Testament 3: Downers Grove, IL: IVP Academic, 2001.

Luther, Martin. *Galatians*. Crossway Classical Commentaries. Wheaton, IL: Crossway, 1998.

———. *Martin Luther's Basic Theological Writings*. 3rd ed. Edited by Timothy F. Lull and William R. Russell. Minneapolis: Fortress, 2012.

Lyonnet, Stanislas, and Léopold Sabourin. *Sin, Redemption, and Sacrifice: A Biblical and Patristic Study*. Rome: Editrice Pontificio Intituto Biblico, 1998.

MacFarland, Ian A. *From Nothing: A Theology of Creation*. Louisville, KY: Westminster John Knox, 2014.

Macina, Robert D. *The Lord's Service: A Ritual Analysis of the Order, Function, and Purpose of the Daily Divine Service in the Pentateuch*. Eugene, OR: Pickwick, 2019.

Macleod, Donald. *The Person of Christ*. Contours of Christian Theology. Downers Grove, IL: InterVarsity Press, 1998.

Maimonides. *The Guide for the Perplexed*. 2nd ed. Translated by M. Friedländer. New York: Dover, 1956.

Marshall, Bruce. "The Unity of the Triune God: Reviving an Ancient Question." *The Thomist* 74, no. 1 (January 2010): 1-32.

Marshall, I. Howard. "Soteriology in Hebrews." In *The Epistle to the Hebrews and Christian Theology*, edited by Richard Bauckham, Daniel R. Driver, Trevor A. Hart, and Nathan MacDonald, 253-77. Grand Rapids, MI: Eerdmans, 2009.

Mascall, E. L. *He Who Is: A Study in Traditional Theism*. London: Longmans, Green, 1943.

———. "Sonship and Sacrifice." *Canadian Journal of Theology* 8, no. 2 (April 1962): 88-101.

Masure, Eugene. *The Christian Sacrifice: The Sacrifice of Christ Our Head*. London: Burns, Oates & Washbourne, 1944.

McNall, Joshua. *The Mosaic of Atonement: An Integrated Approach to Christ's Work*. Grand Rapids, MI: Zondervan, 2019.

Milgrom, Jacob. *Leviticus 1–16: A New Translation with Introduction and Commentary*. Anchor Yale Bible 3. New Haven, CT: Yale University Press, 2009.

Moberly, R. W. L. "The Earliest Commentary on the Akedah." *Vetus Testamentum* 38, no. 3 (1988): 302-23.

———. *The God of the Old Testament: Encountering the Divine in Christian Scripture*. Grand Rapids, MI: Baker Academic, 2020.

———. *Old Testament Theology: Reading the Hebrew Bible as Christian Scripture*. Grand Rapids, MI: Baker Academic, 2013.

Moffitt, David M. *Atonement and the Logic of Resurrection in the Epistle to the Hebrews*. Supplements to Novum Testamentum 141. Leiden: Brill, 2013.

———. *Rethinking the Atonement: New Perspectives on Jesus' Death, Resurrection, and Ascension*. Grand Rapids, MI: Baker Academic, 2022.

Morales, Michael L. "Atonement in Israel: The Whole Burnt Offering as Central to Israel's Cult." In *So Great a Salvation: A Dialogue on the Atonement in Hebrews*, edited by Jon C. Laansma, George H. Guthrie, and Cynthia Long Westfall, 27-39. Library of New Testament Studies 516. London: T&T Clark, 2019.

———. "The Levitical Priesthood." *Southern Baptist Journal of Theology* 23, no.1 (Spring 2019): 7-22.

———. *The Tabernacle Pre-figured: Cosmic Mountain Ideology in Genesis and Exodus*. Biblical Tools and Studies 15. Leuven: Peeters, 2012.

———. *Who Shall Ascend the Mountain of the Lord? A Biblical Theology of the Book of Leviticus*. New Studies in Biblical Theology. Downers Grove, IL: InterVarsity Press, 2015.

Morris, Leon. *The Apostolic Preaching of the Cross*. 3rd ed. Reprint, Grand Rapids, MI: Eerdmans, 1976.

Noble, T. A. *Holy Trinity, Holy People: The Historic Doctrine of Christian Perfecting*. Didsbury Lecture Series. Eugene, OR: Cascade Books, 2013.

Oden, Thomas C. *Classical Christianity: A Systematic Theology*. New York: HarperCollins, 1992.

O'Donovan, Oliver. *Resurrection and Moral Order: An Outline for Evangelical Ethics*. 2nd ed. Grand Rapids, MI: Eerdmans, 1994.

O'Keefe, John J., and R. R. Reno. *Sanctified Vision: An Introduction to Early Christian Interpretation of the Bible*. Baltimore: Johns Hopkins University Press, 2005.

Ortlund, Gavin. "Image of Adam, Son of God: Genesis 5:3 and Luke 3:38 in Interncanonical Dialogue." *Journal of the Evangelical Theological Society* 57, no. 4 (December 2014): 673-78.

———. *Theological Retrieval for Evangelicals: Why We Need Our Past to Have a Future*. Wheaton, IL: Crossway, 2019.

Osborne, Eric. *Irenaeus of Lyons*. Cambridge: Cambridge University Press, 2001.

Owen, John. *Vindiciae Evangelicae, or, The Mystery of the Gospel Vindicated, and Socianisme Examined*. Oxford: Leon Lichfield, Printer to the University, 1655. https://archive.org/details/vindi00owen/page/n7/mode/2up.

Packer, J. I. *God Has Spoken*. Downers Grove, IL: InterVarsity Press, 1979.

———. "What Did the Cross Achieve?" *Tyndale Bulletin* 25 (1974).

Pattillo, Matthew. "Creation and *Akedah*: Blessing and Sacrifice in the Hebrew Scriptures." In *Sacrifice, Scripture, and Substitution: Readings in Ancient Judaism and Christianity*, edited by Ann W. Astell and Sandor Goodhart, 240-60. Notre Dame, IN: University of Notre Dame Press, 2011.

Pelikan, Jaroslav. *The Christian Tradition: A History of the Development of Doctrine*. Vol. 1, *The Emergence of the Catholic Tradition (100–600)*. Chicago: University of Chicago Press, 1971.

———. *The Christian Tradition: A History of the Development of Doctrine*. Vol. 3, *The Growth of Medieval Theology (600–1300)*. Chicago: University of Chicago Press, 1978.

Perrin, Nicholas. *Jesus the Priest*. Grand Rapids, MI: Baker Academic, 2018.

Peterson, Brandon. "Paving the Way? Penalty and Atonement in Thomas Aquinas' Soteriology." *International Journal of Systematic Theology* 15, no. 3 (July 2013): 265-83.

Peterson, David G. *Possessed by God: A New Testament Theology of Sanctification and Holiness*. New Studies in Biblical Theology 1. Downers Grove, IL: InterVarsity Press, 1995.

Plantinga, Cornelius, Jr. *Not the Way It's Supposed to Be: A Breviary of Sin*. Grand Rapids, MI: Eerdmans, 1995.

The Racovian Catechism, with Notes and Illustrations. Translated and edited by Thomas Rees. London, 1818. https://archive.org/details/racoviancatechi00unkngoog/page/n4/mode/2up.

Radner, Ephraim. *Leviticus*. Brazos Theological Commentary on the Bible. Grand Rapids, MI: Brazos, 2008.

———. "Practice Without Purpose." *First Things*, March 2023, 71-72.

Rainey, A. F. "The Order of Sacrifices in Old Testament Ritual Texts." *Biblica* 51, no. 4 (1970): 485-98.

Ratzinger, Joseph. *Behold the Pierced One: An Approach to a Spiritual Christology*. Translated by Graham Harrison. San Francisco: Ignatius, 1986.

———. *Journey Towards Easter: Retreat Given in the Vatican in the Presence of Pope John Paul II*. Translated by Dame Mary Groves. New York: Crossroad, 1987.

Ribbens, Benjamin J. *Levitical Sacrifice and Heavenly Cult in Hebrews*. Boston: de Gruyter, 2016.

Richter, Sandra L. *The Epic of Eden: A Christian Entry into the Old Testament*. Downers Grove, IL: IVP Academic, 2008.

Ross, Allen P. *Holiness to the Lord: A Guide to the Exposition of the Book of Leviticus*. Grand Rapids, MI: Baker Academic, 2002.

Rutledge, Fleming. *The Crucifixion: Understanding the Death of Jesus Christ*. Grand Rapids, MI: Eerdmans, 2015.

Sacks, Jonathan. *Leviticus: The Book of Holiness*. Covenant and Conversation: A Weekly Reading of the Jewish Bible. New Milford, CT: Maggid Books and the Orthodox Union, 2015.

Sanders, Fred. *Fountain of Salvation: Trinity and Soteriology*. Grand Rapids, MI: Eerdmans, 2021.

Scheeben, Matthias Joseph. *The Mysteries of Christianity*. Translated by Cyril Vollert, SJ. New York: Herder & Herder, 1946.

Schmemann, Alexander. *For the Life of the World: Sacraments and Orthodoxy*. Rev. ed. Crestwood, NY: St. Vladimir's Seminary Press, 1973.

Schroeder, H. J. *Disciplinary Decrees of the General Councils: Text, Translation and Commentary*. St. Louis: B. Herder, 1937. https://sourcebooks.fordham.edu/basis/lateran4.asp.

Seitz, Christopher R. *The Character of Christian Scripture: The Significance of a Two-Testament Bible*. Grand Rapids, MI: Baker Academic, 2011.

———. *The Elder Testament: Canon, Theology, Trinity.* Waco, TX: Baylor University Press, 2018.

Sklar, Jay. *Leviticus.* Tyndale Old Testament Commentaries. Downers Grove, IL: IVP Academic, 2014.

———. *Sin, Impurity, Sacrifice, Atonement: The Priestly Conceptions.* Hebrew Bible Monographs 2. Sheffield, UK: Sheffield University Press, 2005.

Sonderegger, Katherine. "Anselmian Atonement." In *T&T Clark Companion to Atonement*, edited by Adam. J. Johnson, 175-93. London: Bloomsbury T&T Clark, 2017.

———. *Systematic Theology.* Vol. 2, *The Doctrine of the Holy Trinity: Processions and Persons.* Minneapolis: Fortress, 2020.

Steinmetz, David. "The Superiority of Pre-critical Exegesis." *Ex auditu* 1 (1985): 74-82.

Stott, John R. W. *The Cross of Christ.* 20th anniversary ed. Downers Grove, IL: InterVarsity Press, 2006.

Stump, Eleonore. *Atonement.* Oxford: Oxford University Press, 2018.

Swain, Scott. *Trinity, Reading, and Revelation: A Theological Introduction to the Bible and Its Interpretation.* London: Bloomsbury T&T Clark, 2011.

———. *The Trinity: An Introduction.* Short Studies in Systematic Theology. Wheaton, IL: Crossway, 2020.

Thiessen, Matthew. *Jesus and the Forces of Death: The Gospels' Portrayal of Ritual Impurity Within First-Century Judaism.* Grand Rapids, MI: Baker Academic, 2020.

Thomas Aquinas. *Commentary on the Letter of Saint Paul to the Hebrews.* Edited by J. Mortensen and E. Alarcón. Translated by F. R. Larcher, OP. In *Biblical Commentaries*, vol. 41, *Latin/English Edition of the Works of St. Thomas Aquinas.* Lander, WY: Aquinas Institute for the Study of Sacred Doctrine, 2012.

———. *Light of Faith: The Compendium of Theology.* Translated by Cyril Vollert. Manchester, NH: Sophia Institute, 1993.

———. *Summa Contra Gentiles.* Book 1, *God.* Translated by Anston C. Pegis. Notre Dame, IN: University of Notre Dame Press, 1975.

———. *Summa Contra Gentiles.* Book 4, *Salvation.* Translated by Charles J. O'Neil. Notre Dame, IN: University of Notre Dame Press, 1975.

———. *The Summa Theologiae of St. Thomas Aquinas.* Translated by the Fathers of the English Dominican Province. 2nd rev. ed. 10 vols. London: Burns, Oates and Washbourne, 1920–1922. Revised and edited for New Advent by Kevin Knight. www.newadvent.org/summa/.

Torrance, Thomas F. *Atonement: The Person and Work of Christ*. Edited by Robert T. Walker. Downers Grove, IL: IVP Academic, 2009.

———. *Incarnation: The Person and Life of Christ*. Edited by Robert T. Walker. Downers Grove, IL: InterVarsity Press, 2008.

Treier, Daniel. *Introducing Theological Interpretation of Scripture: Recovering a Christian Practice*. Grand Rapids, MI: Baker Academic, 2008.

Turretin, Francis. *Institutes of Elenctic Theology*. Vol. 1, *First Through Tenth Topics*. Edited by James T. Dennison. Translated by George Musgrave Giger. Phillipsburg, NJ: P&R, 1992.

———. *Institutes of Elenctic Theology*. Vol. 2, *Eleventh Through Seventeenth Topics*. Edited by James T. Dennison. Translated by George Musgrave Giger. Phillipsburg, NJ: P&R, 1994.

VandenBerg, Mary L. "Christ's Atonement: The Hope of Creation." PhD diss., Calvin Theological Seminary, 2008.

Vanhoozer, Kevin J. "The Atonement in Postmodernity: Guilt, Goats and Gifts." In *The Glory of the Atonement: Biblical, Theological and Practical Perspectives*, edited by Charles E. Hill and Frank A. James III, 367-404. Downers Grove, IL: IVP Academic, 2004.

———. *Biblical Narrative in the Philosophy of Paul Ricoeur: A Study in Hermeneutics and Theology*. Cambridge: Cambridge University Press, 1990.

———. *The Drama of Doctrine: A Canonical Linguistic Approach to Christian Theology*. Louisville, KY: Westminster John Knox, 2005.

———. "Holy Scripture." In *Christian Dogmatics: Reformed Theology for the Church Catholic*, edited by Michael Allen and Scott R. Swain, 30-56. Grand Rapids, MI: Baker Academic, 2016.

———. *Is There a Meaning in This Text?* Grand Rapids, MI: Zondervan, 1998.

———. "Redemption Accomplished: Atonement." In *The Oxford Handbook of Reformed Theology*, edited by Michael Allen and Scott R. Swain, 473-96. Oxford: Oxford University Press, 2020.

———. *Remythologizing Theology: Divine Action, Passion, and Authorship*. Cambridge: Cambridge University Press, 2010.

Venter, P. M. "Atonement Through Blood in Leviticus." *Verbum et Ecclesia* 26, no. 1 (October 2005): 275-92.

Vos, Geerhardus. *Biblical Theology: Old and New Testaments*. Grand Rapids, MI: Eerdmans, 1948.

———. *The Eschatology of the Old Testament*. Phillipsburg, NJ: P&R, 2001.

Waltke, Bruce K. *An Old Testament Theology*. Grand Rapids, MI: Zondervan, 2011.

Walton, John H. *The Lost World of Genesis 1: Ancient Cosmology and the Origins Debate*. Downers Grove, IL: IVP Academic, 2010. Kindle.

Ward, Timothy. *Words of Life: Scripture as the Living and Active Word of God*. Downers Grove, IL: IVP Academic, 2009.

Warfield, B. B. "Christ Our Sacrifice." In *The Person and Work of Christ*, edited by Samuel G. Craig. Phillipsburg, NJ: Presbyterian & Reformed, 1950.

———. *The Person and Work of Christ*. Edited by Samuel G. Craig. Phillipsburg, NJ: Presbyterian & Reformed, 1950.

Watts, James W. "Olah: The Rhetoric of Burnt Offerings." *Vetus Testamentum* 66, no. 1 (2006): 125-37.

Weaver, Denny. *The Nonviolent Atonement*. 2nd ed. Grand Rapids, MI: Eerdmans, 2011.

Webster, John. "Christ, Church, and Reconciliation." In *Word and Church: Essays in Christian Dogmatics*, 2nd ed., 211-30. London: T&T Clark, 2016.

———. *God Without Measure: Working Papers in Christian Theology*. Vol. 1, *God and the Works of God*. London: T&T Clark, 2016.

———. *Holiness*. Grand Rapids, MI: Eerdmans, 2003.

———. "'It Was the Will of the Lord to Bruise Him:' Soteriology and the Doctrine of God." In *God Without Measure*, vol. 1, *God and the Works of God*, 143-57. London: T&T Clark, 2016.

———. "One Who is Son." In *The Epistle to the Hebrews and Christian Theology*, edited by Richard Bauckham, Daniel R. Driver, Trevor A. Hart, and Nathan MacDonald, 69-94. Grand Rapids, MI: Eerdmans, 2009.

Weinandy, Thomas. "Athanasius' Incarnational Soteriology." In *T&T Clark Companion to Atonement*, edited by Adam. J. Johnson, 135-54. London: Bloomsbury T&T Clark, 2017.

———. *Does God Suffer*? Notre Dame, IN: University of Notre Dame Press, 2000.

———. *The Father's Spirit of Sonship: Reconceiving the Trinity*. Reprint, Eugene, OR: Wipf & Stock, 2010.

———. *Jesus Becoming Jesus: A Theological Interpretation of the Synoptic Gospels*. Washington, DC: Catholic University of America Press, 2018.

———. "Trinitarian Theology: The Eternal Son." In *The Oxford Handbook of the Trinity*, edited by Gilles Emery, OP, and Matthew Levering, 387-99. Oxford: Oxford University Press, 2011.

Wenham, Gordon. *The Book of Leviticus*. New International Commentary on the Old Testament. Grand Rapids, MI: Eerdmans, 1979.

———. "The Theology of Old Testament Sacrifice." In *Sacrifice in the Bible*, edited by Roger T. Beckwith and Martin J. Selman, 75-87. Reprint, Eugene, OR: Wipf & Stock, 2004.

The Westminster Confession of Faith and Catechisms, as Adopted by the Presbyterian Church in America, with Proof Texts. Committee on Christian Education of the Orthodox Presbyterian Church, 2007.

Williams, Jarvis. *Maccabean Martyr Traditions in Paul's Theology of Atonement: Did Martyr Theology Shape Paul's Conception of Jesus' Death?* Eugene, OR: Wipf & Stock, 2010.

Williams, Rowan. *Christ the Heart of Creation*. London: Bloomsbury Continuum, 2018.

———. *The Sign and the Sacrifice: The Meaning of the Cross and Resurrection*. Louisville, KY: Westminster John Knox, 2017.

———. *Tokens of Trust*. Louisville, KY: Westminster John Knox, 2007.

Wright, Christopher J. H. *The Mission of God: Unlocking the Bible's Grand Narrative*. Downers Grove, IL: IVP Academic, 2006.

Wright, N. T. *The New Testament and the People of God*. Minneapolis: Fortress, 1992.

Young, Frances. *Sacrifice and the Death of Christ*. Reprint, Eugene, OR: Wipf & Stock, 2009.

General Index

Aaron, 40-41, 107, 121, 144
Abraham, 45, 119-20
acceptation, xviii, 199
Adam
    priestly service of, 32, 77
    sin of, xxiv-xxv, 119-20, 126, 128, 166
    See also Garden of Eden
Alexander of Hales, xxiv-xxv, 168, 195
Allen, Michael, 16, 18, 20
Anatolios, Khaled, 97, 98, 137, 177
Anselm, 87-88, 168, 193-94, 195
appeasement, 145-47, 194
Aquinas. *See* Thomas Aquinas, Saint
Aristotle, 37, 39, 99
ark of the covenant, 10, 28, 30, 66, 118, 165
Arminian theology, 199-200
ascension
    of Jesus, 70-71, 152, 176-79
    of smoke, 69, 103, 109, 138-48, 149-50
ascension offering, xii-xiii, 103, 141
aseity, 16-17, 25
Athanasius, 63-68, 97-98, 135, 175-76
atonement
    definition of, xviii-xx, 41
    mechanism of (*see* mechanism of atonement)
    moral aspects of, 162
    ontological aspects of, 162
    penal substitutionary (*see* penal substitution)
    as purpose of burnt offering, 124-28
    through blood, 60, 112, 130
    through substitution. *See* substitution: atonement through
atoning work of Christ, xxvii, 156, 177
    efficacy of, xv, xvii, 189, 200
Augustine, 99, 111
Aulén, Gustaf, xxi, xxiii

Averbeck, Richard, 47-49, 111
Bauckham, Richard, 19
Beale, G. K., 77, 85-86
Behr, John, 83-84, 135
Belousek, Darrin Snyder, 203
Blocher, Henri, 196
blood, on the altar, 11, 60, 130, 135-37
blood manipulation, 57, 60-62
Boersma, Hans, 145
Bonaventure, 115, 126-27, 194
burning, of offering, 61, 177-78
burning bush, 13-16, 19, 24, 79
Burns, J. Patout, xxiv
burnt offering
    as gift, 110-12
    primacy of, 108-110, 186
    requirements for animal, 112-15, 133, 158-59
    See also ascension offering
Calvin, John, 49, 156, 158, 165, 167, 196-97
Childs, Brevard, xxvii, 82
Clarke, Norris, 96-97
Cockerill, Gareth Lee, 89
communion, 49-50, 60-61, 143, 166
consecration, xx, 31, 55
    Jesus' satisfaction of demands of, 89
    of offering, 133-34, 140-41, 151-52
    of offeror, 141, 177-78
contrition, 137, 173
    doxological, 137, 171
covenant. *See* Mosaic covenant; Mount Sinai: covenant on
creation, 32, 68-69, 113-15
    burnt offering as new, 142
crisis, 61-62, 70, 132, 171
Crisp, Oliver, xix, xx
cultic journey, 43-44, 46, 57, 117
Day of Atonement, 3, 121, 124, 179-80, 192, 197-98

de Vaux, Roland, 111, 133
death
    as crisis, 61-62, 70
    necessity of, 59, 60, 62-70, 93, 133
    of offeror, 134-35
    for sin, 134-35, 149, 163, 174-76, 180-82
    to sin, 134-35, 149, 163, 172-74, 180-82
Derrida, Jacques, 55
divine economy, 65, 68, 69, 74, 82-84
divine fire, 12, 14, 22
Dodd, C. H., 202
Dumbrell, William J., 13
Eberhardt, Christian, 61, 110-11, 140
Eichrodt, Walther, 48, 53
Emery, Gilles, 96, 99-100
esse, 91, 94-95, 101-2
eternal generation, 94-98, 100-101, 188
eucharistic sacrifice, 111-12, 196
exaltation, 156, 165-66, 179-83
exile, 32, 138, 155
expiatory sacrifice, 109, 111-12, 196
filial obedience, 87-89, 167-69, 171-73, 180-81, 187-88
filial satisfaction, xii-xiv, 148, 152, 157, 182-83, 187-89
filial substitute, 151-52, 156-165, 173-74
food offering, 47-51, 142-44
Franks, R. S., 193, 197
Gane, Roy, xix-xx, 3, 58, 138
Garden of Eden, 30-33, 42-44, 46, 77, 117, 166
Gathercole, Simon, 122-23
Gese, Hartmut, 41-42, 123
gift, 55
    burnt offering as, 108-13, 132-33, 170-71 (*see also* food offering)
    cycle, 47, 51, 53-56, 91
    food as, 51-52
    Holy Spirit as, 99-100
Girard, René, 106, 203-4
Gorman, Frank, xxix, 8, 10, 59, 78, 131
gratitude, 46-47
guilt offering, 109-10, 124-25, 132, 168, 186
Gunton, Colin, 80, 176
Halbertal, Moshe, 53, 76
hand-leaning, 58-59, 61-62, 120-23, 150
    See also laying on of hands
Hart, Trevor, xxiv
Hartley, John, 126
Hays, Richard, 80-82, 84-85
Hilary of Poitier, xxii, 17, 193
holiness, divine, 19-21, 26-27, 67, 150-51
    triune, 21-23

Horton, Michael, 172, 202
idolatry, 39-40, 193
impurity, xix-xx, xxi, 67
    See also uncleanness
imputation, 59, 120-21, 128, 150
incarnation
    as act of substitution, 157-60
    Athanasius on, 66
    atonement and, 162-65, 169-70, 181-84, 187-88
    original sin and, 160-62
    sacrifice and, 101-2
incomparability, of God, 17-19
Irenaeus, 47, 82-85, 161, 166, 192
    on recapitulation, xiv, 69
Jamieson, R. B., 179-80
Job, 127
John of Damascus, 164
Johnson, Adam, xxv, 183
journey, 43-44, 57, 70, 117
    cultic (*see* cultic journey)
Justin Martyr, 192
Kiernim, Rolf, 43, 59, 114, 117, 121, 126
kinship, 78, 89
Klawans, Jonathan, 106, 134, 139
Kleinig, John, 45, 50, 106-9, 117, 140
    on animal used for offering, 112-13, 121
laying on of hands, 59, 121, 134, 164-65.
Legge, Dominic, 160
Levenson, John D., 30, 31
Levitical sacrifice
    action of, 105-7 (*see also* ascension; substitution)
    efficacy of, xvii-xviii, 130, 150, 151, 200
    hero of, 72-74 (*see also* filial substitute; offeror; sonship)
    meaning of, 154-56 (*see also* atonement; incarnation)
    Name of God and, 25-28
    plot of, 37-42, 69-71 (*see also* death; return)
    setting of, 3-4, 33-34 (*see also* Mosaic covenant; Mount Sinai; tabernacle; tent of meeting)
    themes of (*see* consecration; covenant; creation)
    See also burnt offering; mechanism of atonement
living sacrifice, 55-56
Luther, Martin, 150, 196-97
Lyonnet, Stanislas, 61
Marshall, Bruce, 101

General Index

Mascall, E. L., 74, 90-94, 99, 101
Masure, Eugene, 92-93, 181
Maximus the Confessor, 115, 162
McNall, Joshua, xxii
mechanism of accomplishment, xxiii
mechanism of atonement, xxi-xxiii, 186
    in the burnt offering, xii, 105, 129, 148, 150
    and Jesus, 162-64, 169, 188
mechanism of relationship, xxiii
Milgrom, Jacob, 50, 53-54, 67, 79, 136
    on purification, xix-xx, 203
    on the tabernacle, 29-30
Moberly, R. W. L., 5, 14, 17, 51
Moffitt, David, 106, 143-44, 151, 176-79
Morales, Michael
    on atonement through blood, 60
    on being "blameless," 116
    on burnt offering, 108-9, 134, 140-41, 145-46
    on cultic journey to God, 57
    on tabernacle, 28-32, 42-43
Morris, Leon, 58, 131, 201-2
Mosaic covenant, 8-12
    See also Mount Sinai: covenant on
Moses, 6-8, 12-13, 18
    See also burning bush; Name of God
Mount Sinai
    covenant on, 8-9, 11, 27, 43, 51 (*see also* Mosaic covenant)
    relationship to tabernacle, 28-30, 40, 125
mutual glorification, 97-99, 100, 101
Name of God
    meaning of, 14-25
    revelation to Moses, 12-14 (*see also* burning bush)
Noah, 68, 128, 142, 146
Noble, T. A., 94
obedience, 44-47, 87-88, 116, 119-20
    filial. *See* filial obedience
    of Jesus. *See* filial obedience
    substitutionary, 137-38
    atoning, 167-69
offeror
    Christ as, 86-89
    as filial figure, 76-80
    as hero, 74-76
O'Keefe, John, 83
Origen, 15
original sin, 126-29, 135, 148, 162, 174-76
    negation of, 160-61
Osborne, Eric, xiv
Owen, John, 198-99

Packer, J. I., xxi, xxvi
peace offering, 10-12, 50, 107, 109, 112
Pelikan, Jaroslav, 194
penal substitution, 120-23, 175, 182, 195-203
perfection, 166
    of offering, 142-45
    through Christ, 70, 142-45, 163-64, 179-83
Perrin, Nicholas, 77
"pleasing aroma," 53-54, 117-18, 128, 144-47
presentation, of offering, 57-58, 61-62, 76, 111, 151
procession of the Spirit, 99-101
propitiation, 145-47, 201-3
purgation, 3, 124
Radner, Ephraim, xxviii
Ratzinger, Joseph, 96, 159-60, 171
recapitulation, xiv, 33-34, 69-70, 105, 148, 187
reception, 51-57, 81-82, 96, 100-101, 142-45
Reformation, 195-97
Reno, R. R., 83
repentance, 44-46, 65, 70, 137
resurrection, 69-71, 143-44, 163-64, 176-84
return
    to the altar, 117-18
    to Eden, 30-33, 42-44
    of gifts, 46-57
    of obedience, 44-46
    of the Son, 97-101
Ribbens, Benjamin, xvii
Sabourin, Léopold, 61
Sacks, Jonathan, 6
Sanders, Fred, 93-94, 162-63
satisfaction, xxiii-xxv, 102, 147-48, 151-52, 178, 202
    in medieval theology, xxiv, 193-95
    and recapitulation, 33-34, 148
    in the Reformation, 195-97
    and Socinians, 197-200
    See also filial satisfaction
Saul, 118-19
Scheeben, Matthias Joseph, 35-36, 126
Seitz, Christopher, xxvi-xxvii
sin offering, 107-10, 124-25, 186, 203
    blood in, 136
    slaughter in, 132
    type of offering used in, 112
Sklar, Jay, xx, 28, 46, 124, 131, 134
slaughter, 57-62, 130-35, 139-40, 151-52, 179-80
smoke, 61-62, 103, 108-9, 117-18, 139-41, 144-45
Socinian challenge, 197-200
Socinus, Faustus, 197, 199
Sonderegger, Katherine, 21-22

sonship
    of Israel, 76-77
    of Jesus, 88-90, 141, 170, 172, 181-83, 187-89
    and sacrifice, 73-74, 88-90 (*see also* "Sonship and Sacrifice" [E. L. Mascall])
"Sonship and Sacrifice" (E. L. Mascall), 90-94
sovereignty, of God, 17-18
Stump, Eleonore, xviii-xix
substitution, xiv, 120-24, 137-38, 149-50
    atonement through, 128-30, 169-70
    filial (*see* filial substitute)
    penal (*see* penal substitution)
    as symbol of death of offeror, 134
    vicarious, 58-59, 140
tabernacle, 6-12, 28-32, 43, 79, 128
    See also tent of meeting
Ten Commandments, 10, 30, 45, 118
tent of meeting, 28-30, 39-40, 42-44, 116-17
    See also tabernacle
testing, 117-20, 163, 165-67
theological exegesis, definition of, xxv-xxix
Thomas Aquinas, Saint, 94-95, 99-100, 126, 182, 194-95
    on corruption, 127, 167-68
Torrance, T. F., xxii, 89, 163

transformation, 61, 138, 140, 142-43, 177-79, 186-87
Turretin, Francis, 198-99
type-antitype relation, xvii, 73, 81-82, 197-98
typology, xvi-xviii, 80-81, 85-86
    prospective, xvii, 73, 80-82
    retrospective, xvii, 73, 80-81
uncleanness, 67, 113-17, 125, 149-50, 179, 203
union
    with Christ, 164-65
    of Christ's human and divine natures, 160, 163, 183, 189
    covenant, 27, 50, 56, 108
Vanhoozer, Kevin, 146-47
Vos, Geerhardus, 20, 85, 140
Warfield, B. B., 42, 191, 200-202
Weaver, Denny, 202-3
Webster, John, 20, 21, 94
Weinandy, Thomas, xxii, 25, 89, 96, 171-72
Wenham, Gordon, 117, 124, 126
    on identification of offering with offeror, 59, 121-22, 131, 134
Williams, Rowan, 22, 56, 95-96
Word of God, 115-16, 129-30, 137, 148-49, 187

Scripture Index

OLD TESTAMENT

Genesis
1, *17, 30, 113, 114*
1:2, *31*
1:14, *31*
1:14-16, *31*
1:29, *51*
1:31, *31*
2–3, *31*
2:3, *19, 31*
2:10-14, *31*
2:15, *32*
2:17, *57, 135, 149, 174*
3, *43*
3:8, *31*
3:17, *128*
3:24, *117*
4, *53*
4:16, *117*
5:29, *142*
6, *128*
6:12, *115*
8, *128, 146*
8:13, *142*
8:20-22, *128*
8:21, *127, 128, 146*
9:1, *142*
12:1, *13*
12:1-3, *9*
13:11, *117*
17:1, *159*
22, *45, 119*
22:2, *119*
22:3, *119*
22:6-8, *119*
22:9, *120*
22:13, *45, 119*
22:16-18, *45, 119*

Exodus
3, *12, 14, 17, 24*
3:1-2, *12*
3:3-5, *12*
3:5, *19*
3:6, *13, 24*
3:7-9, *24*
3:8, *51*
3:12, *13*
3:14, *16*
3:14-15, *13*
3:16-17, *24*
4:22-23, *76*
5, *23*
5:1, *23, 77*
5:2, *23*
6:2-13, *23*
6:6-8, *24*
7:5, *18*
8:10, *18*
8:25-27, *77*
10:9, *77*
15:3, *18*
15:11, *21*
16:4, *8*
17:6, *8*
17:8-13, *8*
19, *14, 125*
19–24, *9*
19:1-2, *9*
19:4-6, *9*
19:8, *9*
19:9, *9*
19:20, *7*
19:21, *11*
19:22, *125*
19:24, *11*
20:1–23:19, *9*
20:19, *27*
20:20, *120, 165*
23:20-33, *9*
24:3, *10*
24:7, *10*
24:8, *10, 108*
24:9-11, *10*
24:11, *49, 51*
24:15, *29*
24:16, *7, 29*
25:1-9, *9*
25:8, *29*
25:9, *29*
25:22, *30*
29:38-45, *104*
29:38-46, *108*
29:42, *108*
29:45, *6, 108*
29:45-46, *7*
31:3, *31*
32, *39*
32:7, *39*
32:35, *39*
34:6-7, *39*
34:23-24, *50*
35–40, *30*
35:30, *31*
39:43, *31*
40:9-11, *31*
40:34, *29*
40:34-38, *5, 107*

Leviticus
1, *7, 47, 53, 73, 74, 76, 78, 87, 117, 131, 138, 142, 146, 152, 154,*
155, 156, 157, 166, 170, 176, 185
1–7, *47, 48, 60, 78, 107*
1–16, *2, 4, 6, 30, 47, 50, 54, 59, 67, 79, 110, 111, 112, 117, 121, 131, 133, 136, 139, 140*
1:1, *4, 5, 7, 12, 28, 38, 40, 66*
1:1-2, *44, 105*
1:1-9, *43, 75, 114, 159*
1:2, *2, 35, 37, 43, 47, 73, 74, 88, 110*
1:2-3, *43*
1:3, *53, 75, 129, 159*
1:3-4, *122, 133, 159*
1:3-9, *7, 104, 105*
1:3-17, *105*
1:3–6:7, *107*
1:4, *76, 112, 124, 129, 148, 159, 178*
1:5, *59, 130, 131*
1:6-8, *138*
1:6-9, *132, 133, 138*
1:9, *47, 48, 53, 87, 111, 117, 128, 144*
1:10, *113*
1:11, *59*
1:13, *47, 53, 76, 117*
1:17, *47, 53, 117*
2, *75*
2:2, *48*
3:1, *59, 113*
3:3, *48*
3:6, *113*
3:9, *113*

3:16, *48*
4, *108*
4–6, *125*
4:3, *113*
4:5-7, *136*
4:11-12, *109, 132*
4:20, *125*
4:20-21, *132*
4:22-31, *112*
4:23, *113*
4:24, *59*
4:25, *136*
4:26, *125*
4:28, *113*
4:31, *109, 125*
4:32, *113*
4:35, *48, 125*
5:10, *125*
5:13, *125*
5:15, *113*
5:16, *125*
5:18, *113*
5:25, *113*
6:1, *168*
6:6, *113, 168*
6:7, *125*
6:8-13, *132*
7:5, *48*
7:7, *109*
7:8, *132*
7:25, *48*
8–10, *5*
9, *11, 40, 107, 108, 144*
9:8-21, *107*
9:22, *107*
9:23, *12, 40*
9:24, *12, 40*
12, *114*
14–15, *107*
14:18, *201*
16:2, *29*
16:10, *201*
16:21, *198*
16:21-22, *121*
16:24, *112, 124*
16:145, *111*
16:147, *112*
17:11, *57, 60, 132, 136, 201*
18, *116*
18:4, *116*
18:20, *116*
18:22, *116*

18:24, *116*
18:27, *116*
18:29, *116*
18:30, *116*
22:17-25, *113*
22:23, *113*
26:3-12, *86*
26:11, *86*
26:12, *31*

Numbers
2:17, *28*
3:7-8, *32*
4:20, *29*
6, *107*
7:89, *29*
8:19, *27*
8:26, *32*
11:24-27, *28*
14:10, *27*
15, *48*
15:1-10, *109*
15:24, *127*
16:19, *27*
16:42, *27*
18:5-6, *32*
20:6, *27*

Deuteronomy
5:25, *8*
5:27, *8*
12:11-12, *14*
16, *54*
23:14, *31*
26, *54*
27:7, *50*

Judges
19–20, *139*

1 Samuel
1, *7*
13, *119*
15, *119*
15:22, *44*

2 Samuel
24, *145*
24:25, *127, 146*

2 Chronicles
3:1, *119*
29:7-8, *127*

Job
1, *127*
1:5, *127*
9:8, *31*
42:8, *127*

Psalms
2:11, *7*
7:9, *139*
11:4, *118*
15:1, *27, 43, 77*
15:1-2, *116, 157*
24:3-4, *27*
27:4, *7, 44*
43:3-4, *7*
43:4, *54*
50:12-13, *48*
50:13, *143*
51, *118*
51:17, *173*
51:17-19, *118*
104:2, *31*
132, *7*
145:15-16, *52*

Proverbs
3:19-20, *31*
8, *97*
8:30, *97*

Isaiah
1:4, *118*
1:11, *118*
1:13, *118*
1:21–2:5, *155*
40:22, *31*

Jeremiah
3:6, *49*
7:22-23, *44*
11:20, *139*

Ezekiel
28:13-14, *31, 77*
40–48, *85*
43–45, *107*
44:11, *131*

Hosea
2:8, *51*

Amos
9:14, *51*

Malachi
1, *113*
1:7, *78, 113*
1:7-8, *118*
1:8, *113*
1:9, *113*

NEW TESTAMENT

Matthew
4:6, *167*
6:9, *167*
6:25-34, *167*
25:21, *118*
27:40, *167, 172*
27:43, *172*
27:46, *172*
27:50, *172*
27:54, *172*

Mark
15:39, *90, 172*

Luke
2:48, *167*
2:49, *167*
3:22, *167*
22:30, *51*
23:46, *172, 188*
24:26, *172, 177*
24:44, *79*

John
1, *92*
1:1, *88*
2:16, *167*
3:3, *135*
3:16, *56*
5:17, *167*
5:19, *56*
5:20, *167*
5:39, *82*
5:46, *82*
6:35, *52*
6:51, *51, 52*
14:12, *88*
15:3, *115*
15:4-7, *115*
16:10, *88*

Acts
2:3, *145*

Scripture Index

2:4, *145*
14:17, *158*

Romans
1:4, *172*
1:18, *158*
1:19, *158*
1:21, *56, 158*
1:24, *56*
3:23, *158*
6, *122, 173*
6:6, *135*
6:10, *172*
6:11, *173*
6:23, *135*
7:4, *174*
7:6, *174*
8:3, *135, 161*
8:4, *174*
11:36, *57, 137, 158*
12:1, *56*

12:1-2, *158*
12:2, *56*

1 Corinthians
10:16, *52*
10:18-20, *49*
15:49, *178*

2 Corinthians
2:16, *157*
5:15, *174*
5:16-17, *174*

Galatians
3:13, *161, 196*

Ephesians
1:3-14, *70*
1:10, *32*
2:5-6, *178*
4, *122*
5:2, *87*

Philippians
2:15-16, *115*

Colossians
2:9, *169*

Hebrews
1:5-9, *181*
2:10, *86, 89, 180, 181, 183*
2:11-12, *87*
2:14, *180*
5:8, *44, 173*
5:8-9, *87, 120*
5:9, *180*
6:19, *120*
7:16, *144*
7:28, *70, 144, 180*
8:5, *85*
9:22, *179*
10, *194*
10:1, *87*

10:10, *181*
10:14, *70*
10:19-23, *156*
10:20, *70, 71, 87, 183*
11:17, *119*
12:4, *173*
12:10, *173*

1 Peter
2:24, *174*
3:18, *175*

1 John
3:2, *145*

Revelation
1:4, *17*
8:3-4, *79*

The Studies in Christian Doctrine and Scripture Series

Studies in Christian Doctrine and Scripture promotes evangelical contributions to systematic theology, seeking fresh understanding of Christian doctrine through creatively faithful engagement with Scripture in dialogue with catholic tradition(s).

Thus: We aim to publish **contributions to systematic theology** rather than merely descriptive rehearsals of biblical theology, historical retrievals of classic or contemporary theologians, or hermeneutical reflections on theological method—volumes that are plentifully and expertly published elsewhere.

We aim to promote **evangelical** contributions, neither retreating from broader dialogue into a narrow version of this identity on the one hand, nor running away from the biblical preoccupation of our heritage on the other hand.

We seek fresh understanding of Christian doctrine **through creatively faithful engagement with Scripture.** To some fellow evangelicals and interested others today, we commend the classic evangelical commitment of engaging Scripture. To other fellow evangelicals today, we commend a contemporary aim to engage Scripture with creative fidelity. The church is to be always reforming—but always reforming according to the Word of God.

We seek **fresh understanding of Christian doctrine.** We do not promote a singular method; we welcome proposals appealing to biblical theology, the history of interpretation, theological interpretation of Scripture, or still other approaches. We welcome projects that engage in detailed exegesis as well as those that appropriate broader biblical themes and patterns. Ultimately, we hope to promote relating Scripture to doctrinal understanding in material, not just formal, ways.

We promote scriptural engagement **in dialogue with catholic tradition(s).** A periodic evangelical weakness is relative disinterest in the church's shared creedal heritage, in churches' particular confessions and more generally in the history of dogmatic reflection. Beyond existing efforts to enhance understanding of themes and corpora in biblical theology, then, we hope to foster engagement with Scripture that bears upon and learns from loci, themes, or crucial questions in classic dogmatics and contemporary systematic theology.